# PASSING THROUGH THE FIRE

## Conscious Imagination and Thinking

## D. C. KERNS

BALBOA.
PRESS
A DIVISION OF HAY HOUSE

Balboa Press books may be ordered through booksellers or by contacting:

Balboa Press
A Division of Hay House
1663 Liberty Drive
Bloomington, IN 47403
www.balboapress.com
1-(877) 407-4847

Because of the dynamic nature of the Internet, any web addresses or links contained in this book may have changed since publication and may no longer be valid. The views expressed in this work are solely those of the author and do not necessarily reflect the views of the publisher, and the publisher hereby disclaims any responsibility for them.

The author of this book does not dispense medical advice or prescribe the use of any technique as a form of treatment for physical, emotional, or medical problems without the advice of a physician, either directly or indirectly. The intent of the author is only to offer information of a general nature to help you in your quest for emotional and spiritual well-being. In the event you use any of the information in this book for yourself, which is your constitutional right, the author and the publisher assume no responsibility for your actions.

Any people depicted in stock imagery provided by Thinkstock are models, and such images are being used for illustrative purposes only.
Certain stock imagery © Thinkstock.

ISBN: 978-1-4525-3597-5 (e)
ISBN: 978-1-4525-3596-8 (sc)
ISBN: 978-1-4525-3598-2 (hc)

Library of Congress Control Number: 2011910514

Printed in the United States of America

Balboa Press rev. date: 7/7/2011

*To the Universal Spirit that Lights*
*The Flame of Life*

*To Life expressing itself as Consciousness*
*In Time, Space, Matter, Spirit, and Fire*

*To the Heart that listens in Silence*
*In you I will remain*
*Forever a Flame lit bright as the Sun that is in me*
*For in the end your Heart will be*
*All I See*

# Contents

# Expressions for "Essence":

All-Embracing Care, Awareness, Being, Book of Life, Burning Flow, Cause, Clarity, Compassion, Consciousness, Contemplative Solitude, Cosmic Awareness, Cosmic Consciousness, Cosmic Light, Creative Power, Creator, Divine, Energy of Time, Essence, Eternal, Event Light, Fire, Fire of Creation, First Cause, First Light, First Principle, Flame, Formless, Freedom, Friendship, Gratitude, Great Circle, Harmony, Heaven, Higher Self, I AM, Imagination, Immeasurable, Immortality, Infinite, Infinite Time, Infinite Circle and Life and Fire, Innateness, Inner Self, Innocence, Intelligence, Intelligent Heart, Intuition, Inviolable, Invisible, Invisible Intelligence, Joy, Kindred Kind, Law of Harmony, Lightness of Being, Limitless Power, Love, Maker, Mystery, One Reality, One Source, One Totality, Origin, Peace, Perfection, Permanency, Pure Consciousness, Rarified Light, Real, Sacred, Self, Serene, Single Eye, Singular, Silence, Soul, Still Small Voice, Sum of Creation, Timeless Now, True Being, True Power, Truth, Unity, Universality, Universal Justice, Universal Love, Voice of Silence, and Wisdom

# *Preface*

*The thoughts expressed in this writing originate from my own awareness and those who have had an impact on me. Each topic presented in <u>Passing through the Fire</u> builds on and supports the other themes. These thoughts are not true or false regarding any person, idea or thing. Rather, they are to stimulate individual imagination and thinking that can lift one above negativity in everyday living. It is up to the reader to determine if these ideas have merit. Anyone is free to take from these words as long as he/she treats these thoughts kindly, either in acceptance or in rejection.*

Everything in the physical universe consists of a gathering process, whether minerals, plants, animals, humans, planets, solar systems or galaxies. This mass that encompasses everything is termed Essence. As humans, we give this Essence various names and forms, which constitute Consciousness. From a physical view, Consciousness is dependent on mind to arrange and produce the view screen onto which the mind records the images. Thus, we have the reality of the human experience: the Invisible becoming visible. Beyond this visibility, we have the Invisible pure quantum state, energy and force or Fire by friction that fuels the totality of time, space and causation. From a single particle of Light, this mass of Invisible Intelligence is constantly in a state of splitting and creating in a furnace of Fire, or Pure Consciousness. As such, there is no beginning or ending, only a gathering of awareness.

No matter what one writes, it will never fully explain our beginnings or endings for that is an ongoing process. The patterns and frictions from life guide and direct each of us through our personal journey. When we are no longer asleep to the ways of the world, we can see the Commonality of each thing and its interconnection with all other things. Through this connection, we come to the place of our own originality. This space forever was, is, and will always be in the Infinite Circle of Life and Fire.

Therefore, to understand the things unknown to us we must peer into the vastness of our individual universe. When we can do this without judgment as to persons, places and things, we will see the manifested patterns of life in, around and everywhere. When we look into the fossil preservations of nature, we gain an understanding of our origin in nature. When we use love and understanding regarding the complexity of man/woman, we find ourselves living and moving with the creation of a wondrous body. This body houses our personal universe and its similarities with nature: the rivers / blood veins, the skin / soil, as well as the atoms, molecules, stars, and galaxies that light up our vision. This understanding is always moving us forward into the Perfect expressions of ourselves beyond earth, air, water and fire and into the One Source from which we all originate.

Every sentient being on this blue-green world, which we call our home, is only here on a short visit: to gather, to learn and to understand its workings in such a way that in the end we are more intelligent or not. The choices made usually dictate the closing stages and end outlook. Each of us is alone in this releasing process. It is my hope that these pages will bring a better understanding to the journey. As I am still passing through the Fire, I am still discharging old patterns and fashioning new ones. Through understanding, I have come to see the things of the past as they are, the past. When we leave this temple-earth and name-body, we will never remember them quite the same way. Therefore, we should honor, respect and surrender back to our earth home the elements it so generously loaned to us. If we can do this in a forgiving way, the Inner Self will be watching, directing, and sheltering us in our future that is to be. We live through Joy and sorrow, and when we come to know this, we will let go of the world rightly. To do this each of us must create our own unique system of believing and imagining.

Eternity is. In its existence all that happens in space, time, energy and matter disappears and returns to Pure Consciousness: Passing through the Fire.

## The Unfettered Reflection

We can never return to the home we left behind! Those former times are only points of reference that give meaning for what we have become. Our life history makes available signals that point us toward future opportunities built on the substance and essence of what was before. Regardless of our nature, each of us stands alone in the judging of our destiny. When the light of life glows dim at the twilight of our time, our hearts will fill with overwhelming gratitude for those memories, and in the Dawn of our New Beginning, we will slowly awaken to a newer and better creation.

The Spirit of life awakens to feel, hope, and dream in the river of Silence and Time. Wisdom of the heart and mind is the Source, the wellspring from which every word and action proceeds. Shaped by desire and recurring awareness, the vast dark sleeping earth and all its rivers, plains, mountains, forests, oceans, plant and animal life awaken from the endless rounds of time. The newness of nature, with its intricate patterns, passes through the senses with fragrant mysterious secrets. From the brown soil, new life and all its numerous familiarities of the senses come into focus from the ancient web of memory.

Our mission begins in this world and we amend it in the next. Our True Power exists when we choose love and kindness over hate and cruelty. The true nature of earth can exist only when discord and tyranny are no longer a part of human consciousness. When we look into the mirror of the Inner Self, we see the face of matter and Spirit. Each came out of the fire of creation. More radiant than fire, more beautiful than the lilies of the field, purer than light, is the Self. The outer world flowers with unfettered reflection when we are at peace with the Inner Self. In the clear crisp blue sky, a baptism of amber light reflects off silvery gray clouds sailing on the breath of life. Floating shadows of light and moisture ripple over the body of earth. New vistas open, new dreams and visions appear. In our doings, we think we have broken the bounds and liberated ourselves only to realize that we have given up an old belief for a new one and forsaken one dream for a wider one.

While on this earth, each of us stands alone in the swarm of human knowledge, an atom in the cosmic chain of events and circumstances. Imbued with an atmosphere of collected noise, we are Everlasting, fixed and unchanged, no matter how we live and die. We visit the million sights, see the endless faces, read mountains of books and data, only to become weary from what we know and see. To assuage ourselves, we strive to hold the earth and its vast swarming riddle in our hands, as we might hold a coin of gold. Yet, we are nothing if we are not mindful of its everlasting unfoldment. We breathe in the certainty of our immortality, drive out and banish confusion when we are aware! Let us embrace the living earth as we do a loved one, unfettered, for there are no limits or restrictions on what love can do.

When we are free from our fears of self-idealized conceptions, the fragrant mysteries of the earth unfold as a flower does in the morning sun.

### Conversation with the Living

Fire, the base, the glowing ember of imagination, is the central point from which all of us have our beginning. From the mind's internal eye, the beginning of life always meets the end in a spiraling awakening. Fire, the principle of heat and light, is the source of all life. Without it, we would be a blank slate. All of the elements that make up the periodic law blend and blaze until the essential elements separate and are withheld at the end, where they subordinate to a greater cause, the system that arranges the classification. This system of cause coordinates these elements according to their atomic number. Likewise, this journal (or conversation) of the human imagination is inherent and latent, manifesting and advancing through a combination of elements in such a way that there is no measurable way for them to occupy or occur in space as to past or future. When we walk out through a sea grass dune that meets the ocean and watch the waves roll in and out, or peer into the vastness of the night sky at the endless points of light, we cannot help but stand and wonder. Are we standing within ourselves?

Most of us, when we think of fire or get too close to its heat, cringe from the thought of pain. This type of fire is the destructive form seen through the workings of nature. The atomic and electrical attributes of fire, if not handled properly, can also be very destructive. However, they are beneficial when controlled wisely. For example, the heat and light of the sun nurture our lives through the workings of the earth from which we get our sustenance. Sentient lives, and all types of animals, know when it is time to move out of the sun into the shade. The fusion of the sun allows us to see, and when we look at a color x-ray of the eye, it bears a resemblance to the sun. In unison with the cosmos, we are constantly generating, assimilating and radiating the elements of fire. Sadly, we use the periodic law of the elements that make up our world to create harmful products. In time, due to friction, these unwise choices will pass because the fire of mind and the fire of matter are always repelling one another. This will allow us to see the wisdom of our actions.

The reality of Cosmic Consciousness consists mostly of energy and love.

## The First Light

The First Light and Darkness, the energy of creation, came out of formlessness and created everything that turns in the universe. Darkness and light create insight into stillness and movement. This insight or perception is the cause of living. The attracting and repelling occurrences in nature produce the effects in the environment. When the mind is hurtful and destructive, the qualities of Light can transform what has been dark! Through action nature passes to human vision, humanism through change passes to spiritual vision, and the social structure through discovery passes to Universal Vision. Darkness and Light are all over our world. Through self-discovery, the nature of Light and Darkness can appeal to the heart and mind to become one receptacle that is inclusive to the waves in nature. Thus, the power of Life has its recognition in the person who begins reflecting on the nature of existence.

Who am I? How did I come about? When did life start? What was the reason? Where am I going in life? What we call Life is just a series of events and circumstances formed by the mind in order to give meaning to our relationship with the outward appearance of the universe. 'Who am I' is the Life, the substance out of which creation started. It can be seen and unseen by the mind during its evolution. The energy of the universe forms life and is the cause of our existence, of space and all that exists in it. Life is everything from the grandest of objects in manifestation to the smallest of particles in their makeup: the tiny loops of vibrating energy strings. Life is the sum of the universe and all that is contained within it. Life is the flow of Light upon darkness. It is the intelligent use of the mind over matter in the working of things seen and unseen in nature. The hidden side of things keeps consciousness evolving. It is the true Self reflecting on its relationships among other forms, animal and human. It is the many dimensions of Spirit, the memory of our loved ones. Life is coming face to face with the One Self that guides us toward our Immortality. It is also more than this! Life came into existence out of each of us! It is the sum of you and me!

When you dream, see in those dreams exquisite forms upon on a wave of Light intended only for your destiny. When you dream of memory's dream, the memory of the Self will awaken. It is a great prism of multicolored circles formed around a great wheel of rotating fire. At the speed of light, this great power field weaves and turns. There is no passage of time here, only Diamond Consciousness expanding forever. Matter, Light and Life, the sum of human life, is but a fragment of something greater, seeking to return to its center of being. Peering into a glass of darkness, we slowly come face to face with the Light that opens our own window to the Soul. We each pass onward to greater dimensions of living. Beauty and splendor are all around us. They fly into our visions, and we touch this glory in a lofty moment, only to lose the contact and to sink back again into the dream of life of the First Light. The sights and smells of persons, places and things always share similarities. It not hard to imagine we have been here before. It is the when and how that is hard to pin down.

Our minds make up the world, the First Light of imagining.

## Persons, Places and Things

Everywhere we go we leave parts of our Essence to flow over persons, places and things that make up our everyday life and world. We choose what we want to keep, agree upon, or discard. We choose the picture; we write the story in our minds about the meaning and the encounters of these people/places/things. What they mean and what we have learned from them forms our awareness of life. A person independently thinks and reacts from his/her own nature, has rights, and communicates feelings, expressions and mannerisms to others. Humans give meaning to places, which are a part of the earth's surface, large or small. Our concept of things results from an action, abstraction, artifact, event, matter, a statement, an entity, self-existence, a feeling, or movable possessions.

Along with thoughts, we shape our lives from the interactions we have with persons, places and things. When we encounter distress, it is how we hold onto it that causes pain. We should not swim around in the murky waters of others. Instead, we should rely on the Good that we encounter. As to the events and circumstances of life and nature, we should always focus on what is pleasing. Where would we be without the bee making honey or the plant that bears our food season after season? Where would we be without thinking about the earth that gives us water and elements for our tools, or the sun that gives us vitality?

We base knowledge on the input we receive from our involvement and reactions to persons, places and things that enter our minds through the physical organs of sense. We enter life blank. The impressions that come before us are of a material nature and are always fleeting. Yet, the experiences we derive makeup our consciousness because the knowledge of sense objects and what we perceive as truth matches our impressions to persons/places/things. Awareness or sense impressions are always duplicating reality, imagination, dreams, or illusions. The sensations of duplication produce intense feelings and the conviction of our essential reality. Whatever image we encounter, the strength and vividness of it establishes the perception. What we have come to know is circular, inherent, latent and electrical. Always transmitting, reflecting and absorbing, this Essence permeates the visible with the invisible qualities of persons, places and things. This fine ether bathes all of us. Only our hearts feel how many persons we have spoken to, how many houses we have lived and congregated in, how many streets we have seen empty or filled.

We cannot wait for another person to hand us the key to the mysteries of life. We have to do it alone, one person at a time. We carry in us our own places of exile, our failures and our own negative effects. It is our duty to fight them in ourselves and not let them loose on the world. In this way, we become a friend to all living things.

Like a daily sunrise, all things take form through us and go beyond the earth as person, places, and things.

## *How We Create*

Through the frictions of life, we create and come into existence. From early dawn, our consciousness has been slowly expanding from darkness into Light. Before we could differentiate, how could we say what was? We can only use our imaginations and produce working models of the cause that may or may not be true. What stirred awareness to be cognizant of things? Only by arriving at the end will we be able to grasp some shadows of the Beginning. For an imaginative person there are no beginnings or endings, only transformation. Pundits of the past and present have imagined much about Light and Life but have shed little insight on the causes of creation.

All any of us can do is realize that we are a part of the Cause of creation. We live and have our being within this Orb of Fire and Awareness. As we move around in this source of Light, we can strive to create and preserve the ideas that come from our imaginations, always moving from our lower beginnings to higher ones. Our current periodic table is the grail for human life. Everything in life begins from a combination of these elements. From the combustion chambers of human feeling, to the shaping of an axe handle, and onward to the creation of space technology, the Fire of friction forges these ideas into material reality.

What is the nature of our inner being and can we share it like the periodic elements? Imagination and memory access the inner world. Pictorially, the inner world of imagination and memory is similar to the outer world in shapes and thoughts. Does this Inner Being survive the breakup of the earthly body and the current definition of death? Do we really need proof that we exist now? If we do not need it now, why should we need proof of our existence when we die? Fire radiates and emulates, giving off and copying from itself. If the imagination faded out, would any of us know the specifics about what was? The Light of the heavens and the earth is the Essence of all existence, the mirror and the culmination of what we choose to sense and believe.

Lift the heart into the Light and let the mind be fearless when it is time to enter the Fire with our minds and hands. Define what it means to be imaginative in the periodicity of cycles. Just like the cells of the body, we are constantly renewing. Is it so difficult to imagine that the inner life does the same? There are elements still undiscovered in the living and forging process. The Wheel of Fire turns and so does the imagination.

This fiery circle encapsulates all that we have done. As we pass through the Fire, we can train our imaginations to learn the lessons needed so that we can stand complete.

The things we create come from the Fire of imagination. We can make them more lively or less.

## What Kind of Image Do We Want to Become?

The process of training and developing knowledge, skill, character and the study of the methods, processes and effects of life start in the womb and end in the mind. All that exists, between the physical universe and our perception of it, is unfolded from within us. Fire can illuminate, deceive, or destroy our learned and inherited complexes. In order to know what is true, we must give the mind/brain methods in order to be active constructors of worldly order. Contrary to belief, the universe/world is not chaotic; our perceptions and actions make it seem that way.

To understand the true nature of Life we must first be aware of the energy that surrounds the natural order of life. Our minds create from the laws of matter, and matter forms the laws of mind. Whether we desire it or not, we create order and meaning out of the complexity of nature. The great thinkers from the past have constructed complex theories of order, yet we now recognize that those accepted ideas are inadequate. The earth is not the center of the universe; we are. Through our abilities and experiences, we are now just beginning to recognize that Universal Center in our hopes and neurological needs.

The invisible glow and warmth of electricity is all around. It fuels our sun and passes through our world, minds and bodies. We often have very little reverence for this power. We seem to want to reserve that reverence for the institutions and their experts, the secondary processes. Society subtly influences the mind to be overly submissive to the class structure. From childhood through adulthood, humans strive to find the meaning and importance of their space. We should attempt to understand what others are doing and saying without resorting to dangerous retaliation. Personal or institutional retribution is a learned tendency inculcated by others. The natural order of energy, the Fire of Life, is not interested in persuasion. This energy merely acts as a builder, a conserver and archetype of our thought processes and cultural inheritances. As receivers, assimilators and transmitters, we are the creators of that legacy.

To become true co-creators with this vast reservoir of living Essence is to absorb that which is benign. We must become the images we make ourselves into by becoming better listeners to the ideas of others. Otherwise, malignant acts set in and hateful attitudes influence the mind. We will enrich our relationships with the natural world and each other when we relate through a higher awareness of conscious thought rather than reacting to the influences of an unconscious immature secondary function. Secondary functions, such as institutions, are more creative when they serve the needs of the many in the ordering of world things.

The events and circumstances in which we find ourselves occur because of the thoughts we have formed. If those thoughts create positive attitudes, the expectations, pleasures, satisfactions and happiness envisioned will attract and create situations, people and events that conform to our positive outlook.

When our acts of creativity are the result of a highly developed purpose, then the world advances through those principles.

### What Kind of House Do We Live In and Upon?

With the discovery of electricity, the human species has harnessed, to some extent, the vast electromagnetic field that surrounds the Principles of creation. As we advance, one window of the mind closes and another opens. We are an adaptable species in the utilization of earthly resources, almost on par with breathing air into the lungs. Gradually we are adapting responsibly to the daily use of these precious resources. The vast reservoir of human knowledge can now be down loaded on streets of silicone chips. Our cities resemble huge motherboards to roam around in, and the inside of our houses bears a resemblance to the inner workings of our bodies.

The fiery essence of technology is fanning the flames of the Infinite. This energy enables the mind, bit by bit, to boost its frequency automatically and enhances its overall knowledge by intelligently participating in the changes occurring on earth. Through thinking and feeling (the freedom of decision or of choice between alternatives), the personal mind consumes the positive/negative occurrences within its atmosphere and reacts by cleansing or contaminating itself. Both of these reactions make up the patterns associated with the atmospheric and ground changes of earth. Personally and universally, there is a symbiotic relationship and a metamorphosis on all levels between all humans and the earth.

The Essence of transformation speaks through birth, youth and maturity. At birth, we are vessels of innocence dependant on others for our security and health. In youth, we are rebellious and spontaneous. In our mature years, we are more reflective of what was and is. Existence has two faces: 1) the gentle side of warmth and love that gives energy, life and passion, 2) the hurtful, wild, indifferent side that has an unsatisfied appetite. This destructive side tears down anything that stands in its way of gain and scars those who survive its passion. A well-prepared mind is attracted by the Fiery Essence, knows or dreams what it can do, and begins it. The principles by which we form choices establish the kind of relationship that will evolve between Fire and life. If we turn our minds toward this Fiery Essence, then the Infinite Energy of Life and all the possibilities of growth will exercise its creation through our imaginations and will. New art, new science, new philosophies, better governments and higher civilizations wait in this ring of Causality. The earth is the beginning and the fullness thereof. From then on, the boldness, power and magic of the laws of nature and the choices we make will give us the kind of house in which we want to live.

What is nature but the transformation of matter/spirit (ether, air, fire, water and earth) into the mind, intellect and ego?

## *Through the Light of the Mind, We See our Lives*

The sunny side of our bodily existence starts surfacing when we think and understand that healthy optimism relates to mental and physical health and success. When it comes to the future, it is far better to be optimistic than pessimistic. Humans expect positive events even when there is no evidence to support such expectations. The brain is a watery, fat, protein-based receiver that converts light and sound into the persons, places and things perceived. Soft and fragile, the brain records who we are, where we have been, and where we will go in our future consciousness. When we sense the brain as being the intelligent camera of our actions, then we are thinking smart and developing our true potential. To make it easy, fill the brain with optimism about the future of life on earth. The sun, the earth and the brain are as much a part of each other as our thinking is to the recognition of our awareness. Everything in the universe is information and all of us can tap into that Invisible knowledge.

We are all participants with the substance that fuels the universe. It is possible to synthesize all the elements of the universe as one whole and look at the form with the mind. In our ongoing currents of thinking, we come to understand the elusive aspects of the mind by removing irrational thoughts. We are all greater than the sum of our individual effects and capabilities, but we are in denial about it. When we start producing pleasing effects in the brain, object recognition will result in a brighter environment. Imagination and imagery have great power to convey information and arouse a sense of excitement. We might even move atoms and molecules around. If we can do it physically, we can do it mentally, even reshape our emotional imagery to take away sadness. Regarding society, we need images that tell a story in a compelling way that instill hope in the future. This will give all humans a purpose for being a part of the intelligent mirror. Our images can go beyond the bounds of logical thinking that is inherent in science. Imagery is more than the grouping of the normal and odd. Our descriptions of what we think and feel can give us a healthy optimism about our reflections and awareness that make us human beings. With the mind, we see and feel the constructs of our lives.

We do not derive happiness by changing the world but by changing the mind rather than the image. Affliction is the result of seeing though an unpolished mind. Cleanse the mind and it will begin to see and feel Joy.

## *Rising and Setting*

From an endless sea of faces, life evolves out of the tears of sorrow and happiness perishing and reappearing upon a landscape of change. Each part of us awakens at a different place and time to a sun shimmering in the sky. This radiance vivifies our every cell by its touch, in a play of building, preserving and casting off. Yet, its brightness is Fixed and Immutable.

Dawn comes over the eastern hills. The golden rays reach out to us to embrace. We welcome its beautiful face. We breathe it, and it covers us in a shimmering glow. Each occurrence is more beautiful than before. More and more, as we see its image, its glow changes our demeanor and we see ourselves becoming like it. The morning and evening sunbeams scatter like pearls over land and sea. Darkness to shadows, shadows to light, in an Infinite mating of rising and setting. Together we gather the Light that is beyond knowing. In and out, around and around we move upon the sea of space.

The universe is a mixture of elements all coming together in an endless portrait of experiences. We think we are separate from the clusters of stars that shine above; but in reality, we are those stars. Those luminaries above us go through the same stages that we humans do. First, they intermingle as dust, gas and invisible particle in a playground of innocence. Then they wed together and form planets and solar systems. Out of the vastness of time they, too, pass into maturity and old age becoming dust once again. Every atom and molecule of our being is a refined copy of the transformations occurring in this vast electrical, magnetic, and gravitational energy field.

In physics, we understand this energy field as quantum mechanics: the relationship between energy quanta, radiation and matter. As a rule, the results of quantum mechanics are not observable to the visible eye, but through the microscope become manifest at the atomic and subatomic level. What lies below these levels only fits in the realm of quantitative inheritance: the leap of the imagination. This realm exists; we can feel it and even measure it. Perhaps it is a variation of colors not distinguishable to the eye. These minute strands of interlacing light currents are the neurons of imagination. By using imagined experiences, or episodes from memories, there is the capacity to construct from this complex spatial context the Light of the First Cause.

There is no passing out of the One Universal Creative Power. Organic and living, the whole world is alive and moves through each of us. The sun and earth are the universal givers of life.

## Work for the Greater Good

Our most powerful desire and motivation is Goodness. It is how the universe is now and how it will unfold in the future. Integrity will bring it into fruition faster. Our family, community, government and institutions can make it so. Outside of our homes, the work place is the second consumer of our time. When we come into life, the means should be there to make it a right to work. The air is for everyone to breathe; work should be equally so. The worker takes the plans of the inventor and brings them into actuality. At the present, technology is assisting the worker to make this happen.

In the future, nanotechnology (a field of applied science and technology whose unifying theme is the control of matter on the atomic and molecular scale and the fabrication of devices within a size range) will interface with the worker and machines in ways that will transform all life. The focus of this science is on the non-covalent bonding interaction of molecules (self-replicating machines). The true nature of this technology rests on the ability of human consciousness to outgrow greed and apply that knowledge to the greater good. However, when matter becomes unbalanced, the sub-atomic level readjusts itself and stimulates the destroying aspect.

It is not hard to imagine the world as being a place where all people enjoy work and rest equally. Our bodies work incessantly on the molecular level. Only when we get sick do we take notice of this marvelous miracle machine. We breathe the air with very little effort. Our voices relate to one another in kindness or in other ways. Our eyes see the sun, the moon and stars, the mountains and extremes of the world. Our blood flows like rivers and our muscles move us about. Our nerves make us aware of what we have created. Work and life are somewhat the same. One cannot exist without the other. Even in retirement, we work to enjoy not working. What is even more wondrous is that the Fire of Life is working and carrying us along in its fullness, from imperfection to perfection. If there are ever any complaints from it, they are of our own making. Whether it is through the acquaintance of letters, words, or applying color to a surface or reshaping molecules with computer programs, our work is a tangible manifestation of creative efforts, individually and in groups. Work unveils the laws of the Greater Good of the universe that is in all of us. Life will eventually call for new types of professionals in the future workplace: those who are honest, dynamic, morally mature, and bold spokespersons for equality of life. As market place leaders, they will raise up the social institutions to work for the common good. Money and job stigma will fade out; the mind will reward the senses with creative releases.

When we look upon ourselves as future beings, we have the ability to gather what belongs to us, i.e., new truths, fullness from want, equanimity, clarity of mind and heart. Whatever our future is to be, we must create it.

## *Family Equals Politics and Money*

Fire is the basic element of the universe. Like the sun, it mystifies and is not limited to one particular group or country; it occurs everywhere as does the human family. Money and politics must be the same nurturing source for all human life. To use the Energy of family, politics and money successfully, we need to operate in both a physical reality and a metaphysical one. Our dreams, visions and altruistic imaginations create these realities. Family is cohesion: the source of human life where all of us get our start. Family is the generator of politics and money. In the free market, money is also the arbitrator of how that market flows because of human purchasing choices.

Money influences most aspects of living: work, leisure, creative activities, home, family, and spiritual pursuits. This powerful form of energy is what lights our political atmosphere. Money is not negative; it can have pitfalls or successes because of the way we use it. Our worry over money can make it a highly emotional spend. We first express the strength and qualities of money in our family life. Money gives value to our time, physical vitality, enjoyment, creativity and friends. The lessons and examples in the use of money have the ability to enrich every aspect of our lives. If politicians would use money selflessly, it could be a candle in dark places.

We use money to control the flow of commodities. Presently leaders use politics to persuade people to act in various ways. The family is the setting that enables the child to go out in society and act responsibly as an adult for the betterment of both. The human family is the economic commodity for the use of money, the success of politics, and should be the persuader of policies. The family gives cohesion to politics and money. The exchange of ideas must persuade and motivate politics to use money wisely. Our natural resources, safety, environmental health, and world family depend on the wise use of money.

The free market must modify and use the resources of the world equally. Then the balanced use of these resources will act as a first strike in the health, education and domestic policies of governments everywhere in the world. Energy follows mind. It is the greatest number of thinkers that ultimately influence the doers that fill the manifested world with events and bring purpose and Light to family, politics and money.

Domestic happiness is the fortune of the family and community: the true destiny of humanity. Happiness does not mean more possessions. Contentment lies in the Joy of achieving through creative effort.

## *Infrastructure of the Mind, Emotions and Body*

The mind and emotions instruct the elements of space, earth, air, fire, and water to provide the framework for our bodies. The Essence of life, energy and force (the Flame of life) is the framework that supports our bodily existence. Likewise, the structural elements that provide the framework for our roads, airports, and utilities may collectively be termed civil infrastructure, which constitute the human living habitat. The processes of energy/force and structural elements begin in the mind and end as our underlying foundation: the basic installations and facilities on which the continuance and growth of community, state, and mind depend. In planning for the needs of public systems, the landscape and culture should agree. The architecture of systems, services and facilities should include the functional characteristics of the places they are to be located.

Human imagination is the property of a complex living system. Society and culture are the scaffolds on which the human body (senses) can gain experience in material form through solids, liquids and gaseous shapes in the attempt to incorporate psychic dimensions of life into a Universal view. The sources of knowledge, the institutional social organizations of life and the environment, are the conceptual supportive structures of images. When we use these systems in a holistic manner to satisfy the various needs of all humans, our thoughts and efforts become examples for others to follow and remain a part of our heritage.

With a good infrastructure, the quality of life increases and life is productive. When we share our thoughts, time and effort with others, we develop the organizational skills to create our surroundings so our minds, bodies and public works function together for the peace and well-being of the human family. The mission of a confident and dynamic world is to build an innovative, growing, smart society that can deliver health and well-being to all parts of the earth. The world that the mind seeks to build must protect the environment by using resources responsibly in its public works, especially in health and education.

The family unit makes up the most important part of a society's endeavors. In order to maintain the public systems, it is important that both families and society are thriving. The cultural roads are like our bodies; if we do not properly maintain them, they run down. The mind and emotions rule the roads that we travel upon, and we must do what it takes to care for them. When we open our eyes in the morning, we want to see a coherent and intelligent world that is rich in experience and one that constitutes the potency of the mind. How we relate to our inner works determines how we plan our outer ones. For example, perception, communication and action provide the means for us to negotiate safely between the inner and outer structures of the mind, the planning and structuring of our world needs, and the right distribution of energy and force in carrying out the organization of the mind, emotions and body.

### The Future is in Time

Imagination is essential to understanding the clarity of life. We sense the surrounding world as a microcosm. The domain of this closed world is unknown and formless but to the imagination, it is alive and filled with regions of beauty and splendor. From this side it is an organized self-conscious macrocosmic space where life and death meet in an endless cycle of historic inhabited transformations. Imagination raises the mind above the archaic traditional societies of then and now. With an acute imagination, we can harness the ability to regain our lost contact with the natural world.

A history of kindness must replace the history of cruelty, thus becoming a paradigm for integrated systems. In the flow of time we live, move, and have being. Then, in an instant, being is gone. However, with our imagination, we can replace form in another nuance of time and charge our being with a new vitality. Will, the strength of mind, sees with clarity once the emotions are not agitated. If we let our imaginations do their work, empty space and immobility become the height of our awareness! Think of this; every moment we reach this serenity in the midst of ordinary life, the Essence, vitality and space are cultivated, and the subatomic world gives us new secrets to behold in the imagination. What do we know about out past and future? We know only what our memory and imagination tell us. Optimism allows us to believe that the vast expanse of the universe and mind act as a set of mirrors within mirrors, a multiplicity of here-and-now that is beyond the history of cruelty.

To some extent, we can see the past through our verbal, written and visual technologies. However, there is a probability that those in power, in order to have a dominant hand over the populace, skewed historic events. So, is the future out of sight? Just because someone tells us that we cannot see it does not mean it is not there. The microscope shows us there is an underlying smallness around everything. Look at it this way; the qualities of the universe are visible and invisible to the eye. Within it, there are two groups of particles; one is made of small particles and the other is made of large particles. Both are whirling around each other in a repelling and attracting dance of strength and vitality that are fused into a stately harmonious whole.

Whether we are aware of it or not, the Inner Learner, our Real Self, does guide us through life. When we allow this psychic double to influence our outer world, past and present, we control the future: our emotional and mental space.

When we remain confident that we are a part of a great whole, unification occurs in consciousness. Then growth of human responsibility will take place globally to meet our earthly needs. Whether they are environmental, humanistic, or economic, the future is in time.

## A Heart of Clay Becoming a Heart of Fire

Everything in the universe happens gradually. First, consciousness as identification comes about and form follows. Next mind and emotions evolve with their scaffolding of ideas for the building of knowledge and wisdom. Whatever the endeavor, gaining knowledge is based on binding the present with that which is believed to exist in the future. The first question one asks in this process is, "Who are we and how do we relate to the sun, the source of our system, be it humans, planets, or solar systems?" We originated from fire, heat, and light and we come from its elements: earth, water, and air. Subjectively, the sun is the sum total of heat and light. This Fire (mind) animates us and demonstrates as consciousness. The coming together of Spirit and matter, not only objectified the solar system, it also brought life and form into manifestation and provides the continuum of all human relationships.

On the lowest level, we are exact replicas in miniature of the universe including the sun. A veil of matter deeply hides everything, but the future is bright! In time and in due process, as the Wheel of Fire turns, all within that fire will correlate and assimilate the Flame of other forms, human or planetary, and all will eventually be complete in kind. We are all solar fires: a heart of clay becoming a Heart of Fire. We need to think optimistically about how we want our future to be. When we think about the future, proactively, it gives us increased power. We should see our planning as already happening and self-knowledge can contribute to that outcome.

What we choose and what we value will create the framework for a stable, peaceful, prosperous, diverse global civilization. This framework will produce 1) respect for freedom of individual belief through a democratic political system 2) high level educational and health care systems 3) an impartial and accessible system of justice 4) basic and advanced technology that is applied in ways that are in balance with the natural environment 5) an evenhanded distribution of social benefits everywhere on the world. When we revamp our social and economic regulatory systems to support the changes in industry and agriculture, we will avoid the disparities of wealth within and between countries. This will result in policies that bring all communities together through demographic changes that bring balance to population growth and material resources.

This future thinking will lead to a new society of individuals who live within democratic governments that are technologically advanced, economically free and environmentally safe. These new priorities will sustain and align communities, corporations and governments around the world. Because of the onward movement of technology and scientific knowledge, humanity will not need increased physical growth to create a sustainable economy. Its basic social beliefs will support interests that are less materialistic. Personal values and a deeper understanding for the world will lead to greater concern about global issues, the environment, and most importantly to new priorities in technological designs and solutions.

When the human mind is on fire, it becomes a powerful weapon. A time will come when the warm breath of Cosmic Awareness will exhaust the dark sea of matter.

## Thinking in the Always is to be Part of its Awareness

There are physical regions in the outer cosmos that are so far out in space that the only way to see into that spectrum lies in the movement of time. Presently, the human form cannot visit those regions. However, the mind has the ability to witness those far away regions through mental imagination. The difficulty on the mental physical plane is the lack of language to express those intuitive impressions. Some of our scientific discoveries and laws have come through this process, but they are only partial derivatives. These visible and invisible fields are fully alive and are the impulses behind our growth. This intense magnetic heat and light originates in both the macrocosm and microcosm, filling the cells in our bodies with self-sustaining processes. Time is the secret to unlocking this vast reservoir of Infinite Awareness.

Futuristic thinking requires removing unorganized thoughts and applying the imagination to parallel qualities that exist with the past and present. The purpose is to evaluate the judgments in the mind's causal field that are negative and replace them with optimistic views. Everything within our individual minds is only a reflection of what has transpired down through the ages through the collective minds in the outer world. Those imprints are at the sub-conscious level and influence our thinking unconsciously in the present moment. They motivate us to act and make choices. From the Cosmic point of union, there is only totality that filters down to the lowest sub-atomic particle into empty space. There this Cosmic point of Light enters the center of the void and works its way back to the periphery where a gradual awakening occurs. This ongoing expansion can only be termed Consciousness. Through this funneled reciprocity, we exist in various forms. We create, live, and die in an endless state of Cosmic vibration.

The more we explore this Inner Light, the more we will see similar parallels with the light of physics. Physical light and Consciousness have no mass; they are not part of the material world. Physical light seems to be necessary to the universe. The light of Consciousness is likewise necessary; without it, we would not be able to experience. The reality of the mind and the reality of the physical world share the same common pathways of the Light of the One Totality. When we return to the quietness of our Being, we are submitting to our future that has always been. We are what we are because of the various aspects that identify our individuality such as our bodies, appearance, history, nationality, how we play, work, our social and financial status, etc. We also develop our identities from our thoughts and feelings, beliefs and values, and from our creative and thinking abilities that give us our character and personality. These aspects play a part in forming our individuality. In the physical world and the mental world, time and space provide the means to fill our minds with the various colors that allow us to see a commonality in all experiences. So, what do we think? To be thinking in the Always is to be part of its awareness.

Here we are among innumerable stars, living as sparks in the right light, at the right time; everything is as it should be.

## Life Does Not Think Us: We Think Life!

Who are we? What is reality? We are more than sub-atomic particles covered in a vacuum of space. We are material in nature and weigh a certain amount based on our eating habits, genetic disposition and body type. However, are we something more that reaches beyond the physical? We are the sum of our thoughts, aspirations and ideas, which are visible only to ourselves. Even though they seem real to us, they do not have weight, color, and texture for others to see.

The great virtue of time is that it shows us where we have been and the probabilities of what the future holds for us. Along its path, we think, learn and act out our life experiences. These become the study of meaning: the principles underlying conduct, thought and knowledge. Time is the analyzer. Through time, we sharpen our ability to question accepted thinking and to express that thinking in a clear way that ultimately becomes our inner world. The essence of our education is to form questions in our individual reality that gives us an advantage of living positively in time's grasp. In addition, there is the probability that there are parallel streams of time flowing in and around us: copies of existence in its various forms. Through our imaginations, we can use those parallels to enhance cognitive abilities. The purpose of life is to be responsible for our choices. Life gives us images to form our actions and relations with others.

Life is a vocation, a calling, which makes us responsible for our decisions. Living is not something we ought to do because we are here; it is a conviction that we are more than our physical attributes. Depending on how we think, life can quickly become a passing motif or a permanent memory by which to live. We are able to live, move and have being based on what we know how to do. In material life, knowing what we are going to do, and how we go about doing it, is fundamental. It is through those choices our vocations and professions are determined. Thinking enables us to bring the abstract into concrete form whether that form is music, art, literature, or our cities and manufacturing necessities. Perception is more than observation; it is a cognitive realization that something is or is not the case. Most likely, if we had no memory of the world when first encountering it, then we would not be able to learn from new information.

When we gain knowledge of the substance from which we surfaced, we can move into the true nature of our relations with fire/electricity. We then comprehend its quantity/quality and utilize it beyond present commercial uses. When we have discovered how to contact and use positive solar electricity in combination with our planetary electricity, human and earthly, we shall then see very benign conditions unfold in that ideal environment for happiness. However, our observations and experiences must be meaningful, even at the sub-atomic level. What we see depends upon what we look at and what our previous visual conceptions have taught us to see from the largest all the way down to the smallest. This will be our reality. Life does not think us: we think life!

When we form an image in our minds as to how we would like that image to be, and hold it firmly and long enough, we will become that expression. Life as change is ongoing and so are our thoughts.

## The Shifting Standards for Change

Poverty, the absence or scarcity of substance, is a condition in which a person or community is deprived of the essentials for a minimum standard of well-being in life. There are many types of poverty: material, emotional, mental and spiritual. However, there is no scarcity in the Essence of life and it has no need to create poverty. Human ignorance, a lack of compassion, and greed in the economic and political fields create poverty. Poverty in the face of affluence is immorality at its worst. If governments and corporations invested in families and communities on the same scale as the stock market, our world would be a financially untroubled world. We all yearn to be free from toil and worry about our physical needs. However, we must relinquish this yearning through the emotional and mental processes rather than through violence. Reality shows us that business and government have a monopoly on the power of money. Poverty will fade when people develop the skills necessary to act in a self-governed way. To be self-governed is to believe that poverty does not exist in the mind's well being. We will overcome the poverty of mind, body, and spirit when we serve to make social justice a part of our collective humanity. As a result, government and business will get in step with civic life.

An individual optimistic view must be adapted in human consciousness for the preventative measures against poverty to take hold. A vibrant citizenry motivated by genuine politics of betterment will lead in finding the practical solutions toward overcoming poverty at all levels of the social stratum. The mind must rise above the concept of failure. Poverty is mirroring our collective social psychosis of wealth. Poverty and wealth both show a dislike for balance in the mutual interplay of the human magnetic field. This magnetic field bridges the underlying fields of the polarity poles of electricity, both large and small.

All conditions in life are temporary, but whether they are favorable or unfavorable, we must view both as passing clouds. Clean clothes, a clean mind and a healthy set of thoughts will go a long way in facing any situation bravely. We must turn our thoughts toward something bright and happy. Our homes, our minds, and emotions must reflect order. The influence of a self-respecting home spreads first to the children who are the inheritors of our wishes and dreams, the framers of future communities.

To bring the form aspect and that which is material into balance requires a sense of right relations with those needs and wants. If we are to overcome the various states of poverty, we must use all expressions of material life prudently, from the tiniest atom to all that waits for us in infinity. Remember, we ourselves evoke and call forth the outcome of our desires. The consciousness of every human being operates from a sense of duality, and the interplay between those dualities leads to all the neuroses and complexes that make up humanity and its shifting standards of change.

When we attempt to attain what we are not, we diminish what we are.

## A Wider Vision for the Right Use of Money

If we are to advance our thinking beyond the ordinary, we need to attach it to the Fire that gives us light and life. One of the 'lights' of human evolution is money. What is money? Classically, money acts as a unit of account, a store of value, and a medium of exchange. What are the types of money? There are commodity moneys, metallic coin, other commodities, fiat money, fiduciary money, bank notes and checking accounts. How should we use money? The right stewardship of money is using it for the betterment of people and the environment. The correct use of money occurs when we use it to influence the values we seek to create.

Our social, economic, and environmental growth determines the quality of community life. A quality life gives serenity to the mind and body and allows us time to contemplate the meaning of the Inner Self. Without a strong outer community for support, our inner pursuits are lacking. Money is a tool, a mechanism, and a measure of how we use our lives. In life, we have choices, but money by itself is morally neutral. Presently, and often, we use money to fulfill excessive desires. As the future advances, government and business enterprises will start using money as a service for the common good. When human ingenuity is rightly used, the definition of money will change. Humans will become its medium of exchange by promoting free enterprise and wealth creation through a focused method of localism and diversity that outweighs rigid targets and controls. When we misuse a form or an activity it is because we lack responsibility and are selfishly motivated. Take away greed and there is enough in the world to meet the needs of everyone.

When we use money equally, we will have a world society where common values and regulatory processes will make the necessary changes in governance, ethics and development in guiding the fundamentals of money. The lessons that we can learn from using money are: 1) human consciousness by choice creates its distresses and successes 2) when we see the form of money as a means to a greater understanding of consciousness, we will become weary and tired of the exploitation of the defenseless and of the growth of centralization of the power of money. When money is rightly organized, the extremes of riches, poverty, and selfishness will fade and a desired wider vision will grasp the right use of money. The meaning of money is coming together to make a community where all people dwell in concert for the common good. Compassion is money used wisely in human affairs. Money is worthy when it enriches peace and stability for all.

If we want to feel the wealth of the world, we must hold a wider vision for the right use of money.

## *Life is an Education of Sorts!*

Education is teaching a body of theoretical and applied research relating to instruction and learning in the preparation of life. The first criterion for learning is to understand where we came from and where we are going. How we got here is theory based. However, there is one certainty; we are a composition of matter and energy. Energy is what equals mass multiplied by the square of the velocity of light. Matter makes up all material things, occupies space, and is perceptible to the senses in some way. We could say that matter is dormant intelligence, activated when it encounters human awareness. Without perception and sense awareness, matter is inert. The various colors of the spectrum differentiate the elemental light, allowing the human eye to see what exists in space as objects. All life is conscious when we are conscious of its various levels through the senses. We feel this contact as power, wisdom, activity, harmony, discord, science, idealism, and order. From these expressions, the human race records its memories that result from cause and effect.

Idealistic minds and skilled scientists have said much about life, but with little purpose other than life being an education of the senses. Science has done little to lift the veil over the First Light of the Cosmos and the mysterious beginnings of life on earth. The more we try to penetrate through its vast levels, the more intense is the learning. Perhaps, somewhere along the way we will find that its mysterious ways lie in our own garden. Every molecule of the living body contains the germ of mortality in itself. It begins fading as soon as it is born so that its successor-molecule can pass on in its turn. Every part of the living being has some specific function in life and is a combination of such molecules. Through education, we transform the natural forces of life into feelings, will, thought, and conscious growth. Life and learning are everywhere and yet they are not permanent. We live and educate ourselves for decades only to find we have slept half of them away in the busyness of learning. However, life as an education becomes beneficial when we sense that space, time, cause and effects are but what we perceive within ourselves.

The cosmos is our university; it consumes itself to light the way. In time, it is like a good teacher who describes the way because it provides the lesson plans for being conscious of Cosmic Light.

## The World in its Many Different Ways

Should we punish and make people libel or should we help them overcome the need to be punished? Punishment is the practice of imposing something unpleasant or aversive onto a person in response to an unwanted or disobedient behavior. A conduct disorder may involve violations of the social norm, often with aggressive threats and destruction. These disorders occur on almost all levels of the social stratum: physical disability, substance abuse, learning or reading disabilities, motor skill disorders, mood/attention or stress related adjustment syndromes. Not only do individuals express such behavior, groups do also. There are abuses of power, of money, and the rules pertaining to the workings of society and its laws. At present, these disorders are ongoing in society.

There is a story of four blind men who were touching an elephant from various angles and describing it to each other. One thought it was a rope since he was holding its tail, the second thought it must be a fan because he was holding its ear. The third one said it felt like a curved stick because he was touching the tusk, and the fourth said it resembled a tree since he was holding a leg. The elephant, a metaphor for performance on how we perceive our surroundings, is similar to how we rationalize disobedient behavior. The causes of disobedience will remain until we learn to see the world and cosmos as our neighborhood and learn to share, to explore, and not to exploit. This world can be a joyous garden, a test, or a vale of tears according to how we conduct ourselves. We are all composites of the stuff of the cosmos. Therefore, it is in our best interest to be aware of that cosmic make up.

Because of our lack of transparency with the natural order of life, we tend to develop behavioral traits that are contrary to its order. As a spark of this order we are producing, evolving, and embodying the Cosmic Principle through the methods of attraction/repulsion and cyclic progress. When active intelligence utilizes the qualities of compassion and wisdom, eventually we will develop full self-consciousness that meets the needs of the indwelling thinker. In our struggles for strength and courage, in our laws to follow and faults to avoid, we will each forge the templates to bring out the best in us. Like the four blind men's differences in touch, we are confused about conduct disorders and our present way of dealing with the principles that apply to penalizing others. When we see the future as clear and bright for everyone, we will no longer need to impose something unpleasant in the human drama.

Like the air we breathe, our neighborhoods and world will be our nourishment from all that is. In our wisdom, we can learn to see the world in its many different ways. Our actions should never control or try to possess others or their things. When we overcome our ignorance, we project ourselves beyond our unlikable behaviors. When we view life as pure gifts of Grace, then there is no conflict. There is no contradiction or problem reconciling human beings to treat others with kindness, generosity, comfort, empathy and Goodwill toward the world and its differences.

The complexes that make us who we are direct our conduct in the world. Truthfulness in life and the conduct of the community reflect what resides in the hearts and minds of the citizens.

## The Human Ways of Life

Conflict is a mental struggle resulting from mismatched or opposing needs, drives, wishes, or external/internal demands as well as the opposition of persons or forces. Conflict, whether person or group orientated, is everywhere. Human action causes conflict and only human action can end conflict. If persisted upon, armed conflict shames us in alarming degrees due to the destruction not only of armies but also of civilians and infrastructure. Conflict acts against the need for durability of infrastructure and its sustainability. Conflict effects even the necessities of life, such as food, water, energy and the quality of air. History reflects the causes of conflict embedded in the people who want to keep the conflict itself alive due to personal interests. Politicians frequently magnify the importance of historical antagonisms for their own gain by playing to the long-standing fears and resentments among their constituents. In doing so, they hope to increase their own power and the appearance of legitimacy.

When we closely examine the substantive issues that create conflict such as unbalanced distribution of wealth and power, fear, hatred and other negative emotions, we begin to eradicate conflict from our daily actions. The purpose and solution is reconciliation through positivism. Addressing the underlying causes is time related; no single visionary can solve the complicated, overlapping, and enduring causes of any conflict in the short term. Nevertheless, there are things that we can do to alleviate the pressures of conflict. So, what can we do? We can address what takes place in our thinking. For example, we can address the values and assumptions that help us decide how we will respond to conflict.

We can urge others to stop confrontational approaches before they start within our social situations by setting the tone for how we will act and think in addressing the root causes. Once we move past the stage of sorting our petty nature and the core issues behind conflict, we come closer to territorial truth where two opposites can exist at the same time. As the architects of quantum theory imply, both the objective and thinking world can be one that is complex and simple at the same time. Another way of looking at it is, do we want to be right or do we want to be happy? There is not any one winner, only increased wisdom and awareness on all sides. When we use compassion, moderation, and humility in resolving issues, it lessens the need for rule and order and leads to a better understanding and receptiveness toward the world. All values are relative concerning the human ways of speaking and guiding behavior, each differs according to circumstances as to persons and cultures. When we step away from conflict we not only strengthen ourselves, we are also defending humanity.

The longer it takes us to get somewhere, the more appreciative we are when we do arrive. A firm heart and a solid conscience take us beyond conflict to values that make our conduct worthy for others to follow.

## *Dimensions of Being*

Whatever we do, say, or think in the physical world also penetrates the invisible world, or parallel universe. That universe becomes real only when consciousness anchors itself within that dimension. Once consciousness is within that dimension, its laws animate and govern, and the thinker awakens, either permanently or as a visitor. When in this earthly dimension, we can only be aware of that parallel universe by thinking about it through meditation, out of body or dream experiences, or perhaps the afterlife state. The afterlife state for the living becomes a memory field for those left behind on the physical world. It is very difficult to anchor oneself in two places at the same time and be aware of both simultaneously. However, some believe that such persons do exist and they are able to do so through out-of-body projection. In this state of awareness, the physical body becomes inert and the thinker separates from the physical and enters the realms of the emotions. In most cases, these higher realms are more vivid. If a person lacks proper training in those techniques, those realms can become addictive and can cause neurosis of the mind. If done selflessly, those experiences can be fulfilling as teaching methods. It is believed by some that the aforementioned realms become real only when a person is permanently anchored there. Until that happens to each of us, they are just realms of the imagination.

When we are awake, walking around in this consciousness, we are creating memories and forms in the parallels that do not exist to the physical eye. When we throw a stone into a body of water, the impact creates ripples that spread out, slowly disappearing as they move outward. Nevertheless, those undulations continue and become invisible to the eye. No matter where we go, we will be followed by our shadows, the invisible becoming the visible and vice versa. Repeatedly our creations enclose the state in which we find ourselves awake. Any image we make remains for the present to see and experience until the image disintegrates or dies. Eventually all persons, places and things pass into the Formless and wait there to be reconstituted by consciousness, as person, places, things and groups.

First imagination creates all things in existence, and then puts into form all persons and groups. Each creation is attractive or unattractive depending on one's magnetism and affiliation to the person or persons doing the creating. Attraction and repulsion, by degree, go through the same process regardless of the plane. Example, if consciousness finds itself enclosed on a world constituted from a gas body, consciousness will then enlace itself in a similar body made of its past memories, even the memories of societal experience. The laws that govern the mass of that world will guide consciousness. The birthing process would be according to that world's natural order. The concept of alternate universes is important to think about because it allows us to become more aware of the universe. If we expect others to set us free and think for us, if not similar to our own thinking, we will only be wrestling with a mixture of his/hers/ mine fixations. Our thoughts and aspirations draw us into the residues that are the recordings of persons, places and things in a time stream. These residues split off from a past event and progress in a different manner from the base time stream. Therefore, it is important that we stretch our own ideas and create our own dimensions of being.

In a mutually supporting awareness, endless levels of vibration and dimensions of inter-connectedness exist.

## The Burning Flow of the Ethereal River

When we come into this world, we tie ourselves to matter, time and space: our temporary nature. There is also another side to us, one that is permanent and made from the matter of Invisible Light. The life that flows into all forms (mineral, plant, animal, human) is an invisible substance that pervades space and serves as a medium for the transmission of light and other forms of radiant energy of the higher regions beyond the earth. This invisible energy shapes consciousness so it can permeate the higher (mind), middle (heart) and lower (body) level of human existence in order for a relationship between oneself and one's environment to take shape. Every person operates from one or a combination of these three parts of the self. Our behavior determines the nature by which we live life. By will we can ascend toward the higher or we can descend to the lower regions of action. When we are just witnesses, we are alert and observe what is happening inside or outside of ourselves. As a result, there is no judgment and no attachment as to how one should be in the world. Our awareness then becomes a reference point of pure insight and not an action state. When we become overly attached to the action state, we fall into the lower self and become earth bound. When we are earth bound there are limitations to this invisible substance. However, when we are in the higher regions of the mind, these restrictions are no longer there and a commonality occurs between the heart and mind with each assisting the other in universal truth and equality.

In this higher state, the will of mind, powerful and rational, is now void of restrictions of matter and space. When consciousness and rationality are free from the web of another's creation, the higher and middle parts can instantaneously create real places of refuge, real mountains and oceans, all from this Invisible substance. When we are free of the restrictions of matter, and in the reflective light, we are alive in a refined copy of the physical body, but much more alive, sensitive and dynamic. When we are awake in this light, we can capture the true memory of nature and our motives, desires, and impulses.

All of us are the products of the opportunities and limitations of our own daily living. How we grasp this source of conscious knowing is how our thoughts will make an impression upon our brains and provide us with the ideas on how to build from our earthly environment. Within all of us, there is this deep well of knowledge and wisdom. In the middle of family, friends and associates, and in the infinity of time, space and the surrounding universe, we stand before the fact of our own existence. From this vantage point, we attempt to find the meaning of our brief existence and all we can do is depend on our own insights. We are conscious as individuals when we travel through life believing that we are more than the body and that we have control over the circumstances of the visible. When we choose to live consciously with the Invisible and recognize we are a part of that

Burning Flow, we are living in the powers that create and re-create our lives: our very presence in this life and the one that is to follow.

When we connect our thoughts to the currents of the universe, we become a part of limitless space and betterment. The past, being our witness to the passing of time, awakens reality, stimulates memory and guides and improves our daily lives. When we view the passing of time as a record of memory, it can illuminate reality and vitalize the present.

## A Set of Feelings

The movement of the world and the springs that set it in motion are justified by our interest or indifference to its actions. Our motivations create attraction or revulsion to our actions. Interest is the power of attracting or holding one's attention due to a state of excitement. Whether good or bad, the objects and ideas presented to us are not important. Rather, it is our feelings that determine the fate of the object or idea. Interest is like the impression that sunlight and air have on a developing plant. If our impression to an idea is one of indifference, the idea withers, as does a plant in confined darkness. Therefore, it is important how we use our feelings concerning persons and things. When our interests are attracted to objects and desires that cause ill will to others, whether intentional or otherwise, they culminate in pain. Our study of the mind has shown that our consciousness acts from a sense of duality. Within us, fueling our complexes, there are two energies, positive and negative, that are at odds with each other. We should not resist our obsessions but focus on the good and so strengthen our clarity of mind and our ability to think clearly with that which we are involved.

Through the forces of the Invisible, the visible earth came into being. Unrestrained, all things come into being spontaneously, as the vital forces of husband and wife unite to produce children. Similarly, we do the same thing with our ideas to bring forth our necessities. From this commingling of ideas, we create the atmosphere of our nature. When we love the good, we will guard and nurture it all about us; if the reverse, we will fall victim to our own negative complexes. The forces of repulsion eventually destroy vise and the forces of attraction build virtue out of the destruction. Contemplate this language of duality. Center thoughts on goodness and the feelings of the heart will open the gates of the Invisible. When our interests and indifferent attitudes have been refined, they return simplicity to us. Our actions are then in accord with our thinking which identifies with our desirable qualities.

The myriad things that make up our differences and indifferent attitudes suit each of our own natures. They regulate the seasons of life and harmonize the elements that make up our existence. When we master our unconscious thoughts, we understand the dimensions of the Invisible. When we think correctly, the potencies of our actions drive activity by the power of thought. It is the duty of each life to train itself to be a creator by taking control and governing one's own destiny. By governing the potencies of thinking in terms of difference and interest with that which produces the objective form, we are working responsibly. Whatever name we give it in mind, it is all light of the Invisible. It is up to each of us to give it a consciousness. Nothing can stop the eventual success of growth; it is just a matter of time. Great things in the world do not determine who we are; it is the direction they take us that matters. When we believe in ourselves, we are never alone. Consciousness is always reminding us that deep inside we are valuable, worthy, trustful and sacred Infinite beings.

## *The Economy of Life*

When we think of economy, our minds turn to the human activity of production, distribution, consumption and the resourceful use of resources through the expenditure of money. For most people material wants come first, followed by our animal, intellectual, and ethical desires. While the body has wants that need material supply, the Inner Self has duties to fulfill and to harmonize those needs. The economy of society is not the satisfaction of appetites; rather it is the need for justice, peace and patience for both the inner and outer worlds. When we seek that inner independence first, then all the necessities of life will manifest. Any economy whether founded on an inner or outer belief cannot be understood until we understand where we came from and where we are going for betterment in the future. When we think of economy, we must include the makeup of our bodies. No component is ever lost; the storehouse of treasures preserves it in the planes that overshadow us. In our transformation, we are always picking up and enhancing extracts preserved there from our imprints. There is no doubt the individual aspect in economy is important, but acknowledging the inner treasures that exist in everyone everywhere is equally important in preserving the economics of life.

The Economy of Life, the material aspects that govern the scattering of atoms of matter and their dissociation from one another, covers a wide distribution in life. This association builds form and adapts it to vibration through group unity and spiraling movement. Each of us is a part of this process. Our wishes, hopes, and dreams move us to blend this economy with the aspirations of the heart and the totality of existence. Our true Essence abstracts and liberates form with the essential qualities of the heart in forward motion as association, unity and maturity of life, the geometry of the cosmos. All of this activity, from the molecule of a salt crystal to the temple of complex organisms of the human body, forms the structures of the great Cosmic Fire. To the thinker, the economy of life blended and focused becomes magic in motion through the elements of air, fire, water, and earth. When we use our power wisely and justly, we can move the different classes of 'quantum' realities hidden in the recesses of the mind to manipulate the economy aspect for the betterment of all and everything.

When we work through those various realities, we will eventually arrive at a place where the mind is not, matter is not, and all that is left is consciousness merged into the Ocean of Consciousness. We are all moving to a certain measure of vibration and progress at a certain speed as we act and react with environmental atoms. When we maintain the principles of economy, life survives as a harmonious system without the excesses of economics such as money, land and property. Through economy, we conserve and protect life and energy with proper care. The mind, having greater value than the body, has its own system of economy and balance concerning all that is on the inside. The mind and body must work together to give life purpose. Thus, each of us adds to the quota of the fire that is the economy of life.

Economy, when ruled by money, reveals another state of poverty, diminished light. Only when we attach ourselves to something larger than ourselves, do we arrive at our actuality.

## *Association through Knowledge*

Association is a connection with a body of people through interests and activities in society. It is a mental connection or relation between thoughts, feelings, ideas, and sensations remembered or imagined that link a person, object or idea. In chemistry, it is the combining of chemicals. In ecology, we signify association by a large number of organisms in a specific geographic area that make up a community with one or two dominant species. We gain knowledge through the association of authority, intuition, experimental inquiry, experimental methods, agreement, difference, uniformity of nature, and the plurality of causes.

Control and power come with understanding. The more we know about a person, place or thing, the more control we have over it, whether it is a human organism or modern technology. When we know our environment, our relationships and ourselves to the movements of the greater whole, the more knowledge we have. When we know our limitations, we know what we can do. Knowledge and association 1) work together in helping us form resemblances and 2) teach us to gather the truth about a phenomena or entity so we can control its influence over us. There are many different forms of knowledge such as reliable knowledge, knowledge in communicating, situated knowledge, partial knowledge, knowledge management, and knowledge of the spirit, etc. Names, association, and knowledge enable us to master our insights into persons and things. Often when we have been in contact with others, the things said and done continue to act on us, even at a distance, after physical contact has been severed, leaving a positive or negative influence.

It is through imagination/creativity that we become intelligent. Intelligence allows us to apply knowledge and mold it to that with which we are associated. The more we know about the characteristics that make up life, the more we are able to imitate its better aspects. This produces a strong association, even becoming that characteristic. This allows us to hold two opposing ideas without feeling anxiety. When a new idea comes up, the mixture of ideas allows the new idea not to be a compromise of the opposing ideas. Physical attraction, chemical uniformity, bodily health, mental sanity, emotional balance, and equality are various forms of the workings of the unity of all life. We are the One Totality in action, revealing its nature in and through its manifestations by degrees of growing together. Through our acts or variances of opinions, outlooks and kindred characteristics, our common bonds will link us into the patterns of the whole. As a part of society, we must come together in a unification of all its parts with the knowledge and association of each particular part. When we unify consciousness, we let go of the results of action and become free of negative causes. Attachments no longer fragment our desires and we become less bound to our work.

Learning breaks the chains of strangeness and sets us free to train our emotions, our minds, our customs, and conventions so that we utilize our associations and environment properly to meet any given circumstance.

## *When We Know Ourselves, We are Total and Natural*

Wrapped in the Invisible upon the darkness of space, we are the cause of our existence whether we choose to accept it or not accept it. We all awaken in time to the things our senses desire. As those things pass from the region of ideals (the future) to the region of memories (the past) that make up each of our experiences, the senses register the things in our present, similar to the sparks on the retina. The real person or thing is not what we see now, but is a composition of the sum of all its various and changing conditions in the material form. From the future eternities to past eternities, we move back and forth as the ocean tides do, dissolving (changing) the dark matter of space with awakened consciousness, reabsorbing the sum-total of existences. Through thought, will and feeling we manifest and enact in nature the meaning and purpose of awareness of the whole of existence.

As we move from darkness to Light we have Being in lesser and greater degrees of reality. We must search for the things we possess in that reality after they pass through the material world. As long as the sense instruments of material awareness are used, we cannot cognize an existence directly. Whatever plane our consciousness is acting on, the things belonging there are our only realties. As we rise in awareness and turn our faces toward the sun of wholeness, our shadows fall behind us. When we recognize something that is familiar that we gained through experience or association, most likely it is something we have already known and what has been set in memory.

We are intelligent when we have the ability to learn or understand new situations, and then successfully apply that knowledge. Knowledge, intelligence and memory become relevant when we apply them to a bigger purpose. Each of us is unique as evidenced by our DNA and fingerprints. Thus, it is reasonable to believe that each of us has a uniquely personal purpose and reason for being a part of the memory of totality: the organized array of individual elements and parts forming and working as an integrated whole. Many of us yearn to find the ideas that will give us meaning. Those ideas do not need to be revolutionary or stand out for others to see and know. All these ideas need to do is come from a commitment to be faithful and apply the best to whatever we do, even the most basic tasks. When we understand that our Intelligent Will is behind our existence, we begin to have faith in ourselves. For faith without will is like a boat without water. Perhaps with this in mind we can gain some idea of what is necessary to use will power properly to understand the naturalness that moves through us.

When we use our desires or aspirations unselfishly, the force that flows through us is universal in its character. With this attitude, we can have the strength to do what is before us. The way to success is the belief in our abilities, the advantage of knowing the rules, and strength of the lessons offered. Are they punishments or rewards? Those who know the way of Life and Self will never be at risk in the total and natural ebb and flow of change and circumstance.

A new truth does not win us over by convincing us that it is reality because Truth is something we grow into.

## Politics, Envy, Money, War and Redemption

In the political arena, words flow like a whistler whistling in the wind. Words glue themselves to the listener as short-lived promises, maddening the brain and will of the Spirit. Any sense of responsibility is similar to oil that is slick and shiny motivated by money and the best way to spend it. In our hearts, we know what is best for society: a sense of purpose, worth and security from fear and want. We are at the whim of the political arena concerning the important matters of equality, opportunity and financial power for every class. Often, however, we choose to accept the 'safety' of desires and fantasies of wealth, power, fame and love in its place. In crowds, we often glare at one another with hard competitive eyes, prancing around like crested cocks. Needing idols to look up to, we allow the wealthy to exert their power and we think it is marvelous.

All of us in one way or another are like rabbits trapped before the fierce yellow eye, the hypnotic stare, of a crouching tiger. Therefore, the past keeps coming back, the voices of the lost. The pain, the pride, the madness and despair, the billions of faces of the buried life fill our streets and homes, again to wonder why, in the darkness of unredeemable wrong. For now, this is the way of the earth: to know pain, death and moments of joy. All must walk in the wilderness upon the savage land where the blood of everyone runs down into the earth without any answers. In this immense land, there is only growth, ripeness, and pollution. We empty the forests and deserts with the heartless silver jingle of a million tongues crying for honey, "This will be mine". With weariness and indifference, words echo forth, and we hold out our hands filling them with dry dust and ashes.

When we go upward in consciousness, we touch the Spirit of Immortality. When we live in the Spirit of the earth, we experience our mortality. Earth, the place to which memory returns repeatedly to live and grasp affections, evolves through each of us and draws out the subtle and gross habits that lay buried in the human warehouse of the psyche. From the centuries of plenty and starvation the poor and wealthy grasp their opportunities memorized with time and money. The memory of all of us, as the centuries roll by, will play the part of 'have and have not'. Consciousness will touch all that is powerful, ugly and beautiful in the enormous works and movements of the earth. At anytime, we are what we are and we remain powerless to do anything about it except move with the earth and its rhythms in the Great Sea of matter. Eventually, ruminant and lost, our habits will begin to bore us. We will reach out for something newer and more powerful than the earth can offer. Suddenly, at water's edge stands the likeness of our True Selves.

The landscape of time is a reflection of our lives. We create myths and concepts to understand ourselves. Sketched from conflict, pain, love and the million faces and words of the sunny and dark, we paint our visions. Sacred, fabulous and dreamlike, the apotheosis of our design is clothed in fresh, glorious light. We turn our eyes upon the image and look full in its wonderful face. We seek forgiveness from our imaginations and the things of the earth grow strangely dim.

Let the mind begin a new journey. Leave the thoughts of fear and wanting behind. Do not lose Inner peace for the short-lived things of the earth. Let the Soul go where it has never lived before. We are all here to give the earth purpose through us and to enable the earth to live more fully in the greater universe.

## A Constant State of Being Intimate

Everyone has a personal definition of what being intimate means to him or her. Some of the things we expect in a relationship are love, intimacy, communication, commitment, equality, respect, compatibility and companionship. Each aspect has a unique meaning to different individuals. The most important form of intimacy for society may be the couple relationship. It is the basis of family, the place where most of us learn about adult love, about negotiation, how to change and how to compromise, and it is often an economic unit. Emotional and mental intimacy occurs when there is a sense and meaning to the relationship of heart to mind. For example, when a couple shares similar morals, values and ethics with others, the future becomes inclusive in both the short term and the long term. Before we can obtain total intimacy, the struggle for identification must be resolved. First, each of us sees, hears, feels, and tastes everything from within. Thus, we learn to know who we are as individuals in the totality before we come together as a common entity. From that point, it is possible for 'you and I to become we'. As a family, all things band together, have a common source, and are similar. Mind and emotions are the recorders of memory and give purpose to the sense of intimacy.

To see clearly one must peer beyond the normal view, which is to look at the shades of darkness and light that surround every object. Whenever one is feeling intimate, learn to feel the energy within as it flows through the skin and nerves. The electric fire of life is what sets the mood for any relationship. Fire is what fashions our dreams and brings them into living matter for expression. This Fire is not the earthy fire, the kind that warms or burns. Rather, it is the Intimate Fire of the heart, the Essence that animates every human to live and move. On all dimensions, this Fire of being is in everything, animate or inanimate. Scientists know it as the tiniest of atoms and particles, to the grandest stars, planets and suns. Imagine this Essence as Omnipotent. Imagine the delight we will feel when that Essence suddenly caresses us. Imagine the feelings and contentment of it becoming each of us, as Omniscient Knowing. Imagine how it will feel to see truthfully. Being intimate is the foundation upon which humanity builds its dreams. Human desires that are not balanced are shadows that fade out when reasoning begins to rule the mind. When flashes of passion do come, think of them as happiness caressing our thoughts with right action; then we will be thinking with the true mind. We will feel whole and unexplainable to those that know us. However, our kind, deep within, will feel these awakenings in us and they will dream with us in a garden of intimacy cultivating Joy. Change, money, race, or dominance has no meaning; they hold no power in this imaginative world. Keep the heart and mind on greener thoughts and as we fulfill each other's wants and needs, we will find things spinning calmly in control.

If we are not at home in ourselves, we cannot invite others in.

## *To Blend is to Create the Story of Life*

When we blend correctly, we are bringing all components of life together completely. Changes are always occurring in human action whether those components are human, chemical, atomic or biological. In human nature, blending is an ongoing process and it encompasses all things that live and move on the earth. Without blending, identification of substance and sustenance would be inhospitable and without meaning. Our concepts and myths of gods, creation and humanity mix in the storytelling of life. Oral and recorded histories express the desire to please something that is beyond humanism. We are always trying to pierce the veil of the Invisible with our insights. We think we are separate from the matter that is all around us as our finite minds indicate, but in reality, we take our nourishment from matter. Settlements, conquests, governments, religions, caste systems, agriculture, technologies and other innovations of life have all come from the past and now reflect our present. We are all becoming intimately familiar with the 'melting pot' way of life. We are a world of immigrants and we began with a blending of cultures. Over the millenniums, we have kept adding to the mixture. Everyone who is born to this world adds something to it. Although there have been struggles along the way, and a lot of angling for control of the story, overall we are doing 'all right'. The most beneficial contributions to society will come when we voluntarily live side by side with other systems of thoughts and endeavors and share the same end goals. Accepting the beauty of the ideas of others does not mean the end of one's own views. It is merely making the world as a whole a more beautiful place. It is a place of mind where the sheer presence of being and its manifold presence experience action and exploration on all levels of creation. When we engage in dialogue and act responsibly toward others, we can then balance the claims of the inner life and outer life with the personal, cultural and planetary life.

The presence of totality, the One Reality, works through our being in a phenomenal, subtle, intermediate, spiritual, situational, immanent and transcendent way of self-inquiry. We each have our own relationship with Being at this time and place. The authority of that knowing is in each of us. We can posture, gesture, move, breathe, and sound out the energies of that embodiment by exploring, expressing, and participating with others and simultaneously be enlivened. Based on our collective worth in blending our creative lives, we form and make our world a better place. Imagine a world built on individuals who consciously activate self-responsibility. Life comes prior to the meaning of it, and we must live life first before we know the why of it. The laws of creation do not determine our lives, living the story does. The only instrument that can take us beyond the five senses is the mind. Only by declaring, "I am It" and holding to the mind can we move beyond height, width, and depth to where time and space blend completely. Only by being true to one's own mind and being faithful to self-discovery can we blend our individual stories with the Greater Story.

When we plant an acorn, it brings forth an oak, not a pine tree. Therefore, whatever thought or idea we sow and nurture, that idea comes forth.

## *Lightness of Being*

We know or derive phenomenal occurrences through the senses rather than through the mind. We experience multi-dimensional reality in various ways. However, we do not always remember those dimensions. By evoking the senses through memory, imagination, and visualization, we can have a sensory interaction with our environment that enhances the experience; this can be physical or non-physical. We do this by remembering the past, by being in the present moment, and by visualizing the future. All three can exist in 'the now'. Seeing, touching, tasting, hearing, smelling, knowing and signaling are the complex physiological methods of perception. The senses operate by using the organs and cells of the body continuously and act as a system of communication. Thus, through our physical bodies, we interact with the world of materiality.

On a level of pure energy, subtle realities saturate the physical world. When we sense these energetic levels of existence, it seems probable that we also have a body of energy with its own structure tuned to this finer interlaced force. Until death, this echo of the physical form works in conjunction with our physical bodies. After death, it can exist for the imagination as mental/emotional memory: the refined portion of our being. Most persons do not see subtle reality the same way. Our brains are used to processing data through the senses. When we perceive something that is distinctly non-physical, we have to select the sense that relates to it in order to understand it. We have to know what we are looking for in order to see clearly. Physical and non-physical seeing depends on the strength of the tools the user employs and his/her ability to perceive accurately. When one studies something as vastly complex as life, it is difficult to see the whole picture, and it is a mistake to think that one opinion is a fixed analysis of the whole. What do we see when we see a face, or a scene, and how do we describe its makeup? Is it from our own Inner Lightness or from that of another? We are always looking from our own particulars of being.

Lying between two extremes in time, space or degree are mortality and immortality, the intermediate, the stuff of individuals and the cosmos. Is there an intermediate state of existence after human life? If we agree with the idea, "I think, therefore I am," we could say yes! Science has taught us a great deal about the functioning of our physical bodies. However, no one has been able to see our thoughts/memories and where they go after we are no longer visible to those left behind. All we can really accept, now, is hope in things Invisible. We are more than our cells, and our mental acuity is more than brain matter. When we view the situations in life as desirable, we can see the means of the transitions of today and what lies in the future. Through self-examination, we can replace fear with confidence, moderation and common sense. This knowing supports the belief that we exist by degrees of conscious awareness in the remarkable Lightness of Being.

An aware person knows that seeing is a two-way path from darkness to Light or from Light to darkness and knows the same is true for the Inner and outer life.

## The Sacred Matters of Life

The sacred matters of life at deeper levels are personal and unique to the individual. Their ways of expression are as numerous as there are minds to contain them. In the final analysis, the relevance of such matters leads to a broader singular awareness for the individual since no two people ever witness the same revelation. Yet, we are all human beings seeking and aspiring toward lives that have meaning and value. Each of us views life from a different perspective based on individual values regarding our own existence, that of humanity and the universe. We live in a vitally connected world that involves moment-to-moment adjustments to suit the moods of our seasons, storms and behaviors. The values we hold are the fundamental building blocks on which we view our experiences, the world, and the elements of our continuation.

The energy and force behind creation are similar to the impartial winds that blow over the surface of the earth or the shade of a tree. Neither are concerned with who is in their presence. This power exists to treat everyone equally and our task is to figure out how to use its nature. When the earth turns, the billions who have departed as particles turn with it. The seas and mountains wither and deserts are flooded. The races march toward extinction, but the great rhythms of the earth remain. In majestic procession, the seasons pass returning forever on the land – new crops, new races, new harvests and new gods. We are the city, the continents, the world, and the distant soaring ranges of nature. What occurs when we pass out of the mixture of darkness and light? Are we still aware? As the ocean is not aware of the raindrops that fall in it, the world does not remember except what we put back into it.

In the final moments of our Silence, when all things on earth, the thousands of images of life, pass as visions of the personal matters of living, it is not difficult to imagine that all shapes and thoughts race back to their proper place. The sounds and sights of the senses take hold and are set in motion; we embrace them again. In the personal, the vital forces, the sensations, the mind, and the intellect still move and live in humanity and the universe.

The big question is, "What form will they take in the remembrance of persons, places and things?" Conceivably, we are all just atoms rotating and changing into ideas, ideas more vast than our capacity to create! Seeping into our consciousness slowly, our beliefs swirl around as patterns built on the foundation of living and creating in unnumbered time. What we shall do and what our future will be in the substance and Essence we can answer only on a personal level regarding the sacred matters of life.

We cannot measure life by where we want to be, but how we act to get there, moment by moment.

## *A Combination of Circumstances*

The general state of things, the combination of circumstances at a given time, is set in motion by how we think, act, and respond to each other. Cooperation, understanding and right responsibility in our situational dealings give meaning for every new social condition. Every moment in our existence challenges us with situations that either give meaning to life or devalue it. Even our dreams confront us with situations. Different situations require an assortment of styles that will direct life to be flexible enough to guide us in problem solving in work, play and at home. When we are flexible with others, we can overcome any situation no matter how stressful or menial it may be.

The world situation needs greater knowledge concerning the prospects and preparation of our future. It is important that integration with the value system of the individual and the value system prevailing in societal situations is an ongoing process of compromise in the patterning of society. What we commonly refer to as culture cannot be limited to what we call a personality. The personality is a one-person interchange from the combination of ideas in the social system that the ego generalizes from the many. A social system does not have an independent source of motivation of its own; its drive comes from the many. We tend to select the particular elements from the available cultural patterns that become a part of our orientation system. A healthy outlook should allow us to change our behavior patterns positively with those of other cultural patterns.

It is our individual responsibility to know ourselves. As to others, their side needs to be unfolded also. On all sides, there can only be increased wisdom and awareness. When we understand others, we are aware of their viewpoints and the effects both sides have on the surrounding field that we observe. Connections pertaining to any situation are both personal and not personal. Therefore, when we use cooperation in dealing with such matters that confront us individually and socially, we are lessening the negative foibles of the world. None of us can be separate from the world because we are always responding to it with our minds. How we resonate with the world discloses it in a particular way. We are always moving from one mood to another. We cannot stop a type of mood; all we can do is transform it into another one. As human beings, we are always responding to the world through our emotions. However, when we reflect on our emotions, we can see things in a new way. We disclose the potential of our being through understanding and that shows us our capabilities. How we relate to others reflects our own personhood. We draw parallels to things like energy and mass as well as time and space. We are all creating a space between one another, and it is in this space that we have true dialogue with one another. When we release our self-reserve and reach out with wholeness, we reflect the circumstances that are going on within us.

The world is a massive place of circumstance and time where sometimes a seemingly petty chance gives life a greater tinge. When we look carefully at the trifles of daily life, the common things that seem to go unnoticed can be the mainsprings of circumstance.

## What We See, Think, and Come to Know

What we see, think and come to know remains within ourselves. The mind controls this knowing and is present throughout the universe. Our impulses, through magnetism, love and desire of the male and female form, manifest and unify the personality with living essence. A calming of self, the All, is mind. It sees its own light and real meaning and everything becomes a miracle in the force of growth. The universe sees us equally. We are already enlightened when we serve others in this intertwined creation. We began in this force, grow in the mental, and manifest in the material. In our patience, we learn to see ourselves, to measure and test our ideals, to use faith and seek understanding. In this understanding, we change our patterns, restructure our lives and behavior, and become more loving, giving, kinder and gentler in the rhythm, ebb and flow of nature's way and its duality. Time does not exist when we become still and know that we are this Energy. When we create order in our lives, we move forward step by step in assimilating the energy immanent in the world and in the individual. We see and know the future of our reality. Each experience assumes its ancient obligation and comes out of negative situations into a newer and stronger beginning. We take full charge of that which is our duty and let go of that which is not. We respect our internal values and find our own point of balance.

Initially, we project our inward ideas into nature, the reality from which our sense of mind shapes the elements into form that give meaning to our existence. In the objective world, individuals are ends in themselves. However, nature gives the individual real existence. We concretize this knowing in our desires and ideals represented by imagination. No matter what form the imaginary object takes, we derive our happiness from human society. In the material sense, we have no regrets when we obtain our happiness through a balanced economical order. However, at some time we must reach for a higher degree of realization.

In human relations, if given enough opportunity, people answer their own questions. The only real control we ever have and need is within. The right to one's own space is an aspect of free will. Each person is free to make career decisions, decide what belief systems one feels comfortable with, and to create the life that will allow one to fulfill his/her imagination. The fundamental methods of growth that make up the universe are evolving. Our expansion of consciousness affects that growth because of our awareness in it. At the end of life, internal aspects, not the physical ones, determine our type of perception. Regardless of beliefs, the Universe of Mind is moving from the indistinct to the distinct. The successive movement of negative and positive action creates the two forces in people and nature that influence our behavior and destiny. We all build our being on these two principles. Above us is the universe, in the middle is humanity, the inner and outer person(s), and below is the earth. From this, we derive the means for our communication. It is from the nature of all things that we fulfill our individual nature. Life is an unfilled container that we use, but we can never fill it totally with the Infinite Source of life. No one knows where the Source of All comes from. The space between the Source and earth is like a blowing wind; its patterns differ but not its form. The more we understand this space, the more it conveys what we see, think and know.

Myriad sparks come from One Flame forming infinity of beings that live, move and have existence in order to return to the Flame.

## *Thoughts are Transcendent*

Thoughts are as much a part of nature as the blood that courses through our veins, which we derive from the elements of the food that comes from the soil. We could call it ecological sustenance. We are all a part of this landscape of thought. Thoughts are the same as seeds planted in the ground. Seeds grow from the soil. Thoughts are lodged in the vital air of our planet's energy field, pass into the brain, and come out as the things we think. Our mental processes allow us to model the world according to our goals, plans, ends and desires. Words and concepts such as cognition, sentience, consciousness, ideas, and imagination can help us go beyond the material universe to gain experience and knowledge of what is outside of the ordinary range of perception. The physical circumstances that produce these mental constructs are representative of the whole community's thoughts and are the best tools for the advancement of our own thoughts.

The earth is a vast intelligence disk. Everything we do, say, think and create is stored on that disk, the electro-magnetic field that surrounds the earth. Thoughts travel with us on our personal journey through time and space. In the material world, they remain in the comfort zone of the head. Unless we are telepathic, these thoughts are of little use until we record them. All the elements of nature work together, and our minds and bodies make use and profit from these elements in their endless circulation of magnetism.

The natural laws are Inviolable and Serene. We can reform nature but only through the redemption of our thoughts. Love is more powerful than any perception. Therefore, in things transcendent, we build our own world. As the world moves and expands with the universe, so will humans. Nature and humans are vital to one another; it is doubtful whether nature and humans can separate permanently from each other. It is through thinking that we remember the things of nature as awareness, and awareness is indicative of our Transcendence. We must remember whatever we destroy in nature we also destroy within us if we do not think positively. Whenever we serve nature's ends, we serve our Life. With awareness and understanding, we create forms, whether they are physical, emotional or mental. It is through subjective conditions that knowledge takes place.

Our relationship to objects is what directs our thoughts toward them. We should think about nature in the same way we think of our loved ones. In our creative pursuits, we must adapt to using its elements wisely for our experiences. The forms in the time concept of the present are the result of developed characteristics latent in the seeds of past thoughts. These forms exist according to the traits dormant in nature and in our perceptions of the consciousness of the dimension(s) beyond our physical one. These thoughts include aspects of earth for us to place in memory. The process of thought is necessary for the Light of Creation to sustain our minds just as we need physical space for physical light to give us our ecological sustenance.

A thought comes first, and then words to describe it. A word never comes before a thought; everything comes afterward.

## A Moment of Cosmic Arousal

Our minds are similar to the Hubble space telescope, an earth-orbiting optical telescope that produces stunning images and observations of space. Time and space as well as light, mass, and energy lock us in concepts as thinking beings. We are but reflections of those attributes. As physical beings, our bodies encapsulate the elements of dark matter that do not visibly radiate and are not observable in or outside of us. This matter is what holds space together and constitutes most of the universe's mass. The Light of Creation skips across its cold dark surface enabling us to see, think, and differentiate between objects. As our mental acuity grows, so will our physical technology. This will occur at some point in the future when we realize our sustainability and the earth is in balance with human needs and wants. We will peer into the vastness of space with our inventions and see the beauty that spontaneously gives us existence. Until that moment arrives, we are just collectors of concepts and theories.

Space is just an enormous house built by our own thinking, just like the houses we build for our comfort. Distinct and unclear at times, this co-mingling of matter and Light is our journey. Caught in the attractiveness of its ebb and flow, we seem helpless in its grasp, which is nothing more than erroneous thinking. This spontaneity did not occur only to end in darkness someday. Space and time are but shadows of the greater reflections that are the impulses behind growth. Nothing in nature or Heaven can stop the progress of awareness on its long journey from darkness to light. Not ignorance, not even death can keep this Greater Light from manifesting in our consciousness. There are no powers on earth that can prevent this inflow. Thoughts and ideas are evolving within each of us and our increasing responsibility for one another will allow us to enter a new era in scientific unfoldment. New discoveries will release new energies with a far-reaching effect that will allow us to penetrate that momentous happening that gave us darkness and Light. This manifestation is the vehicle of thought and will. Along with it are the hosts of human beings who are the intelligent forces that act with nature to enact its laws. At the same time, these hosts are also acting according to the laws imposed upon them by this manifestation in bringing forth the structuring of society and its ways. This large energy field surrounds and influences all things. It is composed of thought energy coming from individuals in a space and time field.

Due to unity of thought, all visible matter sustains a body of expression whether it is an atom, man or solar system. Space and matter have one subject, one goal, and one concept brought about by the Will to live, move and have being. This one moment of cosmic arousal gave us our being. In its infancy, this ongoing surge of energy remains and brings forth information that forms our world intelligence. We cannot discover the secrets of life without the human Spirit arousing the prepared mind. When one feels the awakening in the mind, emotions and body, it is unforgettable.

Our world circulates and turns out stories that have no ending.

## The Thinking and Feeling Dimensions

Our future is our knowledge, our source, and all of us are moving toward it. The rivers, oceans, the earth, the sun, the moon and all of the other planets from the smallest of particles in the expansion of the universe are moving with this Infinite Knowledge. This Infinite Knowledge is the force of our intellect reflecting on various levels in all humans. It is the cause of the progressive development of the world. When we think about this Higher Power by setting higher goals for ourselves, it allows us to discern what is right and best for human life. Infinite Knowledge shapes the mind and disposition to use nature's resources judicially so that consciousness forgoes its excesses. We witness the future in our imagination. Beyond the certainties of this life and probabilities of our faith, we have the wonders of our thoughts. What we prepare the future for is what we will get. The future is waiting to tell a great story, all we need do is listen.

The 'I am' is what forces us to climb out of our external awareness into the internal unity of 'we'. This thinking and feeling dimension interacts with and effects plants, humans, animals and other life forms in the environment. From this nurturing of nature, we form a complex blend that excites or inhibits our reactions. This dimensional loop of thinking and feeling relationships influences and forces our mental nature to process and make sense of the world's past memories with our present dreams, goals and visions. This generates an array of opportunities for a better future. Humanity will continue to preserve and succeed in adding to the understanding of the environment and beyond. When we abandon our preconceived prejudices through science and technology, the outer world will balance with the inner.

We are all aroused in one way or another by this life-giving source of energy every second of our lives. The more we become aware of this energy and force, the more knowledge we gain of our intimate selves, the fountain of our being. In order to be aware of the interplay with cosmic forces, we must be in rhythm with them. Through experiences of the physical, emotional, and mental states, we come to understand that our entire nature is an atomic factory constantly rebuilding and transforming our memories into thought energy that gradually awakens. Every atom of our physical body contains enormous energy. When we understand this energy, as ourselves, we can control its influence in positive ways. The extraordinary phenomena that occur in the universe can then align its power with our everyday needs and uses. Our bodies are the sacred rivers that we swim in, a veritable microcosm, an exact copy of the entire universe. In all the places we have visited in this vast ocean of atoms, none is more beautiful than the reality we are in right now.

Our duty is to the earth and to each other, like the sun and moon that shine and watch over nature. We are similar: the mountains akin to our bones, the wind to our breath, the rivers to our blood, fire to our liquids and in thunder and lightning our thinking and feeling!

When we connect with nature, our senses become more orderly; we are soothed and healed.

## The Space In-Between

We are awake as Consciousness. The space between an object and us is the reflection that gives meaning to our thinking and being. The pulsating grandeur of the cosmos, its solar systems, galaxies, supernovas and dark matter, creates the external light waves that keep us dreaming and awakening. The creation of fire and the Fire of Creation guide and guard our mortality of being and our Immortality. Through our scientific endeavors and cognitive assimilation of energy and force, the elements of creation, we are slowly awakening to greater observations: the arena of the mind. Clarification will lead us on to greater understandings. The goal of discovering the Source of our beginning is a worthy task. However, the mind slowly adjusts to such realizations the same way that a baby slowly adjusts its eyes to light and objects. Clarification of visual forms begins in the womb and integrates as molecular and biological patterns that make up the form that is to enter physical life. Once this body form is independent of the womb, the oxygenation of life begins with the earth's magnetic field that is the training ground of a young mind's conscience.

Much like a baby, we reach out to the Light that contains us. Even if we should ever arrive at how creation started, would the brightness of that Awareness identify with that infantile beginning? Would one want to go back, identify itself as a baby, and follow it through all its foibles? In truth, our beginning is our only real creation. Anything beyond that is just scientific theory, cosmological theory and other stimulants for growth and mental acuity.

In reality, we are all on the journey of aesthetics. We are searching and reaching out to the beauty of Infinity in ways that will awaken our sensitivity to Life. It is something we likely have always carried and are seeking to encounter the latent potentiality that is a part of our selves. Whatever our modes of being, we think in ways that seem important to us: first as individuals, then for others. When we focus on the space in-between, we see shadows first, and then we gain the ability to see deeply into those shadows that become brighter moments. The images that we see are at first small and variegated in size and those encounters often puzzle us. When life articulates something to us as the search for the Source does, it contains psychological cues on what it has done to us and what we are doing to Life. We are the receptacles for the cosmos and through its connection with us - it expands. The seminal factor of creation and its eternity of processions are the concrete occasions that give meaning to our perceptions that we see within creation. This brings about a process of mutual action and reaction between its Essence and the individuals that compose creation.

We are in a process of manifesting our Spiritual Essence. When achieved, it will be the end of the cosmic process for the observer and the beginning of another cosmic process. The cosmic process through scientific insight is equipping the human being to view its unceasing motion as Knowledge and Wisdom of the space in-between. The space in-between is not visible to the naked eye, and when viewed through a telescope, we see only our backyard, our celestial neighborhood. This vastness of space holds a variety of gardens tinted with colors not yet ready for the human eye to view. This Invisibility is there to see when the heart/mind has achieved Unity.

## *The Essence of Relationships*

Imagine you are in a space void of the physical body. In this space, you are conscious of the Self and are aware of your existence. You have a circumferential vision that encompasses boundless freedom and feeling. Imagine yourself standing on an effulgent wave of liquid transparency. In this state, you feel the wave moving you as a boat moves upon the ocean. There is no height, length, width or breadth in your awareness. You feel whole in this space. Without want or need you gaze into this Clarity and witness a kaleidoscope of images that were the persons, places and things that you experienced and with whom you had relationships. From that vision, all you can feel is Compassion. There is no remorse, no judgment and no fear. You are selecting and processing the foibles and strengths of what has been. As this Truth rolls you forward, you see the causes and effects due to past decisions and how they are to be resolved in your consciousness.

In form life, our relationships are rarely as forgiving as is this space. In open thinking and working with relationships, we will find these connections both subtle and complex due to solidified matter that makes up our biological physical nature(s), such as cellular regeneration and hormonal changes. Because of the accumulated experience of countless ages, matter is Eternal, without beginning and end. When we act without examining the effects first, complex situations will arise because of our lack of forethought. When we believe we have a personal Inner Life that is uniquely our own, understanding the distinctions between the thoughts that produce the act will certainly mitigate the effects. When we identify many causes of an effect, the main cause is more important than the contributory causes. Understanding the distinction between the main cause and the less important causes can be vital in planning one's life. How can we tell what is the proper action to take? When relationships and experiences are stress-less and free of conflict, our Inner Essence is online with the Invisible. The contributory causes eventually fade and life becomes clean and clear. Remember, an immediate cause is easy to recognize, such as, a response from a person, or thing. A remote cause is more difficult, especially one that has taken place in the past or is yet to occur in the future. Be somewhat farsighted in dealing with persons, places and things. We err in thinking when we assume that one event must immediately cause another just because the event occurred.

When analyzing cause and effect, we should be aware that event one will produce event two and equates a chronological cycle with causality in a time and place that meets with opportunity. The question to ask the self is, "Do I want my actions and experiences to encompass a positive place of freedom and feeling, or one that is restricted and remorseful?" Cause-and-effect reasoning aids us in seeing why things have happened or will happen. This reasoning can link us to things of higher or lower value in what happens first and what will happen next. Change is everywhere; it occurred in the past and will occur in the future in the Essence of relationships.

History is a reflection of a right or wrong action that has occurred in a relationship!

## The Twofold Perspective

Human nature has a double character and behaves in two very different ways, as do energy and matter. The perspective is that the universe is an arrangement of binary oppositions: Spirit and body, Good and evil, male and female, Creator and created. There is also the mind and body, in addition to emotion and thought, that give us a double view of what is around us. Our surroundings are composed of the laws of the universe and are ever-present. These laws exist in our relationships as awareness, communication and experience.

Through the currents of motion, energy and matter, our actions bring persons, places and things into being. From a two-fold character we create similarities for no two details are alike. Through the art of light and color, we bring about change in our physical, emotional and mental makeup. This creates a common ground in which we review and resolve differences from past periods. Consciousness expands: the past, present and future enlarge to reveal the needs of the universe in a continuous and endless process of creation through cycles. Whatever rises will fall, and whatever falls shall rise again. On the physical plane, we view destiny through the confinement of matter and energy. Everything from an atom to a human being subordinates to this energy force.

Each life assumes its ancient obligation and comes out of positive or negative situations into a newer and stronger beginning when we take full charge of that which is our duty and let go of that which is not. As we progress, our internal values help us find our own point of balance. Everything circles around, rising and falling, always manifesting again in time through rhythmic compensation. We observe these processes in the continuous cycles of life, death, and the rebirth of all things. This rhythm is seen in the growth and decline of governments and nations, and in the constant creation and destruction of suns, worlds, and galaxies. Rhythm perpetuates the phenomenon of the Energy of Time.

Solar evolution is the sum total of all the lesser activities and is the interplay of the suns from the material aspect and from the consciousness aspect. Every living thing in existence has this duality. Through this knowledge, we change and bring about new forms for this medium to express itself.

The conscious act of a person is to create through every thought, word and deed the ability to be the reflection of this solar innateness. The ability to communicate determines the nature of the material world. The physical plane anchors life so that every aspect of bodily life subordinates to the whims of matter and energy. For certain life forms, it is a conscious endeavor. For others, it is subconscious and instinctual. Everything shaped from the earth originates out of an idea. Over time, an idea takes root in the mind and passes on to other minds through communication. A two-fold perspective shapes and makes ideas into different forms from rock tools to the present day computers for humans to use.

In matter, we measure humans as having a two-fold origin of the sexes, out of which the human race reconstitutes itself.

## The Constitution of Comfort

Comfort is the absence of disturbing, painful, or distressing features and is a relaxed and balanced attitude where one feels perfectly at home or at ease.

What are our needs and are they based solely on social, economic and political security? For life to be right, we need comfort in our lives. In order for us to identify those features that compose a comfortable life, we need to look at our cosmic place and the laws that produce those events including the natural and moral principles that apply to beings and things. Having a plentiful supply of material goods and money is not always a sign of great intelligence. We should not understand wealth solely as material assets that become ends to themselves. Knowledge, Friendship and Love, the non-tangibles of life, are equally important. When we form our desires from the wholeness aspect, we are putting an end to the qualities of the limited mind. Universal Freedom is the highest good; it is the meaning of all existence and pursuits. Nevertheless, we are constrained by a body and mind. We must pay attention to what we need to do to meet those needs. The physical body has its needs and the mind has its intellectual and emotional needs. The barest minimum is food and clothing followed by shelter, health, security, social organizational systems, and governmental administration. We must accept all of these necessities into the constitution of Consciousness. We must obtain these essentials in such a way that it is not detrimental to the needs of others and the well-being of the world.

The perception of beauty and the excitement that it produces in the individual is important in the development of both body and mind. When it comes to material comfort, the pleasure of physical ease and desire are not abstained. Love and sexual enjoyment fuel our comfort zone as well. These imagined and realized joys stimulate us to be artistic and aesthetic and exert influential power on the mind regarding our security needs. As we rise in consciousness, the Rule of Life calls for a proper adjustment of the parts to the whole in balancing the features of wealth and desire.

Physical gravitation, chemical coherence, physiological health, mental sanity, emotional balance, and logical consistency hold the workings of life together. When we transfer consciousness from a lower expression into a higher one, we are removing obstacles and preparing the mind to practice new methods that will cause the creative law to move us forward. We enjoy a sense of individuality because Consciousness is responsible for the creation of new causes. The quality of life (political solidarity, social peace, happiness, wealth and desire) depends on the Law of Unity. A harmonious blending of duty is essential to each of us in the wholeness of life. How the forms are created and held together by desire (the basic cause for physical, emotional and mental vitality) constitute our comfort.

The Law of Harmony holds everything in life together. The recognition of this law produces Unity and affection equally.

## *In a Ray of Light*

What are the laws by which we live? The first would be to feel affection for all living things followed by responsibility in using material elements. From this, our minds make the world what it is, and our thoughts make things beautiful or ugly. We lift ourselves into the right light by placing the burden in our own hands. The attributes of feeling, strength, and vitality mold our intellect with Spirit. The moment we realize that Spirit is the temple of the body we have become free. When others need help, we must be there. We must see Truth in our ideals and uphold them by listening to our own Inner Voice. With faith and truth, we have the power to make everything possible by the Inherent Knowledge within. We express the differences in this world by degree. In truth, we are but a fragment of Oneness. The laws of cosmic life bury themselves in the soil of life and take their strength from the elements of life. We bathe in its light and its elements flow through our veins, as the rivers flow to the ocean, becoming our cosmic life stream. Our bodies are the intertwining tissues of Fire and Light. The state of our consciousness determines the strength of this Essence.

In the silence of a clear mind, one can hear the soft whispers of that Essence, the calling of Life, and the projections of our designs. The order of the universe is in this calling: of the parts repeating the whole. Equally, the universe is a model of us. When we rely more on Spirit and less on matter, we are using intuition intelligently. We become less individualized as we replace our atoms in the infinity of a different time continuum. In time, we will become Waves of Light observing our existence and destiny. From the past and present, and in the future civilizations to come, we will live in the history of our earth until we begin to see everything from the Spirit within.

In the still drone of time, exquisitely minute, from the eye of ambition, this landscape lives and moves: prairie, woodland, seas and mountains, beautiful as the flowers that blossom. Man-woman molded and clothed by this land of delight arose. Who are they that flow like honey over this sensuous smelling panorama? Thirst unquenchable, earth, fire and water consume races that fall like autumn leaves. Still not knowing how it all came to be, this milieu beholds all that has been the fate of you and me. Lighting up the night, Sirius, Orion, and Pleiades, marvels of Light you are. One of many pinpoints in an Ocean of Being, soaring. Clouds stir and swirl. What a sight to see, far above the earth, beyond the pale moon and the dazzling globe of light is the velvet robe of many colors. A faint nebulous gleam peaks. Magnetic charm betwixt the eye, invisible realms coat mystifying thoughts that live to grow anew. Infinite Life, whose presence shall you enhance! Where did space come from that makes up time and place and fills each creation with new hope? Arise: sky meets the earth and leaves Eternal footprints in dust and wind. In the Stillness of the Soul, a spark of the Divine gently touches the face and fills the horizon.

As a Ray of light, we live on: you and I. In its essential nature, we refine our own place in its absolute Essence that passes from hand to hand, from age to age, without end.

## The Seasonal Silence of Time and Place

As the seasons of life pass, and the rustle of words end, the need for Silence creeps into the veins, refining the mind's eye. The grandeur of nature comes into bloom in the sanctity of the human heart. When the shadows of the sun's fire fall on the lush meadows and the loom of the wooded hills molds into the form of the turning earth, unfilled dreams awaken to all things. The firmament of Heaven brightens the stillness. Straining to grasp the whole, endless wafting colors fill the eye with magic, blend, and shift the Eternal Harmony of the moving spheres. The vast arena of thoughts seeks to trace Eternity's face upon the infinity of space. The maker of all things, Knowledge and Truth, touches the great and the small, the wise and the unwise, and the bright with the beautiful. It lights the eyes to track the true original Source of the Heart that beats deep within, to know from what place the living come and where they go.

All of us are headed somewhere. Most of us can put a semblance on the material picture of places and things. Where we go when the skin loses its life is a question that only the departed can answer. It is hard not to imagine some form of continuation because we are alive in the present. Nevertheless, each of us has our own individual beliefs when it comes to mortality and immortality. No doubt, the seasons of life will pass, but what is important is what we do while we are passing through those seasons. How we treat one another, and how we help provide for one another in the passing, determines our place in the Stillness that awaits all of us.

We are a culmination of our thoughts, actions and dreams. All of this gives meaning to our lives by polishing the veneer of our constitution: the alert cognitive state in which we are aware of our situation and ourselves. When we see this thought process as the varied forms of the many, it has the ability to move consciousness from a lower expression into a higher part of the great creative development. We are free from the negative aspects of cause and effect when our consciousness dwells on rightful thinking. With reason, we can find a natural and rightful power over our desires and affections. In our thinking, we must do what is right for our consciousness because it is right for our Sanctity of being. We must be the arbitrators of our own inspiration. Life is a starting point from which we may find our own answers to the 'whys' of living. When we believe in our continuation, memory retains its identity with the effect-producing cause even when separated in time and place. How we regulate our desires and affections so they can be beneficial in the higher sense is a long journey of careful thinking. Our judgments must not violate the rights and conditions of other persons, places and things. We are not torches that burn out when we lose our covering. Rather each of us is a boundless fount of Knowledge: an awareness that burns in our children, friends, work, and in our ideas.

We have given nourishment to the earth on which we have walked, the stars that we have gazed into, the rivers that we have crossed, and the countless living things we have encountered in the seasonal Silence of time and place.

## *Clouds of Colors Patterned in the Stars*

Light-drinking eyes see in sunrays from first to last, the Changeless Face of the Universe. A sign above, what does it mean: as Above so Below! Awake, remembering, sensing all that is between. Moving upon the facade of space, a star shines forth within the dark blue vault of Heaven, a point in a great circle of past, present and future. In this change, the great immensity of places and things we remain - a cluster of flowers intertwined upon time. Clouds of colors patterned in the stars. The glory of the eyes is a crystal palace amid Eternal stars. Seeing a single face in every flower, our hearts stir the ever-beating sea. A kindred key winding time seeks out a sun and feeds its Life. The pendulum swings, the universe ticks, magically working for you and me. Look, there above the horizon between the left and right, the Single Eye. Spirit, a beam of Consciousness, moves in all directions upon the void. Driven by the heart, the stars sing the Marriage Song of the Heavens.

We all start from passion, but it is in the warm liquid of our mother's womb that we evolve into an eventual person. It has taken billions of years for the DNA to reach this moment that we are in now. This Essence and life force that flow through our veins came from suns, stars, and planets. It is the heat, light and dust of all this cosmic stuff, animate and inanimate, that makes up the substance of life on the earth; but it is our Consciousness that paints and places the forms that exist in space on the canvas of life. This very moment is the Sum of Creation. No doubt, tomorrow will come and we will continue doing the same thing with various modifications.

Through this unique awareness we all live, move and have being. Is it so difficult to imagine that the contents of this vast creation are but reflections of our Inner Awareness to light/sound, vision and feeling?

Our innate ability to be aware, to comprehend, judge, and infer allows us to be diverse. Through reasoning, we can gain personal experience of the creative force. The objects before us are not really things in themselves, but are only the ideas that the mind conceives. We gain knowledge and perception by agreeing or disagreeing on individual ideas. Ultimately, it is up to each one of us to determine what is self-evident. The uniform Light that shines within holds life, purpose and form together. The more we work together in uniformity, the less friction we create. Should we really trouble ourselves about our existence and its future? We are in the moment. Except in the imagination, can we really be anywhere else? When we are content in our beliefs, the power that is now will continue in the form of existence that we now display. However, it is more productive to see the universe and humankind as co-dependent in the personal observations of laws and designs from which the cosmic manifestation emits. Therefore, each of us is the First Cause that necessitates, imparts, gives and adds to the Essence of the cause and effects of existence regarding the persons, places and things patterned from the stars.

When speaking let personal motives be silent for such reasons will only rob the Light coming from the Soul.

## The Silence of Clarity in the Gray Areas of Living

In silence, Light is everywhere. Fleeting shapes twinkle and dance upon the waves of changing consciousness. Above the reflection, fullness, growth and splendor have no limits. Dance in the arms of Goodness and let life become the stage. The body that is full of Light has no boundary; it is beyond the now, yet of the moment. Energy, time, clarity and compassion are the soother's of confusion. The confines of mind, like stacks of paper with long-ago dates, remain there for one to examine with lingering attention. A life! Swiftly, youth passes among the smiles of daytime, fleeting. Yet, in fond remembrance, see the Greatness that was, even in the ordinary. One life is but a second in the swirl of time. Let the evening slumber of youth go quiet. Cast pity to the flames as it only stiffens and sours the golden years.

Shadows and grayness follow all of us in one form or another. How we look at those areas is a matter of perception. When we look at our motivations for doing something, we are starting the self-search that will lift the fog that surrounds our decisions and actions. No doubt, shades of gray can make us mellower as we age. Especially, when we retrospectively look back on our lives and access our rights and wrongs. We then gain a sense of freedom and value for others as we see the topics of our lives more clearly, and we sort reality into clear-cut categories. Instead of feeling incomplete, we feel whole in our thoughts and memories. We can use our gray space to move around in our feelings so we can brighten our moods. Our form life is composed of dark matter, concrete substance, and our feelings are just shades of that matter. Grayness creates diverging strategies and boundaries. As a result, we can use those areas to create mazes, checkpoints and defensive structures to move around on the board of life.

Through thoughts and words, we become who we are, the logic behind what gives meaning to what we feel and understand. We seldom wake up understanding something; it is when we get into the day that comprehension surfaces. We cannot always be in our perfect mode, or call it up at will. Sometimes we just have to wait for it to surface. When this gray zone appears, take advantage of it by working through it, smoothly and effectively, by not giving into its distractions. Distractions are similar to dreaming with the eyes open. However, when one looks back through the years, life seems to be like a dream; events, relationships, and circumstances come and go. Look upon the gray areas like a cloud fading into the sun. They are but mental commentaries passing in the mind, the storehouse of habits, desires and fears. When we avoid identifying with our thoughts, we are thinking with awareness. Our mental pursuit becomes the object of perception. Time for this experience is limited. We must not let gray days or the results of other people's thinking trap us, for they can dim our clarity and drown out the silent Inner Voice of living. Most of us believe without any proof of that belief. In the end, that tenet often turns out to be but a reflection of our own foolishness. However, we should never be ashamed to accept dreaming; it makes us wiser today and the future times better. Gray times do not stem from the events of our environment that make up our lives; they come from the meaning we attach to them. Consequently, how we see and read them will determine who and what we are today and tomorrow.

Things in themselves do not change: our desires do.

## *Making Connections*

Entering this life, unconscious at first, requires a stop on a long pilgrimage that calls out for a change of what was before. It will be necessary to make connections regarding previous conceptions and modes of awareness. For the first couple of decades, we are acquainting ourselves with the models we see around us, somewhat like putting a jigsaw puzzle together. All of the pieces, events, persons, places and things provide us with information as to how we will fulfill our lives. The completion is a long drawn out process of familiarization and knowledge recorded in consciousness. We begin in a state of isolation and slowly proceed to a condition of integration with the elements that make up the form life. From this movement we organize our various traits, feelings, and attitudes into one harmonious personality that constitutes each of us. In order for our bodies to work properly, all of its systems must work together. In a similar fashion, we should integrate culture agreeably and functionally as a system, where all of its facets meld together. Thus, cultural integration is dependent upon the mutual support of customs, beliefs, values, and skills.

The collective mass of society, similar to the neurons in our brains, gives sustenance and support for the existence of the earth. Without our awareness, the earth would not be; and without earth, for the present, we would not be. As the past gives purpose to our present, society gives meaning to Light and dense matter. These elements move through our bodies as a combination of foodstuff which combusts into heat and energy. They radiate our minds as consciousness. This world, in which we feel, see, enjoy and suffer as matter bound beings, has a greater working value when we balance our emotional and mental integrity by improving our relationships with others. Gradually, when we look carefully, we see that each event leaves greater beauty in its wake. As we cycle through creation, one world at a time, we are externalizing the greater parts of ourselves upon that world to be. Newer and better tasks await us; they are the basis for our dreams and aspirations. For the present, our world is one world. When we look rationally at how it works, how can we deny its Unity with the cosmic picture that we observe?

Earth, space and we are One. As we merge with the future, our goal should be to become One Great Human Family. We must set ourselves against all separation and materialistic attitudes that cause the misunderstandings of right values. Through true integration, we will participate in world conditions, not from force, but on our own accord. Nevertheless, we must be rational in our thinking for standards are always shifting. As we grow in consciousness, life varies according to our fate. How we think and act in assessing our experiences with time, place and age show us our point of attainment in the life of Consciousness. Most likely, when we are in the future, the truths of today may be only simple aspects of greater truths. We will interpret the important aspects of truth as widely different from what we presumed in making connections. How we touch the world with our lives reverberates in our consciousness and can never be denied or repressed. Therefore, we must keep searching in ourselves for a deeper desire for genuine Love to balance the world that we may have harmed by our touch. Every time we are able to see beyond our own limited vision, we are moving toward equality and Unity.

## *Smoothing Away the Friction*

As we move on through life, each of us is increasing the size, volume, quantity and scope of our awareness. We are always adding detail and providing additional information to that movement. As we smooth away the frictions, the expansion of matter results in an increased molecular vibration of light: the magnitude of vibration that affects the atomic layers that open new dimensions in the mind. At this point, we become aware of the treasured moments in life. These moments transcend everyday living in a dreamland that opens the mind to its unique clarity. What we call life is just a series of events and circumstances formed by the mind in order to give meaning to our relationship with the outward appearance of the universe. The voice of consciousness, the electrical connection to life, receives impressions registered on the brain in its appropriate cell or nerve center. Communication is going on endlessly, day and night, between the physical world and the inner world. The complexity of the brain both physically and metaphysically is similar to the rings of a tree that expand layer by layer. Each layer, being different from all the others, has its own special work, function and properties. To understand the many facets of creation is the same process. Matter is always in a state of expansion and the human mind is no exception.

When we see, hear, and touch we perceive and interpret according to the stage of development of the mental principle within us. This is how we relate to the world of cause and effect. It is that which fuels our imagination, the electric impulses of cosmic fire, or that which we call mind. We are containers of this self-knowing Essence of life. Fire, heat and radiation embrace all that is and all that will be. It is our goal to actualize this in our consciousness. However, from our present awareness it is impossible for us to know the origin of mind from which the systems of space manifested. We can only theorize about this mind as our life waves pass through the various systems of generated thoughts, or awareness, which make up our systems of human development. Human aspects impregnate every atom in existence. Many are dormant and many are alive with activity, gaseous, liquid, or solid, as well as those parts of creation that we have yet to realize. The expression of the realized identity of each of us colors our lives with purpose and swings us into active co-operation with lesser lives still to be. This is how we originated; this is our process and goal for this one of many systems of life. There are two types of knowledge. One is the type we have gained, and the one about which we are inquiring. It is up to each of us to find the meaning to life and the parts we will play. Only by understanding the Greater Self can we remove the frictions that hinder our betterment. When we forget the frictions of the things that are behind us, we are moving into that which radiates our greater being. Movement and change work together producing friction. Friction is absent only in a vacuum of non-existent awareness of which duality is mute. Only in theory, can we make adjustments in movement and change without the abrasive friction of conflict. We might be equating corporeal conflict to habits of moral friction where the mind is so busy that it passes over things that would enable it to discriminate between what is right and wrong. This failure to discriminate makes it difficult to soothe away the frictions gathered while living in the world.

Humans and jewels are alike. To shine we must polish both by friction.

## The Politics of Living

All life is political in some form or other. The moment we place our feet on the floor, we base life on making decisions such as what we will have for breakfast and how we will go about meeting the needs of the day. We are always making decisions whether they concern other people or what color garments we will wear. In human relations, politics as group interaction reflects the allocation of values whether they are corporate, academic or religious. When we study our surroundings and ourselves, we are using authority and power in our individual lives. These values also apply when we scrutinize governments and other political units. However, for us to comprehend fully the purpose of politics requires a different type of self-responsibility. For example, how does our thinking and acting influence the nature of politics? Are we acting responsibly in the shifting patterns that shape our lives? What kinds of thought processes are we attaching ourselves to in the ebb and flow of political ideals? Are we passive or proactive when we aware of those ideals? We can only answer these questions when we choose to live consciously. We must face the facts that are before our senses so that we are not living in a fog of political charisma. We must be willing to stand up for our own value systems. We must live responsibly and with purpose and act according to our deepest beliefs when it comes to actions and choices. When we become self-responsible, we gain control over our own lives.

Our self-responsibility influences the social system in which we work and live. Without it, we become followers, dependent, giving our lives to those who lead. Instead of being self-assertive, we become fear oriented and can never be free to create the lives we want for our children and ourselves. The methods used by many politicians are entirely in keeping with their own goals and the few that elevated them; their methods are seldom for the many. Not only should every country have a Declaration of Independence, but every person should also have one. Political service is not about the few; it is about the inalienable rights of the individual. Presently, government programs do not improve conditions, they entrench them, absent of long lasting outcomes. Look at the greater painting; we etch it with crime, runaway debt, insensitivity to human suffering, widespread cynicism, antagonism between races and groups framed by political imbalance. The creeds of politics are more than words. Politics must be consistent with compassion and respect for others in its affairs. It is difficult for most people to act without interference because there are few in authority promoting responsibility, individually or collectively. A culture of self-responsibility is the only chance we have for creating a self-sustaining social system. When we raise our responsibility, we are also influencing the Greater Will that is in each of us. Remember, by our actions we call forth that type of leadership. Whatever our life calling is, when we are authentic, we are dealing with others and their values in a positive social context. Thus, we cannot help but be true to ourselves. Without any type of falseness to get in our way, we have the confidence to stand up for our ideas in appropriate ways so we can meet our life circumstances in a fair and honest way.

No combination of powers can hold us back when our goals are to improve the politics of living by self-responsibility.

## *Looking Through the Glass*

We are all mirroring each other in one form or another. Whether it is in our writing, acting, or learning, our knowledge data bank comes from many sources. However, the energy remains the same: a fragment of the One Light. The mind is a way of projecting creation within a Greater creation called a looking glass. It has a surface that can reflect light to form an image of an object placed in front of it that reflects or gives a true picture of something worthy of imitation. Knowledge is a mental mirroring of our mind's external world that we construct from imagery. It is an internal world of principles underlying conduct, thought and the nature of the universe as a living process. Through this, the mind goes beyond the controlling and predicting of things. The mind does not move; it creates through the objective world.

The parallels of life, intentional or otherwise, are there for us to construct living copies of various modes of being. What we allow in our psychological or physical world should be there because we have determined what the desired outcome and next step should be. Anything beyond that is due to controlling influences that sway us. This is similar to sprinting from fire to fire, forgetting self-creativity in order to adapt to someone else's knowledge. Influences, even from family or friends, can become a virus diffusing our own-mirrored light with theirs. However, the right influences are worthy when they support our values consistently. We are seeing clearly, when we close the negative loops and we identify with the true objectives of our lives. This moment is our time, our energy, and reflects our true character. We must keep on keeping that which has a clear reason for being a part of life.

Every part of life, situations, persons, places or things are but a mirror to see reflections on an inner level: one that is beyond the physical. Those likenesses are all there so that each of us can come to know ourselves better. From this knowledge, we can honor the parts that are appealing and transform those that are not of service to us. The sun reflects in a cup of water as a faint image; but if we were to look at it directly for too long, it would blind. How we see the light as receivers makes the difference in how we view the imagery. Light remains unaffected as to how we see. Reality is made of different grades of mind; all are reflections of the Ultimate Reality toward which we journey. The Light we see in our own mirror is the essential light. It is shining in everything, in all living creatures. It shines as Consciousness in all individuals. It shines through the universe and gives sustenance to it so we can form our experiences as persons. All things proceed out of this mirror. In this reflection, we may know the truth. Looking into the mirror is about asking what we truly see there. As we look through the glass of our own expanse, what are we seeing, and what do we need to claim or release?

By cleansing our own perceptions, we are able to open the door to the Infinite and there feel the Invisible Heart that sees rightly. When we come to know the Self, we know our place in the universe, why it is as it is, and why we are looking through it.

Do not be disturbed by the examples of others. Rather look for the reflections of our actions in their eyes and words.

## The Inner Journey

When we are boundless, without expectations, and compassionate toward everything, we are nurturing Heaven and earth. Then life grows through balance and harmony. Heaven, earth, sun, moon, the elements and a myriad of beings therein complement each other.

For all of us, life is a journey, even when we are unaware. On this path, we are building memories from a combination of persons, places and things. Along the way, we occupy ourselves with work, play, learning, creating and the combination of necessities that fuel our lives. We live through troubles, successes and a variety of mental and emotional needs that wear on us as well as enliven our spirits. In our striving and seeking, it is not hard to imagine that there is a little of everyone else in each of us. How we got here and what propelled us to seek out this physical life will most likely remain a mystery. Nevertheless, we are here so why not make the most of it. Once we open the door to this physical journey and peer inside, a good part of the journey is already behind us. Why not look at life as a loop within many loops, where the end is always meeting the beginning. When we look at the choices we have made on this journey, we can begin to answer the question 'Who am I'. Through our Inner world, we define the meaning of life and what occurs at death. Do not doubt the reality of this Inner world for it is as real as the one we are now visiting. The Inner world is the sanctuary of our own being; no power can enter except our own.

When we complete this journey, one of many, it will be a part of our consciousness to visit at will. This journey begins because of the Inner self. The body comes into being because this Inner Essence deemed it so. The outer body is a covering for the Inner self within. The day we were born the Inner self became active to this world, and the role of the mind and senses started. Through its long journey, the Inner person can cleanse the dross choices of the past. Within the domain of creation, every living thing has a right to life. As humans, we have the power to discriminate between what is acceptable and what is not. How we act toward others and how we care for the world determines the nature of memories we will revisit on the journey. We must remember that in the created world there is only energy in motion. Every thought and act directs some aspect of that energy. Therefore, when we experience with our bodies we are working with that energy. Any right or wrong activity on the physical plane is due to the force currents within us and has nothing to do with the inherent nature of energy. From journey to journey, we gain more understanding of our Greater Purpose. From perception to perception, from force to energy, from outer to Inner focus, we explore all the avenues of knowledge. We descend into the depths of what is right and wrong. From the valley floor to the mountaintop, we climb until we lose ourselves in the journey of time and space. Here we find purpose and realize the uniqueness of every journey that becomes our Inner design. We see the journey as a relationship; the elements of life exist in everything and are everywhere. This creative flow becomes our blood, our bones, and our minds. In its Stillness, we call the quiet place home.

Once we awaken the mind to a new idea, it can never return permanently to what was.

# The Painting of Contentment

There are many levels of contentment. What we do in life allows us to be happy or unhappy. The encounters that we experience depend on to what extent we are at ease in body and mind situations. When we multiply our daily wants beyond our needs, we are falling from the grace of plain living and altruistic being. Whatever our endeavors we only get out of them exactly what we put into them. Some people want to walk on a beach. Others want a whole world. When we can walk balanced in the world with our minds, emotions and bodies, we are content, confident and filled with wealth and happiness. Contentment does not come in using people and things but is in wanting only what one has. When we give up trying to be free, we are more at ease. When we develop worthy purposes, we are enriching our self-esteem. With confidence in our own innate abilities, we can change our expectation of the pictures before us. We can paint rationality with tranquility. When we are comfortable with ourselves, we are living positively.

When we paint our actions with appreciation and compassion, we are living for others. When we are intensely alive, consciousness is stimulated and we see events and circumstances differently. We do not live life the way we want it to be; rather we live life as currents in motion. In contentment, we overcome the blockages that impede the currents of happiness. When we are happy, we are being what we are. Contentment draws forth sympathy, tenderness, steadiness of purpose and indifference to pleasure or pain and all forms of good and bad.

When we see each moment, each hour and each day as an opportunity to be content, we are moving toward greater development of our minds and emotions. This is using imagination and memory as an opportunity to grace the 'now' with happiness. The avenues by which the Essence of creation can evolve are through our thoughts, our inclinations, our interests and feelings. When we are not fully present, we are out of harmony and cannot feel the perfectness of the moment. When we take time to be in that harmony we keep in touch with the world we all share. True contentment has an all-encompassing foundation that is always present within as a state of heart and mind. It thrives only in the now. When we are in that moment, we are at the place meant for us in the Universe of Consciousness. How do we make contentment a part of our daily lives with its various swings? We must see contentment as serenity, but not complacency. We can be comfortable without over-submission to it. Make it a mental decision, a moral choice, in observing the reality of the cosmos and our place in that abiding reality. When we paint our life canvas with joy, our mood swings leave us. We are improving the world, not harming it. We are empowering our experiences with elegance instead of discomforts. Contentment is a doorway that leads all of us into a greater portrait of ourselves.

In ourselves, we are the Truth: our own mystery, our own accord, a whirling mass with varying degrees of rhythm in unison with matter and Spirit.

## The Use of Time

Time, what is time? In terms of Eternity, time is immeasurable. However, the concrete mind views time as part of the fundamental structure of the universe. It is the occurrence of events in sequence and can be measured to separate those events. Each of us measures time as we go about our daily lives. In some ways, we have become slaves to time. Throughout humanity's existence, we have seen time in the rising and setting of the sun, in the phases of the moon, and even in the wrinkles on the skin. However, when we view time as a part of our Greater Being we can become its master. From our human minds, we see persons, places, and things as transient, as ongoing changes of what we see before us. Time is not something that we can place in a container; events and objects cannot move through it. Time is an intellectual structure whereby humans can sequence and compare events with space and number. It is doubtful that we can measure the full length of time. On the physical plane, we view time as a social value and as an economic importance; time is money. Time reflects an awareness of the limited periods in each day, as in human longevity.

In the realm of positive imagination, time is Eternal and youthful. In this realm, time is no longer an aspect of consciousness because of the absence of atoms. In blending our imagination with physical reality, we gain the power to expand our consciousness. We are living in the timelessness of right now. In this part of the imagination, we are not interested in the petty aspects of a bound personality. Rather, we immerse ourselves in an instantaneous reflection of wakefulness. Time and space are no obstacles to this alert imagination. In this reality, existence is inseparable from the Eternal. In the now, we have the ability to tune our human minds to this imaginary realm and make it a part of the Greater Life that stretches forward and backward in our experiences. Once we connect to this type of imaginative thinking, it does not matter if we leave family and friends behind because in the blink of an eye they are with us. Space and time hold us to physical existence; but in the imagination, all is present simultaneously because time does not apply. In the imagination there are no forms of measurement of past, present or future; everything simply happens.

In earth time the physical phase passes and is laid low. The breath that moves our crimson risings and settings changes color. The waters ebb and flow as we embrace the awareness that was our mother earth, a temporal border in that mysterious flow. There is more beyond the third dimension of thinking, and it lies in the imagination of feeling, seeing and experiencing that which is beyond this everyday world. The imagination is a universal system of communication seen as visions, symbols, colors, numbers, sound, and other beings. Regardless of how we use time or how we view it, it comes and goes. On and on we are. When life flows by, imaginatively, the Soul graces us with a smile. Setting things right in the heart is an effort only time can heal. The Joys of the Heart come with years and as such, lessen our tears.

We are born at a definite time. Our bodies move in it for a certain number of years and our greatest truths live in it, on and on. In time, we discover all things that lie hidden.

## The Cleavages of Life

Knowledge, wisdom, and power are the Spirits of our children that light the veil of night, the birthright of wholeness. Oh, what delight, shaped by moisture and heat! A gift entering this life wrinkled and crying is a joy to see. It is love shaped like a golden ring, never ending. Human life is always breaking up, the large into the small, and the small into the large. This splitting runs throughout Creation: in minerals, in cell divisions, in creating life, in the chemical processes of complex molecules and even in sexual appeal. Without this splitting process, movement would cease. Cleavage subdivides and interacts to produce wholeness that accounts for the various lines of differentiation in our humanistic society. The result of splitting is unification because the genetic content of all cells is identical. The 'in-between' of the occurrence and the end accounts for all the variances in nature: human, systemic and cosmic. This middle ground is where we all evolve. The commonality from where we start and where we end applies to all of us. Each of us is a river that ends in an ocean. Through our own reasoning, we become movers of that fullness. In this 'in-between' state what anyone has felt we can feel, what anyone has thought we can think, and what has befallen anyone can befall each and everyone. This universal splitting is in all of us. Our DNA, genetic processes, and recorded histories reveal the knowledge of what we have been. Through this cleaving, we are explicable. We go forth embodying every sense, every thought, and every emotion that has been a part of all events. In this vestibule, we gather the data that create our causes and discover our laws that unite us with nature. From the first person onward all contain the stardust of past planetary systems, our forests, rivers, and oceans. All of the great empires rest within the cleavage through which we all flow and grow.

The human mind is what we have written, pictured and thought. Mind will solve its own mysteries. Our individual and collective lives will explain the essence of the All of Life that is in each of us. In this stream, centuries are like seconds. The fire, air, water and earth, in which we circulate as our systems, draw from this vast Essence. Each of us is but one more birth of it, and all of the properties of fire, air, water, and earth exist in us. From our first steps to our last, we strive toward betterment in this quantum field of laws and fate. When we understand its power and its energy, we are utilizing the thoughts of others wisely; their riddles will become our private solutions in the structuring of character. The cleavages of life, the 'in-between' of life and consciousness, can guide and set us free, if we would only listen and see. Each life is a quest for that place. The visibility of our search is somewhere between the old and new; it is a halfway moment where the old can be reconciled with the new. We choose human life as a vessel to mold our earthly form by splitting one into the many. We clothe the stormy torrent of our foolishness with the tender side of our nature. As we fall through uncounted centuries, we shape our character with clarity, derived in the Silence of the Soul, and arrive at a place within ourselves where we are free from anything that darkens or obscures our happiness.

My son, a stone worker by trade, carved a facial image of Queen Nefertiti from sandstone as a gift for me. He hammered away, slowly and cautiously, until it was finished without producing a single crack in the stone. When nothing seems to help, I sometimes look at this carving for it reminds me that I must carve life in the same way.

## *Life is Only What We Accept it to Be*

The universe is expanding and so are we. One of the difficulties of life is figuring out what is acceptable as belief or truth. Rational persons want others to accept them in the situations in which they find themselves immersed. We seek approval and reception on all levels of the social stratum from one-on-one encounters to the interactions of groups within organizations. Even our domesticated animals want acceptance. The world has a way of making us feel stressed about things such as our health, money, relationships, work, religion, and politics. We must be mindful of those areas in our lives but not so excessively that they block out our Inner Peace. Our outer ego loves getting us worked up over what is to be accepted. Do we really need to prove anything to anyone? When we look at our lives at this moment, regardless of the circumstances, we have the power to understand that some things we can change and others we cannot. To make our physical goals a reality, we must believe in ourselves as being worthy. We are fine! Acceptance will not come from without; rather it will arise from within. If we cannot find it where we are, where else do we expect to find it? No one except ourselves can bestow our tranquility. We must insist on it ourselves and never copy it from someone else. Trust in the Self for each of us vibrates to that chord. Accept the mind and heart. The Great Immensity has bestowed the connection of events that create acceptance.

There are negatives in life that happen to all of us. We should avoid trying to judge those events. Rather, we should practice accepting who we are and how we resolve these negative issues. We can never expect the ideas of others to always flow concurrently with ours. Understanding and support do not always go well with someone who is in the negative wave. Often he/she will react with resistance, anger, and ridicule to higher ideals. For selfish reasons the outer world has its fears and insecurities that can cement us to points of view making it difficult to recognize a common ground. When we are fair with one another in viewing differences, each of us can enter our own moral state of acceptance. In any relationship, we must show respect. To understand the circumstances of others, we must show dignity, kindness, earnestness, sincerity and openness. Acting this way will still any thunderstorm and bring a new season to life. Alone or together when we accept who we are, we can accept others for who they are. The outer appearance has very little to do with the Inner Essence and mindset of another as he/she unfolds different attitudes about issues in this changing world. We are free when we approve of ourselves. It is the dialogue of the ego of another that disapproves, usually by wanting to be in control. Make a decision to let go of the need for that kind of influence. When we look beyond the expectations of others, we are in our own approval zone: a place of Peace within ourselves in which we can live and accept others for who they are.

We have already gained approval or we would not be here.

## *Memories*

We are always searching around in a storehouse of mental imagery gathering the information that is permanently stored there. Within seconds, we sense a memory and just as quickly, we lose it. Memories can be short or long in duration. The personal experiences, skills and habits that are gathered are the foundation on which we shape our growth and process. However, there is very little agreement on how memory works. Our present needs, desires, influences, etc., all come from memories and often accompany feelings and emotions that call into being the awareness of memory. It is possible when experiences have been abusive, they can be unconsciously repressed which often allows adult problems to surface. Our minds, when remembering, are like jigsaw puzzles and what we retrieve are mostly fragments of experiences.

When the body is at rest or asleep, the brain may turn our life experiences into dreams. It is through this relaxation mode that we can examine those events and even gain an understanding of them. In this storage room, we can erase and add memories. In the arena of the imagination, memories are independent of the body. From the realm of the objective, we form memories from words, sounds, pictures, feelings and actions, forging material things, the necessities of life. When we dwell on memory feelings, we can prolong those impressions. We have the ability to turn them into great novels, art images, audio and video recordings that even those not yet born can enjoy and learn from, i.e., enhancing memory while still in the womb through machine miniaturization.

There is the possibility that memory can access the true history of humanity through a subtle state of consciousness. This knowledge, encoded on a physical atom, is a reflection of a non-physical plane of existence: an energy atom that records every whim, every thought, every action and reaction to events and circumstances that a person has experienced. This dynamic force streams through the ages framing all things that constitute and inhabit the universe. Our memory records are the Books of Life where each of us writes all the information that we gather during our development. This book contains every deed, word, feeling, thought, and intent that we have had or will have. This memory storehouse influences our everyday lives, our relationships, feelings, beliefs and the realities we form. Memories are transforming; we pass on knowledge in various forms as technology of which computers are just a small part. This universal collectivity will become even more enhanced as we remove negative traits that hinder reception.

Memories, time and space, action, reaction, hereditary influence, and judgments form our ideals of what gives life meaning. The home that is farther away from the one we are now in is our treasure house of real memories where we are as little children. It is a time and place of long ago before the sounds of this world came to our senses. What we remember from our childhood we will remember forever stamped, eternally to see. We never leave behind what we imprint on another person's heart and it never dies. In the end memories are the only things that we own as true possessions and true wealth; they are our freedom from poverty. In our visits with persons, place and things, our rewards are what we carry in our hearts and minds.

The people, their language, their country of origin and all the memories we hold of those visitations, we carry in our travel sack.

### Large versus Small

Nothing is inner, nothing is outer, nothing is great, and nothing is small. Nothing is high; nothing is low in the Divine Economy of Change. On and on change flows until at last the mind and its pictures enter the world of Light where all forms are narrow reflections on an Eternal atom. What is loved can never, never be lost in the Great Change.

Large is being more than usual size, amount or number, opposite small, which is below average in number or quantity or magnitude or extent. In the world of relativity, we are always comparing things whether they are values, judgments, or objects. We can do this by thinking or by attraction and repulsion. The law of gravity is universal in dealing with persons, places and things and allows for reconstructing. Life is an ongoing expression of opposites, good/bad, weak/strong, small/large and love/hate, etc. The Soul is so small that we can never view it while embodied, whereas the ego/personality is so large that it is uncontainable. There are many explicit comparatives in the writings of history on the destructiveness associated with the need to be great. Comparatives permeate many aspects of our thoughts and experiences and provide the framework for how we view life. We form cognitive habits so that we can investigate, understand, change or abandon how we view life.

As observers, we each perceive the objective world differently. We can describe persons, places, and things to others but we cannot evaluate those things completely for them. We each have different standards for reasoning. Our ways of knowing and our morality can be true or false since each is vastly different. Culture, language, education do not completely determine how we think. In human relations, size can produce anxieties: how much hair we have, our height, weight, girth and bank accounts define our preferences for one another. Presently, it seems our population is out sizing our world's ability to be sustainable. We all may need to downsize or face the possibility of removal similar to the dinosaurs.

We may flatter ourselves into thinking that size matters in forming our conceptions of reality. Beneath this constantly changing physical universe, tiny particles of Light make up the underlying fabric of space: the Invisible containing the visible. Is the universe conscious and is it trying to connect to human thinking by paring the small to the large? Consciousness must be the focal point of becoming more conscious through separation and division. Size is a matter of perception. The further we are from an object the smaller it seems, the closer we are to the object the bigger it appears. Regardless of the size of something, until its nature speaks to the imagination, it is only a mental compass to help map out a course to follow.

Large or small, worlds within worlds fill Space, one within another.

## A State of Loyalty

Loyalty is a state of being faithful to commitments or obligations, or a committed adherence to a sovereign government, or its leaders. However, loyalty can change with time and circumstances. Educational methods and public opinion have enormous influence as to how we gauge loyalty. As humans, we must first be honest and true to ourselves. There is loyalty to one's belief in a Creator, to one's parents, and to country of origin. However, depending on the circumstances, those loyalties are often contingent on opportunities of give and take. When we are loyal, we should use awareness and discrimination in what is lasting and real, absent of personal advantage. History has shown that loyalty sometimes means going against what we often see as law, especially when we overlook the well-being of minorities. It is ill advised to place one's security in the hands of someone who says they will protect others at all cost. To believe in perfect loyalty without testing it can be wishful thinking. Few truly remain faithful. The closest thing to true fidelity is Unconditional Love.

As we grow in life, we learn to assess the games that people and governments play and how they use others to meet their own ends. Growth and honesty are easy to speak of but can be difficult to put into practice when it comes to being truly faithful, especially when there is a refusal to look at something and see it the way it really is. What are the real priorities of our loyalty? Are they to family, ethnic groups, community, state, political party, profession, country or religion? In this modern age, it is difficult to know. Laws, humanism, and loyalties do not make us free. It is our faith and belief in our own Innate selves that fosters freedom. The triumphs of society as the end, the obedience to authority as abundant faith in its leadership, can have long lasting effects for the world when we use misguided devotion for entering another person's domain. When we do not ask the 'whys' in gathering loyalties, they can become covertly tangible and stifle self-reliance. The integrity of one's mind is more sacred. Our thoughts are more authentic and in due time they become our outer convictions. Envy and imitation of others only weaken discrimination.

When we gather our own portion of what is true for each of us, better or worse, we are sheltered from misguided devotion. When we are loyal to ourselves, we move beyond convictions (laws and ideas that we must obey and follow) to an enlightened system of justice, charity, industry, wisdom, and self-awareness. We can never substantiate devotion to an idea or ideal as long as there is a motivation toward capital gain. Nor can we rationalize the use of force by taking something that belongs to another person, group, or country through nationalism. This type of action goes against the loyal qualities of nature and faith in our own innate selves.

Opinions hankered from others are not always valid; it is often easier to live after one's own.

## The Use of Information

When we gather information, we are processing and organizing the data that adds to our knowledge. When there is uncertainty concerning a question, information is what changes our point of view. We receive and understand a message through statistical data, experience, study or communication. Information is an ongoing stimulation of the mind and emotions. Without adding information, our steps would be small ones. This all-important Light of knowledge defines our goals and provides the framework for documenting data. Can we be traveling too fast on the highways of information and can too much information make us weary of what we realize? Ideas, methods, research and development procedures, techniques, tools, and technology are the factors that move information. These tools can provide us with a process for growing. When we balance the input of information, it can be an initiative for change that will help us create a higher level of excellence in our everyday lives. Rightly used, information is a service for betterment of the social infrastructure. There is also the potential to use information to overpower. Thus, it is essential that we carefully consider information if it is a prescription for change, either individually or for the public. Will it alter what is best for all people, or give too much to a select few who sway public opinion?

Life, the force that animates each of us, is integrating into us as information. It has been doing this since the beginning of civilization. Along the way, we have shut many people out of the integrating process due to the misuse of power and force. Historically, the use of race and color has been an educational negative. Comprehensive education for all can be the supreme use of information. It passes on to the next generation all that the past generations have actuated. Information about history, geography, government, etc must be real. Power users often distort information when they can use it to shape and change events for their own ends. Twenty-first century information must rise above this type of skewed data. Vital information provides for justice, domestic tranquility, and security from fear and need resulting in greater enjoyment, increased harmony, and faster expansion of the heart and mind. Information is the product of laws and ideas for the common person: a testament that allows one to gain the knowledge and experience of the social whole. When it comes to information, the mind is the architect, the heart is the doer, and the hand is the builder. From these three we create the blueprint for existence. Information in the right hands is a benefit for decision-making that allows us to live more abundantly.

## *History's Innumerable Variations*

History is a detailed record of what has occurred, an aggregate of past events remembered, written, or visually recorded. In accessing historical records, it is important to know what is factual and what is not. Do we embellish the facts of history to meet the ends of persons or governments? Do we manipulate history in order to sway public opinion? Can one ever know the truth concerning historical events? For the near future, the feasibility of attaining the real facts of history will remain closed to most because we can never go back to the past thing in itself. In the duration of time, pictures, words and sound can give us glimpses of historical persons, events and actions, but they can never give us a true look at the inner thoughts, reasons, and motivations of historical persons. What is truth today can turn out to be incorrect for the future. However, when the records agree with all the sources available, most historians view history as correct. For consciousness to remain awake, it is wise to be discriminatory about past events. For example, what are the positions adopted and what are the sources in determining the nature of human history? How do we go about connecting the events and conclusions with written history? Who is it for and is it biased against the weaker? Did gender play a role in narratives and was race an issue in shaping past reality? It is up to each of us to keep our minds and emotions psychically strong when determining the realism of history.

When we think about history, we must imagine what occurred and place ourselves there. Let us feel what was going on and what had befallen those who were a part of it, because the mind is the record of history. Our emotions and the human Spirit embody and belong to those events. All the facts of times past, in some form, are the laws that govern our minds: the library of facts. The landscapes of nature are in the seeds of its plants and forests. All the ideas of past nations lie folded in each of us. The human mind wrote history and each of us must read it and solve our own mysteries that we see in it. In understanding the lives that comprise history, are there any differences between days or centuries and the place we are now? Our identity reflects the past and is similar to the present and the future in a variety of ways. We are the ages and we will be the future. Our private experiences are like flashes of light that came from the past, both individually and collectively. Reforms, private opinions, and revolutions all circle around to solve the problems of the present. Long ago, we labored the soil in different shoes. When we read history, we must place ourselves in the shoes of those who walked in the great ages of the past and see their actions in the imagination of our personal experience. Behind the present, we must go over the whole ground to see and live the fullness that is to be. Only then, will we succeed and thus change our vices in the distant persons and things to be. Thoughts go back into the womb of things, and from the rays of the One Flame, those thoughts fall into the Infinite.

Although not obvious to the senses, every time we pass someone, we pass into history; every time we converse with someone, we are conversing with history's innumerable variations.

## *The Face of Depression*

I am glad that my name is in your book. I am thankful that I walked this path of dust with Thee and all its ways. You have made my freedom and Spirit complete as the sky above; of this, I am certain.

The outward appearance that belongs to persons, places and things carries nuances that contain patterns of similarities. As we stand before the patterns each of us is projecting the presentation of the self we want to put forward in interacting with others and life. Mingling with others creates difficulties that can change behavior on all levels of human stratification: physically, emotionally and mentally. Difficulties, if not balanced, can affect the infrastructure of persons and cultures. Because the human mind is in its infancy, we do not know all the causes for the mood swings it goes through. There seems to be a biological and emotional connection, even a genetic link, to disorders of the mind. If depression can run in a family, it makes sense it can also run in institutions and groups. It might even affect the environment. For example, if the people of a nation are depressed over its leadership, there is the possibility that depression can move into the flow of economic patterns, weather patterns etc. Poor performance, personality patterns, lack of optimism, and low self-esteem can relate to depression. Therefore, it is vital that we know the character and strength of those individuals we choose to manage our general welfare.

Just like fear, anger and love, depression is an emotional expression. It leaves an imprint on the psyche after a traumatic experience. When we use self-reliance in forming images, compassion becomes an aspect of will that culminates in peace and creativity. As such, the freedom that is the human spirit responds to our difficulties; we are then creating a new social identity rooted in self-acceptance that will weaken trauma. We each have our reality, the way we see the world. Regardless of what is going on in the outer world, there is still the Inner world. In the Inner world, we have the ability to see other possibilities that can take us beyond the anti-depressants of society. Whether it is a person or a group, communication is important in helping remove those dark and deep shadows that come with life. Our polarity, the tendency to change, grow, think and feel determines our conduct in life, and how we live and care for one another. Through the mind, we shape our own place, our sex, our temperament, talents, and the vital powers that give us direction for being. However, when the patterns of physical life end, it is our knowing that links us to our Essential nature.

Each time we shed a layer of uncertainty about the place we find ourselves, we are coming closer to the True self. Awareness is what transforms the face of depression.

### *Living in Patience*

Nature is slow and its meaning is even slower; the seasons are its testament. As we move through the seasons of our lives, we must endure much to arrive at the place we want to be. We wait. We try to avoid being annoyed or upset with what faces us and to persevere with tolerance. Patience can be a form of mental art. After all, it is more than doing nothing while time passes. When society was more agrarian, it was a slower pace. Now that we are technological, we move faster and we are motivated to link achievement and success with personal worth. We have placed value on time. We must not let the quick temper of folly take over the occasion; it only weakens insight. Always think about the outcome positively. When we combine understanding and patience, they are more beneficial to our makeup. We must be serene with the self and the remedies for the events that appear will be resolved with good judgment. When anxiety seeps into our thoughts, we must apply discipline. We can replace fear and discouragement with a confident and decisive outlook.

All of us want to believe that we have a part in determining the meaning of life. We have pierced the objective world with telescopes in an attempt to document its patterns of existence. We rearrange atoms and molecules only to discover viruses and plasmids. In the enduring process, if we are infinitely patient, the answers will come. Can we rely on artificial concepts developed in the laboratory to discover the slow evolving process of creation? There is a probability for this because physicality is made of matter. Matter is constantly rearranging. What is the Source and power that fuels this process? We cannot confuse life, as we know it with the lifetime of an individual. By tradition, science characterizes life as growth, reproduction, metabolism, motion, and response. In time, each of us, in our own place, will witness the inertness and passing that comes to another. This is the supreme moment, the appointed hour, for gathering the meaning of patience, even life. When the end of life comes to another, it is vitally important to remain calm as nature reclaims its innocence. The form that we have witnessed becomes a perception of matter in our inner awareness.

The meaning of life is about being patient. If we are to gather life's Greater meaning, one cannot exist without the other. When impatience dominates, the more destructive attributes of nature's laws come into being. We are constantly exchanging matter and energy with the surroundings, disorder with order. Everything comes gradually and patience enhances our clarity, wisdom, and power.

Through patience and blending the laws of life with healthy living, right human interaction will result in a continuity of consciousness with the living and non-living.

## *Commitment*

When we are steadfast, sincere and purposeful, we bind ourselves mentally and emotionally to a course of action such as a pledge, promise or affirmation of agreement. Commitment is the Light of Spirit, an inner reflection of consciousness, which sets in motion the outer living of cause and effect.

Commitments come in all sizes and shapes regarding persons, places and things. Events in life are not always colorful and romantic. Nevertheless, there are many moments when we fill life with passion and excitement. However, we should never think that a person, idea or community promise could fill our expectations. Only when we look to ourselves for fulfillment can we avoid the failings in relationships. If there are disappointments, the other person is seldom the source of the problem. One pledge that can bring about inner satisfaction is to be true to oneself. By being honest and true when we search into the nature of our difficulties, we can grasp the clues that others are saying about their disappointments. This truth is as applicable to groups and institutions as it is to persons. When we commit to withholding judgment, we are acting with maturity in an accepting integrated manner. When we entrust ourselves with maintaining a sense of perspective by not taking another person's behavior personally, we learn to remain calm in the face of disagreement; then we are rightly assisting others and ourselves in our inner growth.

Commitment is a conscious journey that takes us beyond the senses to that of intuition and correct perception. When we make a commitment, we are choosing to align ourselves with the energy of others and the embodiment of their views. This is embracing others and every form of life in totality without judgment, thus seeing each life with purpose and meaningfulness. As we consciously co-create with the universe, the earth and each other, we are utilizing experience wisely, releasing the petty traits of the ego for that of a higher frequency of acceptance. This allows us to recognize our reactions so we can join each other freely without shifting motives.

When we freely merge the different elements of a relationship into a union, we form a stronger life view. We begin to release energy spontaneously. The road of understanding allows us to move in the same direction. This permits the thoughts and ideas of others to pass through the private heart that is in all of us. Except by permission, nothing lasting can enter the heart and mind. Eventually, pain and suffering will bring about a reconciliation of any effect not comprehended and washed away by cooperation and Goodwill. Commitment is the force that lifts the mind away from the elements of division. Thus, we become flexible and fluid in assisting others with empowering insight.

When we are voluntary in our affections, wisdom and insight, the higher laws of commitment, work in and through us.

## Consequences of Age and Consciousness

How long have we existed? Does age have a distinctive feature or power we can utilize?

From a scientific view, aging occurs when matter breaks down and decays. For humans it takes place through cellular degeneration. In terms of consciousness, we should view age as a long line of events. The advantage of age is that at a certain point the psyche wears down when healthy glands and cells no longer fuel it, bringing inertia to the physical body. Then the Inner person releases itself from the mortal decaying process. The fact of this process plays out repeatedly in the physical phase. To go beyond the mortal requires a healthy imagination based on faith and belief. In the final analysis this all any of us have.

The play of life and our attachment to it do not work well with aging. We try our best to slow the body and its component parts down with pills, exercise and longevity therapy. All have their benefits, but physical time is not partial to age and the natural wear and tear of the body. A hundred years from now only a very few of the same faces will remain and they will be very aged. When we think in terms of consciousness there is no age, only a rising and setting of awareness. Consciousness keeps track of what it experiences because of the Essence that animates it. Consciousness is always working at remembering and knowing its own pure fundamental nature. In the continuity of continuing, when there is clarity of Goodness, the will of consciousness always unites with this kindness as ageless memory of truth and virtue. For better or worse, life is an education. When we look into the mirror of everyday living and see youth replaced with maturity, and maturity replaced with old age, if we are lucky to arrive at that final place, our real nature will slip inward. We cannot avoid age related changes to the body, but we can minimize many problems related to aging by thinking and believing in the power of imagining.

The key to our longevity is knowing the place where we exist and ourselves. Most people see aging as the culmination of life. A more positive attitude would be to live denying any concept of finality. No one becomes great at his or her work without striving toward being Eternal. It is the same with life; we must live as if we never stop living by transforming our thinking being into something better. According to science, during our lifetime the vast majority of cells in our bodies replace themselves continually. We know, we think and exist because of our thoughts. Therefore, if we could think differently and see ourselves as Immortal, we could exist endlessly. Science and concrete knowledge explain the material side. Consciousness and imagination are the powers that give us being and project our Immortality.

There comes a time in our lives when we must stop believing what others say and embrace our own life knowing.

## *Purposeful Being*

When this existence passes into another phase is there a prior planned reason behind its being? Did we reach the goals and aims of that existence? Good or bad, how do we know if we realized the intentions of that existence? Life did not suddenly appear, not the way in which we perceive it presently. In the beginning, there was no instruction book. We are writing it, as we exist. We plant a seed first in order for a plant to appear. For it to continue, its leaves and sap, along with other elements, must provide the fertilizer. We are seeds, too, from the Creative Tree of Life and our thoughts and actions are its nourishment. Most likely, the seed at its infancy was a Permanent Atom of energy. The mystery behind this early stage is what drives the imagination. Imagination is the ability to process and invent personal realms within the mind. We derive these realms from sense perceptions of the shared world. The sharing of these personal realms with others has created humankind in which we all live and have being. In this creative imagination, we leave nothing out. It is up to each of us to discover the content within it. We have a very long time to accomplish this. The beauty of it all is that we control the hands of the clock. The Singular Creative Happening was an unconditionally fettered release of energy and force. We sense its swell in our imagination. If we could ever contain it, it would be paralyzing and the cause for procreation would cease for physical life.

When we live with purpose, we are using our powers with a reverence for all life. Then, we are expressing the Great Naturalness that is in each of us. As a result, we are enhancing life, not destroying and limiting it. Since physical life is a process of becoming, we cannot remain in any particular state indefinitely. There are dismays inherent in life. Within and without, shadows and darkness are a part of the expressions. When we accept responsibility for our daily work of living, especially in the middle of all the inconsistencies that unfold, we are upholding the worthiness of the Light of being. When we choose to see, it becomes as miraculous as the miracle of a single flower. When looking back, we must see through sadness with Love. We must be unashamed of what was or was not and know in the end that Love is present.

There are tremendous reasons for life. Whether we choose to believe it or not, every time we pass another person we are weaving our purpose out of the existence of that person. Even with all of our trappings, the differences in all of us are miniscule. When we meet life with concern for indifferent attitudes, we are using our experiences wisely. Existence is only a happening, an unfolding of one's understanding of the Inner Life with the discovery and transformation of the outer life and its reality.

Out of our existence, we will continuously ascertain that the essential Essence, the center focus for our being and purpose, originates from our Inner World.

## *Intimidation*

Fear and intimidation are twin allies used by the stronger over the weaker to accomplish an end. When someone feels superior and their fame, wealth or status is over-bearing, it can make others feel discouraged. In communication, intimidation is a deterrent used to make others afraid to try something. Intimidation uses control, coercion, forcefulness, abusive behavior, punishment, making one seem uneducated, withholding love to obtain loyalty, and autocratic behavior. All of us have experienced intimidation in one form or other. When we look rationally at the workings of society, it is not hard to see that individuals, groups and/or governments are intimidating us on a massive and very effective scale to prevent unwanted actions.

Intimidation is a destructive practice that shuts out the Light of progress. It uses religion, economics, and government policies to enforce the strong over the weaker. A vibrant and healthy society would diagnose intimidation as a disease. Intimidation prevents healthy relations from developing, creates isolation, and passive aggressiveness. It diminishes power, causes rigidity in exercising power, creates loss of acceptance, untruthfulness, and lowers self-esteem. Great societies and their dreams lay upon the ashes of time all destroyed by this yet undiagnosed disease. Individuals, groups and nations need to assess what they do, how they behave, who they are and why they need to use intimidating practices. We must carefully examine the actions, traits, and attitudes of a person or group before we allow them to influence, guide, or rule others.

When we learn to be true and trust ourselves, the society of our equals and the events that we create will be trustful; the whips of intimidation will cease to strike out. It is up to each of us to recognize a displeased face. When we look to our own constitution, we will find what is right and our oppressors will seem fleeting like clouds to the wind. Let the world live after its own opinions. Each person's duty is his own and no one knows it better than he or she. When we know we are being intimidated, we have the ability to do something about it. We are not willows in the wind. We each have a choice to bend to intimidation or not to bend. Stand fast in the liberty of the Inner Being that has endowed us with the freedom of choice. Do not become entangled with oppression. Do not be enticed or misled, and do not let others abuse based on external behavior. Inspiration and cooperation are the signs of beneficial leadership, not intimidation. We do not require others to compare and estimate how we must behave. Those who believe they are higher than others are intimidators fanned with ambition, not aspiration.

When the mind is confident, positive and filled with friendliness toward all, there is no room for fear.

## Transition

In our everyday lives, we are passing from one state or place to the next. Whether it is emotional, mental or physical, often an event results in transformation. In physical life, we are always planning the future by moving from one area of life to the next: from high school to college, from one work field to the next, from being single to a committed dual relationship. In addition, parents help their children through the many changes while they are growing up; then the reverse occurs. The children help the parents move into old age. Planning the future is mostly contained in the here and now. We strive to provide information and resources for everyday physical transitions. However, very little thought is devoted to the Ultimate Transition from living life to passing out of physical life.

Passing out of life is a clinical process well documented and can be observed from this side. What we have as evidence for the out–of–life phase comes from opinions and information gathered from those who have entered this imaginary phase. For this kind of information to remain valid for a person, it must remain in the realm of the imagination. What happens to us depends on each one of us. Is this state an ending or a beginning? If one does not devote a part of everyday to reflect on this after–life phase, any awareness of it could be dimming and confusing. Similar to the birth process it could contain the confusion, the light and the same restructuring examples we experience in growing. When we pass away from physicality, the view screen or brain of our reality could begin to fade if we have not taught ourselves to be aware of the light screen of awareness in the new transpersonal realm.

While we are living in physical reality, we must instill it with the expectations of what will happen when we make this transition. We are beings of energy. Even though the mind fades, it is still energy, feeling and desiring to bring to Light what one remembers. Energy is always filtering and shaping information to present to our awareness in ways that we can understand. We can experience glimpses of transition if we open our minds to that possibility. These glimpses can occur in the dream state or in moments when our physical reality is at risk, or when a loved one has passed on. These moments are important if we are to maintain control and balance in life and the transition that is to follow. If we do not take the steps necessary while in the now, our minds could simply project the experiences that meet our fixed expectations of what we believe will happen. The mind is the energy field of the whole being; it retains the patterns, programs, and tendencies that we have developed during physical life. Even though we are experiencing the light images, consciousness remains, interprets and refines the experiences by presenting the pictures that meet our needs.

We are what we practice: we move ahead, arrange, and select the beliefs that are to our liking.

## Interaction

When we interact, we influence one variable on another; both the actor and reactor are engaged in a mutually affecting experience. On the subatomic level, it is the interaction and mediation of the forces of nature where a particle has energy and momentum but no mass. When we relate on a human level, we are also relating in a subatomic manner, 'As Above, So Below'. Through interaction, we employ perception, cognition, emotion, personality, behavior and interpersonal relationships. We make contact by speech, eye contact, touch and other physical means using the senses. In the social process, it is either one-on-one or group-to-group interaction. Is it possible that we interact with each other in order to rediscover the wholeness of being beyond the physical? No matter how we view interaction, if not done carefully, we will almost certainly create consequences on which to reflect. For the present, physical life interaction immerses in duality, not integration. Interaction produces all the various levels of conflict; some are passive and others are proactive. Only when we become indifferent do relationships cease. We must forget areas of conflict so that we may see the Light that another expresses. We may not see the sun that is in us or in others, but we can sense its Light and that is the true purpose of interaction.

When we are in the presence of another, we are sensing the electric fluid of creation that passes through the nerve systems of the body. Interactive contact is either attracting or repelling. Because of individual consciousness, we all orient ourselves differently to the actions of another. Just as the light of the sun strikes the earth at varying angles, our attitudes and behaviors toward others strike different nerves. Likewise, our attitudes toward our Higher Source vary throughout life. From purity to passion, passion to purity, energy directed by patterns of thought shape our relationships. Self-expression and fulfillment are the reasons we live and have purpose and we each cultivate our own mode. The differences between those who are attracted to one another are small and they are in the beholder. When we are interacting with others, we should see life as genderless. Life is not manly nor is womanly: it is lived with the strength and Grace of both. All of the adversities and failures that lay upon the landscape of history are due to the lack of skill in interaction. The external world is an interaction between opposites. Relationships are like rivers of passing events, and strong are its currents. As soon as we form one event through interaction and bring it into focus, it is swept by and another takes its place.

Through interaction, we learn our lessons with persons, places, and things!

## *Involvement*

Realistically, life is uncertain because we cannot determine what the outcome of a course of action will be, but we can hypothesize. That is why we are always taking part, engaging or sharing in the activities of a person(s) or group(s). Involvement provides us with a sense of inclusion in our everyday lives. When we are involved with others, we must listen and respect all opinions. If a view is opposing, we ought not to take it personally. In the decision process, we should integrate economic, social, and technological concepts with political ideas. We can identify and achieve common goals and mutual gains by putting ourselves in another person's shoes. Understanding the ideas of others, no matter how diverse, shows a willingness to include those concepts in the association.

As we grow, develop, and move into involvement with our peers, we discover that our identification with them increases. This brings about physical, emotional and social changes that can be reassuring or disturbing. With differences, use sympathy because all of us face similar dilemmas. In some form or other, we all belong to a family and are always searching for new members to replace those who have moved on to other areas of life, away from everyday contact. New interpersonal involvements are important especially when these relationships share similar beliefs and common interests. The company we keep tells us a lot about ourselves. When we are equal, it is true participation. It is not the size of the involvement that is important, but the worth and choices made from that connection. To receive the full measure of life's joys, we must have others with whom to share those pleasures.

We are all intimate guides when we are involved with the feelings of others. As we seek ways to live more fully, we cannot help but include others in that great drama of improving the mind, heart and body. This need is in everyone and everything. From a single cell, the Essence that we call us has evolved into the face we see in the mirror. All of the seeds of life, including minerals, plants, animals, humans and the cosmos, find their fulfillment through involvement: the compelling push toward expression with others. We cannot escape from this process because we are a part of it. Belonging to the universe, we seek our fulfillment through the universe and our minds are its outlet.

When we look at the larger vision, we see that many people have inspired us to move forward by drawing the visible from the Invisible. Thus, we can find our own doorway that leads to greater promise. This picture of ourselves is fashioned out of our involvement with the efforts, hopes, dreams, longing, inspirations, doubts, fears and the faith of others. If there are any barriers that keep us back, we create them from our own lack of understanding. We should not judge the harvest of others. Rather, we should judge the seeds that we plant as thoughts in ourselves.

Our existence has brought its own peculiar lessons of strengths and weaknesses. Everything in us evolves, as it should.

## *Acknowledgement*

It is difficult to accept responsibility not only for ourselves, but also for others. Often it is easier to focus on other issues instead of the more pressing ones that concern the bigger picture. It is difficult to let go of our comfort zone from which we derive a sense of security. This is especially so when it comes to admitting the existence of truth or reality of what exists beyond that comfort zone. To be conscious means hanging out with other consciousness. In a sense, we can never be completely free from the enticements that exist on another person's menu. As long as we are in physical life, we will be at their table selecting and choosing what others serve. When it comes to the big earthly table, the menu choices are enormous. We cannot control the forces of earth, but we can harness its magnetism and energy wisely by thinking about a more balanced plate. Many of us feel powerless when it comes to influencing public opinion about ongoing issues. However, we do have minds and those minds exist out of memory and thought. When we understand consciousness as a form of magnetism in the same way quantum particles behave, we may find that consciousness acts the same way. Once we connect with other consciousness, we may stay united and influence one another, no matter how far apart we are. It is possible that the whole chain of cause and effect, the history of life and the universe, stops when we ponder on what to choose. However, the effects of the choices made are not random.

What we choose to do or not to do is of our own making. Good or bad, we will be part of the outcome. Big and small exist in the same paradigm. When we perceive an action in our thinking, then a decision comes about. That outcome may not appear in physical reality but it may help balance our Inner qualities. We may not always be able to solve the physical drama of others, but we can open our mental eyes and behold the treasure house of Infinity within them. Most people are sound asleep in the glamour of reality and our thoughts can help awaken that reality. There is a way to transform the workings of society without the use of violence and weapons. That way is by demagnetizing the selfish thoughts of the power movers. When we carefully scrutinize their words and actions to see if they reflect betterment for all, we are using the power of magnetism in the same way light penetrates darkness by diffusing it. When we acknowledge thought as the mover of persons, places and things, and that it is our duty to improve these thoughts, we are practicing the best type of citizenship. Through correct acknowledgement, we appeal to our better selves to work in uniformity with the laws of nature so that Truth is working through all. When we accept our fate with persons, places and things compassionately, we are bettering the inclusive fate of everyone.

Physically, we all exist so that others may exist. We may never be in their presence except through the imagination, but we have the power to see them Perfect as they are.

# Synchronicity

Life, quality and appearance are the three experiences (the gears or wheels of being) that make existence what it is; they occur as conscious awareness. First, we are aware of life: the familiarity of being alive, the course of human events and activities. Next is quality: the characteristic property that defines the individual nature of something. Last is appearance: the outward or visible aspect of a person or thing. These three aspects give us the ability to pattern our behavior in the creation that takes us on the many journeys that we desire. Through this triple interconnectedness, we harness the means to understand our journey, our humanity and our place in the vastness of Creation, the focus of our imagination. Then we connect to the people, places, and things that attracted us in life. When a sense of betterment motivates us, our Higher Consciousness positively creates the synchronistic situations that will play out in our evolutionary process. When we think optimistically, this is how our reality works.

We are the designers of our reality. The strengths and weaknesses of that reality depend on what we allow to influence us. Our fate and the wheels of time play an important part in the architecture of our lives: those coincidences that have a special meaning. The wheels of causality exist outside of our physical reality because we cannot see where that Invisibility takes us or where the Original Cause resides. This is the cause and effect of the past, present and future, inserted into the timeline of now, synchronized by the choices we make. Each of us in our own way is best qualified to understand those moments. Those precious miracles that enter our lives and give us purpose are the aspects of the Higher Self. We must come to understand the coincidental events that manifest in our lives as Inner and outer occurrences in our own unique way even if we do not have the ability to explain them.

Regardless of the depth and insight we get through synchronizing life, quality and appearance, as individuals we choose our own level of response to those patterns. We fashion the relationship. With regard to personal experience, we determine our behavior by our response to the event. The universe characterizes through us. The universe of our world is not how the universe itself is, but how we perceive it. In our conceiving of it, the universe catches us in its grip and the occurrences that link us together.

Drawn to its Light, we cannot avoid its synchronism. From the reflections of the patterns of the living, we shape the universe in our own image as we swirl around in its forms of energy. In the stillness of the imagination, the other parallels are there; we do not have to search for anything, they move into us. We must stay open to the guidance of synchronicity and not let negative viewpoints hinder the path.

Though we may not see it at the time, with the right perspective, synchronicity guides us in the coming together of Spirit and matter.

## *Togetherness*

Togetherness is the concept of being close to another person emotionally and physically. This state makes one feel warm on the inside and creates a positive desire for those who want to be in each other's company. Togetherness is not limited to two persons but includes cultures, societies, institutions, governments and the workings of the animal, plant and mineral kingdoms. All of the parts that make up the wholeness of life jointly indwell and fuse together to create our existence. Thus, we color the whole and its parts by the qualities of one another. When we are together in harmony, we absorb, interpenetrate and mutually infuse each other while remaining open to receptivity. When we follow the natural trend of things, always taking things in the light of the greater community, we are shaping priorities of togetherness.

Conflict-ridden issues lower our sense of togetherness. When we lack togetherness, we often fall victim to the concept, "My views are true, therefore yours must be a lie, so I must protect myself and those I care about from the effects of your lie." This type of reasoning often leads to disagreements and war. When we view all of life as One Family, we will see all of its various parts as separate but equal in its daily interfacing. This type of thinking will keep us feeling close to others. It is through togetherness that we have existence. It also reveals character and understanding. If we did not exist together, we would be alone without knowing we were alone. We are always in the way of one another in some form or other. When our sense of togetherness is strong, we shape our cultures together in positive ways. We should value the cultures we were born in, and respect other cultures through which we did not evolve. We can enjoy persons, places and things in the same way the body enjoys health or the mind discernment. We must care for others the same way our minds do our bodies. From this natural togetherness there is no place for aloneness; we simply take care of each other with full uncompromising respect.

In the same way we view our culture of togetherness, those who follow us will inherit this view also. The way we interact and describe the world to each other influences us the same way we pass on the tendencies of our genes. A good sense of togetherness that rearranges life with beauty, harmony, humor and health can neutralize inherent negative responses. Everything that moves in the universe from thought forms to physical forms acts through interconnectedness. Togetherness can be wonderful when it instills unity without babble and violence. In order for us to understand and shape non-violent cultures, societies, and the people within them, we must value the diversity of others for the Greater Good of the community, thus creating harmony and togetherness.

Our togetherness should be a moving Wisdom that has no boundaries.

### Growth without Suffering

Most belief systems hold to the idea that through suffering we redeem ourselves of the acts committed against persons and things. Is suffering inherent or self-induced? None of us starts out wanting to suffer; yet many of us grow to feel this condition. We accept this state as a part of the everyday life. We are involved in suffering when we have a negative emotion or pain that involves a subjective character of unpleasantness, aversion, harm or threat of harm. What we believe and how other persons and groups think and act motivate and instill in us an ongoing belief in suffering as a redemptive process. The rationale for suffering lies in the belief that if we had not created the cause, we would not feel an effect. When we control our minds, we can diminish what is occurring in our immediate environment. As such, are we responsible for the choices that others make concerning our environment, our politics, our economy, etc? The rules and laws established within any system of government are reflective of the dispositions of those who preside over its workings. Its power comes from the consent of the people. When we give someone permission to act in another person's name by voice or vote, it carries with it the law of cause and effect. We are responsible for the thoughts and ideas that we allow to influence our minds. When we understand this, we will be more vigilant in our responses. As we expand our mental abilities, we learn to wake up and see things as they are. This is the first step toward diminishing suffering from our experiences.

We cannot avoid the pain when atoms, chemicals and neurons of our physical make up go through their separation process anymore than a fetus can shun the uniting of cells for its growth and development. Both are the natural positive ways of nature. Our minds and emotions commence at birth and where they go at death is a question answered only in that state. Our physical life separates through disease, accidents or old age and none of them are without some sort of pain. However, we can lessen the effects that come our way by being harmless in thought and deed. Suffering is not a thing of the future. Rather it is a process of the present. Some want us to hold onto the belief that suffering awaits us in the future. Why would we want to hold such a view since we cannot establish how our future will be, especially since we are in this physical time? We can develop a positive imagination as to how we want to develop our minds and emotions. Causes create a corresponding effect. When we practice empathy, mental suffering melts away. Violent causes bring violent effects. As we overcome the causes of suffering, we are increasing the process of becoming larger, more flexible in our space in an expansive universe

We have options in life, so choose wisely now.

## *Re-Entry*

Is there a repeated entry, a coming into possession again of awareness after departing the physical body? Do we return to earth or elsewhere? When we look at awareness as a state of being conscious of Consciousness, it is easier to accept the belief in such a process. Why would we want to deny our continuation? If a person does deny it, then those of us who do believe in a continuum would not know that others refute it, nor would they know that we do believe in it! As long as there is no harm involved, it is of no great concern what someone else believes or thinks. We are in the moment now, and most likely, those moments go on even if we are not here. Because we exist now gives credence to the possibility of our continuation. It makes sense that if we have particles of physical existence, we must have particles of conscious existence from which we retain our memories of what we have been or done. This is an awareness that is dependent on individual aspects such as relation, quantity, time and place: the categories that make up existence. How those particles reconstitute themselves in time in space is most likely unfathomable to the human intellect.

We can review recorded history through books, paintings, and other various records and see that people and things existed in the past. We can also project that those in the future will be viewing our present in the same manner we are now viewing our past. Hence, re-existence does not necessarily mean a recollection of those past events! Without the element of awareness, no memory objects would exist. However, there is life: the experience in the moment. As long as there is birth and death going on around us, we are still here, wherever here is, i.e., wakefulness. How can anyone with certainty say we fade out completely? Just because awareness is not fixed does not mean a lack of permanence. For example, the fire of a candle can light another candle. A fire spreading from one source to another is dependent on the original fire. Therefore, there must be a conditional relationship between one life and the next: Wakefulness. They are probably not identical nor are they completely separate. If you find yourself existing somewhere, there you are. In what soil do the roots of life have hold but in Consciousness?

Consciousness receives its nourishment and strength from the whole of life. What is concealed in memory enters the soil of life and lives from the roots of its past. The strength that supports the whole tree comes from the basic elements of existence. In whatever manner we perceive or interpret existence whether as Spirit, matter, force, idea, will, substance, subject, or as the eternal recurrence of the same 'Event-light', life is appearing as Being. Whatever represents Being has arrived covertly.

How the force of existence evolved from its concealment and how it manifests remains obscure as a fact in re-entering physical awareness.

### Spirit: a Metaphor for Sustainability

The universe is our playground where the mind acts out its dramas. The mind has its own entrance and exit and each of us sees, feels and realizes our bliss according to our own inclinations. We determine our receptivity for bliss by the amount of effort we put toward unfolding knowledge and wisdom. Our surroundings reflect how we utilize that wisdom. Self-discovery is the open door into that knowing. As long as we depend on others to define our Divinity, we will feel distant from that Truth. In order to understand our Inner and outer nature, we must empower our own being with that Infinite Source. For this Inner reality to remain unshakable, its quest must remain constant even in the difficulties of everyday experiences. Each little spark must connect to the next bigger one, on and on into Infinity.

Physical life is short-lived. What we feel and realize continue forever. In realization, the Inner Life remains constant. The outer life with all its variances is constantly changing its patterns with persons, places and things. At this moment, we have to accept life as it is. The physical world constitutes life as we play it out. Essence or energy gives memory momentum which enables us to have being in time and space. Therefore, we have to keep that energy alive with Spirit and believe that its power animates all. This goal aims at preserving quality interactions with the life processes. By staying the course, we create a strong Will for a productive existence.

We invoke pure Will through truth and virtue. Virtue is the resolve to love selflessly; it originates and terminates in the Spirit. To the thinker, Spirit is nothing material. In its involvement, Spirit resolves to love by means of memory of its own truth. Part of this resolve is also to love other beings. Spirit is by its nature a thinking substance. Spirit originates events that are neither determined nor random. The spiritual journey is about giving meaning to its thinking, not blind utterances in exchange for rewards. Because Spirit remembers and knows its own Pure Essence, it remembers sensations without details as they come around. First Spirit remembers its own pure memory. Spirit is always remembering what it knows. It is always intuitively aware of the Higher Source because Spirit is devoid of a body that acts as an impediment to the immediate Intuition of purely intelligible beings. The body expresses the things of the senses whereas Spirit feels the sensations of those experiences, the only Essence that is sustainable. Universal Spirit cooperates endlessly with the heat, light, luster and action of all things.

# *Transformation in Infinity*

In our own mysterious way, a qualitative change is occurring in each of us as we move through the Eternal processes of Infinity. Repeated in persons, places and things this illuminating Essence permeates all according to the ability to sustain an attraction with it. Free will and free choice shape our existence. This existence requires different strategies, plans and degrees of engagement as we move in the mix. Environment, heredity, family and social pressure move with and against us in our development, transition and transformation. In the developmental phase, we enter and interact with persons and groups that set the standards for our accomplishments. Then we go through the transitional change that replaces what already exists with something very new. We gain new knowledge; we reorganize our thought processes and plan where we want to go and be before the transition. This planning is beyond the more personal levels of skill, action, approaches, behavior and cultural traits; this mindset is personal and timeless. Without this inner shift of mind, we cannot sustain the internal achievements of new structures and systems of information and awareness. Overcoming external causes of the developmental stage of life is the basis of this new state of mind. Because the transformational stage is largely unknown, it rests on imagining the change and believing that we can reach it.

There are always new and beautiful things on the horizon when we release ourselves from our external trappings. Life can trap us in a web of limiting beliefs that keep us stuck. We do not need to be of the world but we need to move through it intelligently as we live in it. When we limit our beliefs, we are slowing the revolution of Infinity in our views. We can always find time to go shopping in the world of causes, but there never seems to be enough time to strive to understand the effects of our actions. When we put our hearts and minds into the working of Infinity, we have risen above fear and wanting to that of doing. There are many situations in the world, both good and unpleasant. The world can provide us with wisdom and motivation when we desire to transform our character with the Higher Self. We do most of our daily actions without thinking; we seem to act unknowingly. When we use wisdom, the dark clouds dissipate and we expose the glow of the Self. As a result, things cannot hide their true outline. When we return to the place of the Self, we will perceive the ways in which to transform circumstances. We must believe in the Essence of who we are: a continuous process unfolding.

Mystery abounds in each of us; to unlock those mysteries is why we are here.

## Shifting Images of Time and Space

As we live and move through time and space, we are always stirring from one state or place to the next. Conceived first in the womb, we then grow into infancy, childhood, youth, and from maturity into old age. At the end of life, elemental nature reabsorbs the elements that make up the physical part of our being. This ongoing change from one place, state, subject, or stage to another is the action of the substance that pervades existence and its core. As we merge with the various attributes that make up existence, it is difficult not to imagine all those appearances are more than what they appear to be. We (plants, animals, and humans) are like beautiful butterflies struggling to set ourselves free from the cocoon of existence. Today and the moment are important, but also it is vital to see life's situational changes the same way we watch the seasons pass: every shift begins with an ending. When we develop lasting relationships, we are creating enduring images that are ongoing even though the physical part is no longer visible. Thus, we are shifting from the familiar to the unfamiliar as we re-examine our values and venues of awareness.

When we look into our past reflectively, we can undo unfinished business with others; we can set those difficulties right. When we call upon the Higher Self, we learn to see things as they are with other human beings in handling present and future shifts. We start using those insights to further our advancements in the Eternal flow. Whatever unknowable fate we face, it is our strength and belief in our survival that give credence to the imagination. The scientific world has its methods for actualizing the material world. The mind that fades away from the physical also has its method for maintaining its reality. Like the clouds that dissipate in the air, the mind dispels its association with the elements. It takes on a new knowing that dissolves previous connections. Change can be our greatest teacher if we but learn from its patterns and alter our erroneous perceptions that limit real human power. Human fate is transferable; it reappears in new places. When we leap, the net will appear. Creation is the net, but we must be aware of what we are doing and being when we leap into it. Like the instinctual caterpillar that goes through its stages to become a beautiful butterfly, we also shift from one stage to the next. Generally, our awakened intuition guards our stages. We facilitate this ongoing process by valuing the past before letting go of obsolete concepts, expectations and behaviors. Whether in the now or in a new place that has meaning, the aspects of creativity, confidence, and optimism are always reconstructing and adapting to new realities.

From wakefulness we progress forward and find new ways to express Being on the changing face of time and space.

## Our Right Humanistic Ways

When we expand our consciousness, we are grasping the Good life, the life that is worthy and satisfying. Life then becomes an ethical process based on universal human qualities that dignify the worth of all people through rightness and rationalism. Rightness is the most powerful way of manipulating creative substance of mind and feeling. This energy mass is available to all living creatures. It molds and builds the stuff of life and opens the door to true humanism. To allow true humanism to surface, we must remove the self-destructing attitudes and primitive reasoning of the inner and outer world's selfishness from consciousness. When we direct our lives through reasoning, our lives become more secure and unified. When we allow unbalanced factors outside of ourselves to sway us, we are preventing the 'Beautiful Life' from expressing itself. As we delve deeper into our own rationality, we will see that we reject the Good life because of the lack of self-determination and discrimination.

Humanism is what gives meaning to all of creation and has a special relationship to it. This relationship is expressed through 'selfness' and should be the main ingredient in every component of the educational curriculum. This is contrary to the belief that the progress of life occurs through struggle. Rather, we manifest humanism by wisdom, virtue and balanced pleasure. Self-sustaining progress brings lasting forms of happiness. Constant partying after material gain does not instill goodness. It only diminishes and hinders the flow of creative substance. Right human character (honesty, caring, harmlessness and self-responsibility) prepares people to lead others and allows for ongoing participation in public life that does not breach the common good.

Civic humanism is best when it stresses eloquence through all social endeavors. When we are responsible for one another, whether in the family, city, state or country, we are defining our duty and humanity. This quest for the Good life when used with a sense of balance can create better community Goodwill. It is the best chance for a constructive multicultural and internationally sustainable world. Everything in the world has its own way. We are practicing humanism when we understand human nature; humanism is about being human. Our pursuit of it is best when we use virtue in attaining it. In the long term it will makes us a true, knowledgeable, kind and courageous humanity. We are expressing true humanism when we strive to better ourselves through study, health and love. We are then using reason and free inquiry and creative substance, thus wisely shaping our human works.

Humanism is a way of life that brings Joy to others in the natural world through reason, science and democracy.

## *Ideals and Reality*

In our physical, emotional and mental states and as individuals within society we are always reaching for something that goes beyond the routine of the moment. An ideal reflects absolute perfection, one that we regard as a standard or model of excellence. In reality, is there a divergence between personal and professional ideals? In the everyday world, there is situational reality like family, marriage and happiness. Then there are professional ideals that include the values passed on to students, work force and the populace. We often express these in character traits of kindness, hard work and honesty, or their opposites. However, in reality do ideals fully encompass a state of things as they actually exist? When we look at our observable state of government, it seems that the experiences that we create by thought, belief and concepts are often contradictory to the stated laws of society, such as justice, equality, domestic tranquility and the general welfare of our succeeding generations. In the actuality of consciousness, life is effortless, especially, when we allow it to be as it is. Consciousness is a natural flow of energy passing through our systems of belief and action. To blend ideals with reality, a person and an event must show the quality of expressive realism. When we examine the moment-by-moment aspects of life with jurisprudence, whether scientific, philosophical, political, or religious, all life benefits equally.

Reality is composed of planning and thinking. Ideals infuse space with existence or Essence. Behind this is our culture and society. Go back farther and we have substance, principle or Spirit: the sum that is absolute and unchangeable. How we handle this constant force reflects in the moments of persons and things. Distortion is in the eye of the beholder; objective reality corresponds to what we paint on the inside. When the mind thinks with the term 'impossible' there will be obstructions to objects, people and scenes. However, when the mind focuses on 'the common good' our potentiality immensely increases. Life's resources become sustainable when we defuse impossible thinking with quality thinking. The ways of society are filled with disruptive patterns (spells of inertia, charms affecting the eye) making it difficult for all but a few to remain focused. This type of action causes things to appear differently from what they are.

In choosing between what is ideal and what we perceive now as reality, we forgo knowledge and equal betterment for the instant fix. We want to do what is right, but we seem powerless to take the right path.

It is up to each of us, in our own particular way, to interpret through our beliefs, attitudes and values how ideals and reality mix in us.

### *Imitative Behavior*

Family interactions, peer pressure, and societal input instill our mannerisms and the way we act to control ourselves at a young age. As a result, the vast majority of society mimics or attempts to copy the appearance or character of others. In our world pursuits, we are following those models or examples often without any attempt at enhancing our own originality. This type of association goes against one's original patterns of self-processing. Consequently, the knowledge, skills, or attitudes of society as a whole become a planned set of reinforcements, thus strengthening and heightening political agendas, productivity and commercialization. Unknowingly, we become followers instead of leaders for each other and society.

How are we to overcome those mesmerizing influences? First, we have to remove ourselves from the box! Then we look toward our health and well-being and ask, "How do I go about removing undesirable behaviors?" We start by removing the maladaptive patterns of self-importance exhibited by others with a more balanced importance of the self. When we voluntarily switch on the light and turn up the thinking about the self, the Inner person, we alter our social environment and our moral values that allowed other persons and things to sway us. In doing this, we are creating a model of the self and its world. Human life is dauntingly complex with all its economic and cultural diversities. However, when we simplify our bodily needs, our private relationships and our broader social endeavors, our internal outlook transcends imitation.

The self in its beginning is shapeless. Only through the imagination and self-inquiry can its light become compassionately indifferent to what is. Without the aid of intuition, the self is 'sleep walking' through material life, swayed by the impulses of the more awakened materialists. The more that the self imitates the substance of its Source, the more individual it becomes in forming its own patterns of doing and becoming. The more the self imitates this Inner substance the more alive it becomes in its individual imagination. It learns to dance in step with the concept of the abstract to the concrete, the concrete to the subtle. When we attempt to understand life through the imitation of others, we are seeing with collective eyes what we have forgotten. When we see that all life is what we have come to know through our own awareness, we start wondering at our own marvelous originality.

Learning is taking advice from others, but real awareness results from understanding one's own feelings about persons, places and things. We must listen to our own echo for when we follow others, we will likely fall behind. No doubt, we all need community, but to those of us who need our own path, we must constantly remind ourselves to put aside the imitations of the establishment and to believe in the self. When we live in the Self, we bring Life to life.

When we seek excessive approval from others, we could be closing our own doors of self-inquiry.

# Identification

The prime mover of human process is identification with oneself (consciously or unconsciously) or with another person or group(s). From a corporal point of view, without identifying with others, human consciousness would be mostly blank. Identification also creates remembrances of persons, places and things. If we are limited in our movements (to speak freely, to converse with others as freedom of action) we are limited in identifying with others. Imagine finding oneself all alone. No matter where one looked or traveled, one could not find a single person with which to relate. One would be in a place of singularity. It would be very difficult to create a volume of human identification from that place.

How did consciousness become aware of itself? Could consciousness have formed when unconsciousness collapsed upon itself due to inertia? We will probably never know with certainty. At some point, we came upon a reflection, a stirring of Light and space, which gave us a mirror image. From that point, we are as we are now. Our moods, sorrows, pains or excitements occur because we identify with the material form aspect. Creation could not be static. Nor could it remain idle. The first birthing process will most likely remain unknowable. The awareness of that process is ongoing; from wonder to wonder, we are sensing its pulsating grandeur. There is no passing out of it.

When we are identifying with others, the goals for our endeavors should be to develop right relations between all points of view in expressing life, regardless of how life may have evolved. What is and what we would like to be can be codependent – for without mutual support life would vanish. It is not likely any of us would want to return to that point. Identifying with life is about fitting the body to the world and life's recognitions to the mind. Systematically, one recall after another and from place to place, we are always at the center of that progression. As we move through our various forms of expression, it is up to each of us to manifest its Goodness for those we leave behind. This should be our task, our dream and aspiration. When we identify with others with compassion and truthfulness, we are grasping the best for the future and understanding what is occurring in this progression of beauty. The grand and intimate aspects of life can continue as memory. They can awaken us with lasting testimony, discoveries, and purpose behind that first identification.

Identification is a process of mental configuration. From these patterns, we form ideals and desires and deem them as our own. The effective ones should be the ones with which we identify. When we look at the world around us with understanding, we shift our identification to think and dream of a healthier present and future. When we live a life full of positive identification there is no ending, only a full self!

When time and circumstance warrant, the identification of persons, places and things, the energy of mind projects onto the substance of space. In that space, we enter the power of the laws and dimensions that are identifiable to us.

## *Adaptability and Contentment*

Because of our bodies, we are able to move around and experience various persons, places and things. We then digest those familiarities into mental factors as consciousness. This gives us the ability to fit or be versatile in the material process. All of us, regardless of our place or status, want to fit in even if it is at the most basic levels of existence. The key is to discover what our expectations will be in that fitting process. We can have guides to help us tune ourselves so we have that ability. However, adaptability is more than living for the day; it is also about the future. When we are loaded with rules and regulations that govern life, they can often offset our rational experience of happiness, satisfaction, and ease in our situation of body, mind and emotions. We need to adapt constantly to our circumstances with contentment. This adaptation is a reward for depth of character that serves society and avoids selfishness.

When we fail to see the wholeness of life expressed through ceaseless currents of motion, we are not adapting but rebelling against selflessness. We are maximizing our material importance while minimizing our personal contentment. When we express balance in all circumstances, in whatever state we are in, we are sustaining our productivity and will have plenty without craving for more. Through this type of thinking, we are content. When we move above 'value importance' in our everyday living, we are flexible. Then we look at what lies beneath our feet as well as what lies on the horizon. To be fully adaptable, we must remove doubts from the mind. Any uncertainty about our existence, our purpose and meaning is futility at its worst. It is far better to go with existence without attempting to stop or hinder its flow. Existence is! We are adapting when we drop the illusion of others. Contentment is a connectedness to the sudden flashes of the Self to solve and fix its own illusions.

Our initial state was one of well-being. When we came to this life, we became 'unplugged' from that state as we grew into this one. When we have satisfied our needs and dreams, passed through the pains and stresses of physical existence, we begin the process of familiarizing ourselves with the True Self and start to 'hardwire' ourselves back to that initial state. It is through attraction and repulsion that we develop our economy of being which is inherent in matter. When we fuse our Essence with material stuff, activity blends harmony with knowledge and idealism with conditions of living. As a result, we will develop the air that passes through our lungs and the electrical phenomena that enters through the brain. Once developed, these phenomena will vitalize the infrastructure of society. It will build forms, create machines to contain and distribute the electrical forces of the atmosphere. It will harness the activity of matter, and form it into better physical life with the Spirit of fire, air and water.

We are at our best when we adapt through matter that is energetic, heated, lighted, glorious, moving, positive and alive.

## *Perfection*

We can strive to be perfect and without flaws. A slow and ordered process is the best method to realize perfection. Is there such a state of being? Most likely, there are only degrees of rightness. No matter how hard we try to live a life of perfection, there is an opposite side confronting us. The best we can do is to take each day and do what we can to be harmless on our path. When our hearts say we are doing something right, we are working toward perfection. Do not waste moments being disappointed on what you can or cannot do. Is there anyone among us who can truly define perfection? If so, would that description match ours? Who decides what is accurate or mistaken? Some people believe in imperfection and that we come here to become perfect. Perhaps when we think things are not perfect just as they are, we are uncertain about our place in the scheme of things.

Thus, we create a negative image of persons, places and things. It does not take much observation to realize that everything is in a constant state of flux and change. Because the world is changing around us daily does not mean we are becoming perfect. We are always making new choices, changing, dropping old ways, and creating anew. True awareness is not necessarily a criterion for perfection. When we think we are imperfect, we are in the grind of habits that we do not want to remove or transform. Perfection is not about control, perspective, or the definition we might put on it. Through perfection, we see all as it really is: a state of becoming, suited to fit our beliefs and needs.

When we work with correctness, we are changing ourselves. As a result, we will view the world around us as more balanced. Whatever we want to achieve, there must be a means to bring it about. We begin with understanding why we do certain things. Most of us in the world act in a mechanical way. Each day seems to be a repetition of the one before. To make each day different we must change ourselves/viewpoints from the unconscious to the Conscious. Then the Inner Self endows us with a higher state of compassion. We learn to see perfection by being better at what we do each day. When we dust off the dirt on the surface of a mirror, we disclose the essential nature of the clear mirror. The dusting of the mirror does not diminish the reflective clarity of the mirror that was behind the dust.

Are we making excuses when we say, "Nobody's perfect" and that we are beyond improvement; or is it just a concept of culture? When we are motivated to seek perfection, goals set on righteous positive behavior instill truth and compassion for others to follow. Some believe that we cannot be perfect and that to be so would be boring. Nevertheless, to give up on being perfect is like giving up on time that is always evolving. To transcend our humanness, we must become conscious of Consciousness. This becomes the path to Perfection.

Our purpose is to work toward aligning the means of existence that is already perfect with our everyday life.

## *Justification of Belief*

Each of us is a belief in the making: a justification for our being that answers why, how and what we know. Many aspects of our lives are justified by beliefs, actions, emotions, laws, theories, intellectuality and so on. If our beliefs are to be accepted, we need to validate them. For example, as a nation, our early founders believed in individual freedom without monarchy, so they created a Declaration of Independence to bring about separation. Thus, the enactment of the Constitution established the justification for such an action. Those early intellectual seeds are still growing in us as 'We the People'. Equality, fairness, security and expression are still without full validation for many because beliefs and other conscious mental states are justified by some in power to prevent the full expression of equality and justice from occurring. Do justification and knowledge work together, or is each a separate entity with its own internal and external agreements and disagreements? When a belief is justified, it becomes knowledge. When we find something does not work, it becomes non-justified belief.

In material science, the outer pursuit of knowledge works from the particular to universal whereas the inner means for obtaining knowledge work from the universal to the particular. When we believe that the process of life is one continuous whole working from end to end, on and on, our material justifications become learning tools for our choices. Humanity in all times and in the most diverse conditions is trying to justify one commonality: the reality behind perception and its relation with it. We utilize all kinds of justifications to uplift society, mostly by selfish means. History is drenched in violence, and barriers of bigotry and hate are still waiting for their resolution. However, when the higher justifications for truth, wisdom and compassion are present in our affairs, negative desires will decline and our justification for existence will align with the One Reality.

We do not find the justification of Infinite Reality in wrath or desire. It lies in moving out of the qualities inherent in matter to those of Spirit: the true objective of human existence. However, through our justifications, we are still piling words upon words and still building alters to our own thinking in an attempt to throw light upon our self-made fears. Declarations are for the people; governments are of The People. Neither is to restrain, but are to improve our lives and interests.

No matter how hard we attempt to justify it, the causes that link us to the One Reality will never fully unravel by material pursuits. Knowledge and Wisdom are the only connections to it.

## *Alone and Together*

The moment we enter life each of us has a set of instructions programmed to enable us to cope with life situations and circumstances that at times seem beyond our power to control. Yet, we somehow manage to progress through this seemingly chaotic world. When we look around, the vast arena of circumstances varies for each person as greatly as the stars above us. These vast differences can seem overwhelming to a mind that does not think holistically. To be conscious of Consciousness we think with wholeness of our being rather than with the parts of our being. No person is just the sum of his/her parts. Although we are by nature individuals, the vast systems of institutions program us throughout life by shaping culture and society according to their set of instructions. We pass on the collection of information from generation to generation. This information has an effect on who we are and what we will become in material life. When we lack intuition and discrimination, that information can become counterproductive to our Higher awareness. This information can keep us enthralled in our senses and can block out holistic impressions where we view nature as an integrated system rather than as a collection of individual aspects. Thus, some think the idea of social holism is a rival to the concept of individualism.

The aspects of human life evolve by studying and learning from other humans. The images and metaphors we use to describe our existence should be universal in our common culture. Across time and space, each of us is a coherent, interconnected system of body, mind and emotion. Space, time, matter, energy, force and Spirit pervade human consciousness in order to gather data to fill us with life, quality and appearance. Therefore, our narrative of individual and relational aspects of expression should be the same when shaping human behavior. Our identification with space and time generates continuous, recurrent pathways of existence. It is through our nervous systems that we induce and control behavior for the physical plane. Time and space are indifferent to behavior and learning. Decision-making and reinforcement of learning techniques are sub-conscious by nature and through our senses; we apply, control and learn behavior. We can only know and learn by stages. Regardless of what we place before the five senses and the mind, we can only view, realize and know Essence if there is a consciousness to recognize and record it.

The vast majority of human problems could be alleviated if society thought in terms of nature/existence as a unified whole rather than seeing people as divided.

## *Realization of Thoughts*

We are always waking up in our thoughts. Our thoughts make us. Through thoughts, we realize and appreciate everything we have in life such as altruism, faith, family, nationality and the world. In our realizations can we be free of thoughts, or is our awareness just a thought? Through growth, we come to understand persons, places, and things clearly and distinctly as well as recognizing what we have created from our thoughts. Each of us is responsible for the kind of thoughts on which we dwell. No matter what we create in the beginning stage, its form is imperfect. Nevertheless, through our senses, we gather more data, information, and in time, the form becomes perfect. Hence, our realizations propel us onward through either bodily sensations or intuition. Realization can be internal and external, or in combination. We are awake when we realize and sense forms. From sound, color, shapes, and movement we produce words and from words, we create the forms that give us pictures to keep the mind awake.

Thoughts and feelings give us a realization of being. Light is the basis for human consciousness and the structure of our world. What we see and what we sense informs us that we are alive. Light or Spirit activates the nervous system to respond. Thought in Essence is the evolutionary response to what we know as consciousness. The more we know the more conscious we become in the Higher Self.

Consciousness is not always aware of its bodily complexes. When the mind is clearly discriminatory in the use of its five senses, it becomes interactive with the substance that pervades the world: Light/matter, the primary requisite for realization. Our nervous system is the backbone that alerts form activity to come into being. All of our urges, desires and needs are set in motion by this neural system. We feed it by modifying our thinking and feeling until we find the right balance. Through realization, we solve what is true and not true. We see and know the differences between our thought processes and learning processes. We evaluate thoughts to see if they are correct and either continue thinking about them or not. When we approach each thought with clarity, we see things as they are and irrational thoughts do not surface. We are all born in Truth. Because of attractive digressions as we grow, we dive into life forgetting the One Reality, the wholeness that gave us being. When we constantly go from one fulfillment to the next, unknowingly we can place unnecessary negative energy in the currents of earth.

We are on the path of self-realization when we hold fast to the natural and moral principles that apply to all beings. This is the most important of all life's realizations because it turns away the thoughts that feed negativity. Self-realization is a synonym for Joyful living. When conflicting opinions and actions in life confuse the mind and emotions, we must stay steady and firm in the belief of the Higher Self.

Consciousness contains an Infinite surplus of creativity that overflows time and space in its pursuit of self-realization.

## The Sun, the Earth and Everything

When this life has run its course and our bodies cease to move in time and space, does the earth end, too? Do we divide and go our separate ways? Will the stars and moon still light the night sky? The only knowing we have about Immortality rests on belief and faith that are not tangible observances of existence. Nevertheless, Consciousness is, and to grasp existence fully, we must view life and substance as One Reality. We can only know the attributes of our new awakening when we are there. Most likely, we will never visualize its reality or communicate factually with anyone from the other side. However, this seems insignificant to a potent imagination. Light is all there is and that could be our make-up and even our Immortality. We understand our world through scientific methods such as the collection of data through observation, experimentation, formulation and testing of hypotheses. When those methods establish facts, they are collectively apparent. There is no clear-cut way of observing Infinity as a fact. For this, we rely on the imagination: the mind's ability to form an image of something not visible to the senses. Imagination is an image of something that is unlike things that one has seen and sparks a new creativity in understanding existence.

Imagination is the creative power of the Higher Self, a reflection of the Ultimate Light. This reflection forms us out of the clay in the garden of earth. This creativity goes with us when we leave this garden to do something, be something and make something happen. It is a sense of being in a rightful relationship with the rest of existence. Its very nature is spiritual and intangible thus making us more patient and alive. If one needs proof of this imagination, it will dissolve as mist does in the presence of sunlight. On earth, harmony is difficult in a system where we identify things as individual. To have merit persons, places and things must conform to a set of laws that govern the tangible by attraction and repulsion. In the spiritual imagination, we retain the better parts of nature and improve it. Time, space and reality exist because of awareness. Regardless of the methods employed to substantiate our existence, without awareness nothing would exist. How life came to earth will remain a mystery. This mystery drives the imagination onward and brings the cosmos into view. Life is the process of thought. Life exists in the universe and is Eternal. In the endless flow of time, life spreads from old planets to new ones. The energy patterns of life constantly rearrange themselves in the light spectrum. This Ultimate Light is the source for Consciousness as we experience it in this frame of knowing. When we leave this reality, what we have come to know exists because of what we have witnessed and recorded in our wakefulness, sleep, dreams or fantasy: imagination!

The sun, the earth and everything including ourselves have meaning because we are able to think and form thoughts.

## *Recall*

Remembering is recalling knowledge from memory. When we recall something, it is the ability to retrieve from memory a representation of prior learning or experience by images or words. Do we have the same kind of memory when the physical part of us passes on? Is recollection innate? Life is about discovering what we already know. Infinite knowledge is proactive and each of us in our own time, space, place and circumstance has access to that base. However, that knowledge is reciprocal. Our actions determine the makeup and manner in which we participate with persons, places, and things. This knowledge base can remain passive or proactive for long periods depending on the lessons that we learn individually and collectively. It is instinctive in the animal, plant and mineral kingdoms; it is conscious in humans.

Physical life is making choices as to what exists in the space between two objects. In the arena of the Higher Self, total recall is a kaleidoscope of color and pattern. Our senses are the prompts that give us clues to help us retrieve that for which we are searching. Because of the power of the senses and our addictions to them, they are not always reliable in forming the correct outlook about physical life. When the time, place and circumstance are not in accord, we experience the feeling that we know the right course to take but are powerless to act. The mind characterizes by the feeling of familiarity. It forms things when we remember something previously, but in the absence of stimulus, a correct response may not be identifiable. We can then remain indifferent and bide our time until the unique recollection occurs.

Consciousness is always relearning previous material. The more conscious, the faster we learn things and gather the information already stored. When we have input from the Higher Self, we revive memories that enliven and refresh our relearning. When we recollect the Higher way, we are providing ourselves solace in times of stress, insight into the higher heart and mind. Life and substance become expressions of intelligent love when we remember the Greater Awareness. When we are responsive to that knowledge, we are facing each other not as opposites but as complements. The deeper we remember, the more complex the mind and universe is. Therefore, the more precise we are in maintaining valid circumstances, the more we prevent confusion in moving among persons, places and things. We cannot be responsible for what is in another person's heart or mind. Nor can we step inside others and change their inner perspectives; but we can become a reflection.

Remembering is recalling knowledge from memory and selecting the thoughts that are of our own choosing.

# Truth of Consequence

To identify a consequence one must track a result of an action, process, outcome or cause to effect. Consequences, the building blocks for the universe, keep physical life encapsulated upon the planet earth. Thus, life is a game of sorts. How we play it, the choices we make, good, or bad constitute the relation of cause to effect. We work out cause and effect when time, place and circumstance meet with similar persons, places and things. Age and time factors vary for each cause and effect. From birth, childhood, youth, maturity, or old age, we change and play out the roles. This applies to individuals, groups, communities, societies, cultural types, races, and nations. All stem from the same force that binds us to the courses of action that force demands. When we plant an orange tree, we get oranges and the whole tree as well. The longer we go on making the same mistakes, the more we accumulate consequences and pain.

When we take a path of action that results in unpredictable events, the perpetrators often explain those results as unintended consequences. Often, this is just an attempt to clear those involved in all interactions of any personal responsibility for the outcome of the original action taken. What we observe is not always typical of what is happening. Often, there are accurate explanations, but we are unable to understand them through direct learned observation. For example, it is easier to see problems as individual when it comes to complex interaction. Blame the victim when it comes to cause and effect. We have allowed the ruling systems that give knowledge to explain away their failures rather than taking responsibility for the choices made. Rewards and punishments are forms of equal cause and effect. We all have the potential to become better persons that will result in better institutions and a more wholesome nation. All we have to do is use free will wisely in making choices that will determine our rewards.

Who and what influences our lives? Negative consequences can happen when we give up control over our lives and allow others to make choices for us. To get in control requires one to take inventory of what is controlling. This marks the path toward a self-responsible destiny that brings about the best results. Unlike animals, humans have the capacity to understand who they are and what will make their lives better. Whatever the causes, past or present, we set in motion the effects that come back. When actions are of a positive nature, we will always get a good return. Cause and effect will always be around; as long as we can look in the mirror and see ourselves, we have not gone beyond their influence.

When we do something that will carry a sweet Harmony in our actions, we are procuring a harmless destiny of change.

## *Forgiveness*

When we forgive, does it prevent cause and effect from reoccurring? Atonement is difficult at the end stages of physical release. It is best to practice it daily when we are dealing with persons, places and things. Forgiveness, the act of excusing a mistake or offense, occurs through loving kindness, compassion, and equanimity. By not accepting personal responsibility for acts and offenses, history has shown us that negative actions often repeat themselves. We do away with negative causes when we prevent harmful thoughts from influencing our mental well-being. The self forgives when we cultivate thoughts that leave a wholesome effect. When we fail to forgive our wrong thoughts, we create an identity around our unhappiness and those traits can return in life. It is impossible and fruitless to try to identify the acts we have committed with each other in humanity's immeasurable past. Forgiveness is a daily exercise in identifying our human limitations, treating others the same way that we would like to be treated, and seeing life as an interchange of forces and energy.

Inner forgiveness and outer forgiveness work from two different levels: On the outer (physical side), the laws of society demand a consequence for a wrongful deed. It is a collective vision or knowing that says to the populace 'this is the result'. The inner side requires reflection by the perceiver. There is no evidence that punishment occurs for any act once we leave physical life. This is strictly a faith issue. The basis for religion, spiritualism, or any concept that relates to an afterlife is faith and belief. We believe these concepts through someone else's views or ideas, or our own imagination. From a certain perspective, we all carry around a knapsack full of actions. What we know, see and experience represents our good or bad ways. Reflective forgiveness is not cause and effect. Through spiritual maturity, we seek wisdom concerning the fundamental values and goals of life.

Life has meaning because we are living it. Are we really learning anything? Does someone else's belief system affect our learning? Society deals with that information according to its paradigms. However, once we depart, the Vital Essence we will function in will be reflective and not of a material nature. It is certain that we pass from this life through accident, disease or old age. The real meaning of action implies the potential for change. Then we will understand that our life is energy and force. We will also accept that our own thoughts make us who we are. We then know what we want to experience, feel, know and see. We understand that we are that vibration working within that energy and force, from our own physical bodies, to every aspect of the external world. All plants, animals, people, and the cosmos itself become a reflection of forgiveness in action.

Forgiveness is a part of living. At the end of life, all we have is acceptance.

## Spiritualism, Science, and Hypocrisy

When we think of Spirit, we cannot help but tie it to religious belief and faith. It is an idea that we cannot prove formally because it exceeds physical reality. Though improvable, spiritualism is self-evident. It takes us beyond the natural world, physical universe, and the occurrences of the physical world and life in general. We take spiritualism and its truth for granted. It is a starting point for gathering other truths. Spiritual matters are concerned with humankind's ultimate nature and purpose, not only as material, biological organisms, but also as beings with a unique relationship to that which we perceive to be beyond both time and the material world. With the Self, it is more important symbolically to ask the right questions than to seek definite answers concerning being. We are constantly dressing ourselves in this arena of spiritual knowledge and rearranging it to meet our own plans.

We attain knowledge as science through study and practice. This knowledge covers universal truths of the operation of general laws obtained and tested through scientific methods concerning the physical world. Science is an organized body of past and present knowledge. It produces useful models of reality through the study of the natural world and human behavior in society. Often we view spiritualism and science as independent of one another, but actually, they are codependent. Realistically, science as material information is only provable as long as we have a life with which to understand it. Does such a field exist after life? It is possible that whatever follows us after this life will reproduce from our recorded memories. There is no clear and valid explanation of how any set of laws can arise spontaneously. Through time-lapse photography, we are able to see the exquisite petals on a rose unfold. Such is the nature of Spirit and science.

Hypocrisy occurs when people pretend to be something they are not, especially in the area of morals or religion, and have a false presentation of belief and feeling. When we look at what is presently occurring on planet earth, the inequalities, the misuse of resources and priorities, we certainly see hypocrisy at work. People and groups are warring against one another, both thinking they are right. Dressing up in false spontaneity and pride of accomplishments is not the natural use of nature's laws. When not used correctly, the laws of nature can become poison, or instruments of death. When used spiritually and scientifically, nature's laws become a medicine for well-being. Policies that simulate goodness without true inclusiveness (hypocrisy in action) become self-destructive and are not the right use of force and energy, or spiritualism and science.

Wherever we go, we will come out of it, whatever 'it' is.

## The One Body

How should people of the world guide, direct and guard its resources? How should we divide the system of production and distribution to provide sustainability? How should groups go about making decisions allocating values in government, corporate, academic and religious settings? Who shall have the power or right to give orders and make decisions? The Will of the people should be the power and source behind any decision concerning the solidarity and sustainability of the earth.

When we look at the earth from space, we see none of the interactions that are occurring below. All the earth does is move around the sun so that we may have the days, nights, and seasons. The earth is more collective than individual and it knows its place in the center of its system. The earth is indifferent to the moral, political or social outlook that occurs on its surface and the control and administration of the resources it provides through governments. The earth is impervious to the politics that disturb its balance. Regardless of their style of governing, almost every country on earth has similar agendas regarding the use of their resources that cause this unbalance. Nevertheless, the One Body, earth, keeps moving.

Until each of us can picture this unique Oneness of earth from space and make it a part of our mind-set, the human patterns of earth will remain unbalanced. We will constantly see its natural formations change above and below the surface. There is only energy and force and only humans have the capacity to understand that. Until each of us accepts the responsibility of our actions, not only as individuals, but also collectively, there will be a governing body or organization controlling our destiny, not cooperating with it. Just as the earth is working in uniformity with other universal bodies that allow the cosmos to expand, humans must work in cooperation, also.

From the inner workings of the body to the social patterns of a nation, humans should work together worldwide, side-by-side to produce harmony and expansion for all. We recognize that every star in the vastness of space has a purpose in the greater scheme. Since made from the same stuff, we should grant every human the same opportunities in the sharing of society. In this age, individual concerns are important but only if people act in the best interest of the sustainability of earth; our physical survival depends on it.

In order for the earth to remain sustainable, governments must act responsibly in making decisions regarding the right use of resources.

## Futurism

Though we live in the now, we also have an eye on tomorrow. Most of us cannot help but believe that the meaning of life and one's personal fulfillment reside in the future. Our growth, advancement, or development is always mindful of the future. Currently, we do not have the ability to peer into the future. In the time to come our imaginations will be out in front of us. The future can alter undetermined events, the condition of a person or thing, and any impending prospects. Life and belief depend on one another via a Permanent Atom where all experiences are stored. The computer world labels it the hard drive. In the human world, it is the Golden Disk of memory where all the thoughts and actions of the past and the future meet in the present. The present is wherever Consciousness is. The brain has the capacity to recall both the past and the future: the past more so than what is to come. What keeps us from focusing fully on the future is the lack of stimulating words and images that could open the regions of the brain involved in envisioning future events. Eventually, neuroscience will be able to use brain imaging to unlock that area of the brain. In the world of imagining there is the belief that all persons, places and things are interconnected and the universe and all dimensions are encapsulated within our Permanent Self, that tiny particle of Light that is Infinite and indestructible.

As the future appears visual technology will stimulate the brain bringing to life those dormant memories recorded in the light frequency spectrum. Those images in the spectrum lie there just like broadcasting images do for our audio and video transmits. When appropriate, in time and space, and according to universal law, the human brain will become the receiver for such light patterns lying in the spectrum. We just need to keep in mind that growth is slow.

In order to have access to those portals, responsible thinking and action are prerequisites, not only in the use of our inventions, but also in the use of force, energy and thought. At the present, we jump around unconsciously from one experience of living to another experience. As our mental abilities evolve, somewhere in the future, we will be able to jump from one dimension to another, from one level of consciousness to another, making the past, present and future one living reality. Except in the imagination that time has not yet come.

Inspirational imagining surpasses physical existence and rests in the totality of things whether discovered or not. We usually conceive this 'Place of Being' as the First Original Cause of existence. The future is our guarantee that we will acknowledge its presence through knowledge and wisdom. In front of us is our recognition of living Spirit, Infinite and always present. If we continue our technology quest, human beings are destined to become spiritual 'machines' in this present solar system. There are future solar systems yet to be! In the state we find ourselves, we will always be simultaneously pervading and surpassing the past, present, and future.

## *Indifference*

As we turn the pages in our everyday life, the people we pass are similar to the letters written on the pages of a book. We are either impartial or not as to the fonts or meaning of the words. We choose to be emotional or not. The faces and words that describe persons, places and things express the traits and interests that attract us or make us indifferent in the story of life. When we pass someone, do we acknowledge him or her? When it comes to the face of another human being, we often question its appearance with our preconceived ideas. To be politically correct, we often rationalize that the opposite of love is not hate, but indifference. Most of our reactions are unconscious ones instilled in us by our past association with others.

We usually go through life without questioning the motives for our reactions toward others. We are not 'islands onto ourselves'; all of us are connected in one way or another. When we fail to acknowledge another Soul, we are missing an important opportunity to greet another part of our humanity. However, we certainly are not required to accept a part of the individual responsibility of others regarding the choices they make in life. To a certain degree, the appearance of another human reflects the quality of our Inner humanity. When we respond to other people with apathy, it surely affects their feelings in an adverse way. When we greet others with a smile of warmth and kindness, this small gesture becomes a page written with hope, optimism, compassion and concern. When we address others, we are really treating them the way we want to be treated.

No doubt, there are things happening in the world that are beyond our control and we are powerless to do anything about them except to remain positive in writing our own story. We may need to practice neutrality until we are able to play a part in eradicating those things. When we find a cure to apathy, we will cure most evils. We are all different when it comes to the answers regarding the Great Mysteries of life! Each of us must seek our own way to the highest, our own sense of supreme loyalty in life, and our own ideal of life. Such a philosophy and worldview will bring forth its Truth and Beauty so that people may grow in vision, stature and dedication.

Most of us believe that indifference is a negative quality. However, when we look at the universe and the workings of nature what do we see:

indifference! There is only energy and force. Floods, accidents, disease, microbes and earthquakes are impervious to our well-being. There is no providence in those works of nature. Nevertheless, when we breathe the air and feel the power of nature nurtured by its plant and animal life, it is difficult not to imagine providence at work. Most scenarios of life compel us to see indifference differently when it comes to energy/ force/ gravity.

All any of us can really do, as a part of nature, is to make things better for ourselves and others until we each run our course. With indifference, nature will take care of the rest.

## *Permanence*

As conscious beings, do we have the necessary information within us to be able to exist for an indefinite duration? Consciousness is dependent on growth, improvement, knowledge, and the ability to accept influences from persons, places, and things to keep awareness evolving; otherwise, consciousness becomes stagnant. Conscious endurance occurs through independent choice making and information gathering in order for it to shape its reunification with its essential Essence. Though each of us is independent from others in appearance and quality, the total life Essence is of the same source. Nevertheless, we are radically different in our momentum and advancement toward it.

Time exists only in the created universe. Therefore, memory exists outside of time as Consciousness. Since memory gives each of us the ability to be, we can say that each of us has already existed for an infinite amount of time and because of that awareness, we will continue to exist. Accordingly, each of us exists inside of time as well as outside of it. If this were not so, the essential Essence and all life would not be in a perpetual state of existence as the 'many in one'.

Persons, places and things provide us with information which enables us to make choices as to who, how, when, where and what we are to be. Mental identification with matter confirms our individual awareness. In wakefulness, we gather information. In daydreaming, we do the same, and while we sleep, we process that information to associate it with the presence that is. In the moments of now and during the future that is to be, we will continue in some way or another. Because we are conscious now, we must have always been so in some form or other; the circle symbolizes this. When we walk within it, we will always pass through where we started. Information tells us who we are as individuals and in time, we become conscious as ourselves. The shapes that we navigate will change, but our true identity remains the same. As we move around in the Infinite circle that has no end, we also realize that it had no beginning, only starting points.

We are forever beyond the reach of change, time, and phenomena. If we are aware of 'wherever and whatever' we can be certain that we are conscious. This consciousness that desires, feels, thinks and wills the body to act is not of the body, but is in it. Consciousness, our separate self, manifests as physical activity, the externalization of inner activity. According to thought, no matter where we may find ourselves in existence, our identity will persist. We cannot comprehend fully the mystery that is the real person in each of us, yet we are conscious of its presence. Memory encodes our living experiences. We relish in both pleasure and pain from one moment to another and live in them until we become weary and seek something more permanent.

Whatever and wherever we are in our moments, know that 'we are'.

## *The Emotional World*

The emotional world is the Heart for the physical world, and through our imaginations, we manifest those emotions. Our talents, strengths, ideas, passions, and desires reflect out from the emotional plane and overshadow creative pursuits and other activities on the physical plane. Presently, the emotional plane is inaccessible to experimental research and we can access it only through a potent imagination. We are all products of the physical world, the constructor of the body, which houses our emotional and mental natures. The emotional and mental worlds are not always dependant on the physical body and can be independent from that body. Awareness of the emotional plane's divisions can come through sleep, daydreaming, drugs or sudden accidental shocks to the body.

Refined thoughts are the key to mastering the emotional plane. When we use our thoughts wisely, we can rewrite our fate. Then we not only become beneficial to ourselves but to our culture and humanity. When our emotions are selfless, we avoid the unwholesome or befogging atmosphere and influences of the emotional plane. When our emotions control, we are wide open to those energies. The sense of pleasure, pain, and living produce feelings of synergistic intoxication. After we pass through our weaker experiences and the influences of others, we can access the higher emotional energies that the Self possesses. At these higher levels, the lower desires resulting in pain and suffering dissipate and the environment of loftier thoughts and aspirations are the standard. When we practice these higher principles, our release from earth becomes a Summerland. It is a place where the entire atmosphere, the cities and their contents, and the scenery of life take shape through the influence of thought. In the present or the future, we are the products of our thoughts. Creeds and beliefs are often the results of lower levels of emotional perception. This emotional energy plane influences all persons from the literary man, artist, scholar, preacher, scientist, laborer etc. When our noble aims become free from selfishness, we will use imagination and emotional energy inclusively.

We must remember that we are the sole translators of our emotions. We can act automatically or unconsciously in experiencing them. Our consciousness will dictate how we will respond to those emotions. Language, education and experience shape the world(s) on which we each find ourselves aware. In our creative fancy, we evoke the real along with the unreal. Emotions carry our positive and negative actions as we create relationships with others. The Soul translates the waves of emotions that form our thoughts into conscious being and doing.

When we have sufficiently mastered our emotions, life becomes a Summerland.

### Silence

Is Silence the art of true listening? When we silence our thoughts, the Inner Voice can speak with clarity. The absence of sound or noise brings forth the mirror of the Soul. Silence as a personal form of communication allows the inner workings to happen; this gets us in touch with who we really are. When we remain quiet we are not only being respectful of ourselves but of those with whom we have dialogue. In our discussions with others, we form our thoughts and emotions. Silence gives us time to reflect and respond. It keeps the moment going by not speaking too quickly. When we hear and listen to the myriad wonders of life, they show us that we have worth, purpose and trust in relationships. We must take time out to be silent with our thoughts and let them pass over us like water flows over rocks. In Stillness, we can observe what is going on around us without any attachment. The more chatter, the more we evoke the elements of fear that keep us stuck in patterns of worry.

Most of our world problems will dissolve once we know how to use silence wisely. In silence, we attain harmony and quell negativity. We model the images and sounds before us from the Light of the Soul, the Voice of Silence. In stillness, we appreciate the energies of life that give us a greater command of language and expression. Silence allows us to think through our thoughts and beliefs and see ourselves more clearly as we grow. To some extent, when we speak, we are judging ourselves; we are painting a portrait of our Inner being for our companions to see.

Words are opinions that influence the persons to whom we direct them. When we do not weigh words carefully, they fall silent to the ears leaving us to judge our own thoughts. Words by themselves are nothing. Our resulting actions bring joy or pain. Silence is the ability to quiet the emotions. Let go of doubt and fear before any event is undertaken. When we are silent, we can direct our thoughts to matters that pertain to the past or future. We are then in our own space that allows the Self to be there without memory or expectation. In the present, this allows us to enhance and balance our daily interchanges in an agreeable manner. In quietness, it is easier to accept the flow of creation and remove all doubts about our continuum. Silence and action each have their moments in expressing ourselves. The strength of our calmness helps in shaping the thoughts that keep us evolving. We come from Silence and by returning to it, we quell our thoughts. This allows us the time to form the appropriate words that we vocalize to others.

Quietness and self-reliance are necessary if we want to remove our tensions and develop the full faculties of the forces of body, emotions and mind. Silence sets us free from all forms of bondage, custom, dependence, superstition and the crippling influences of fear. In this solitude, we gain the strength to accept responsibility for our own individual lives. In silence, we find our self-sovereignty. At the end of this experience, we will, for a time, return to the Solitude of the Self.

In the Still Small Voice of Silence, we respect and acknowledge the virtue of the Higher Self.

## Patterns of Being

All human life experience is set in motion to help individuals explore and develop their potential. Imbedded in time, we imprint these experiences as copies so that persons, places and things become elements in the whole. The themes, images, and characters of what is familiar eventually become symbols. They evoke deep and sometimes unconscious responses to the perceiver by forming meanings to experiences shared by diverse cultures. All things of the same type are representations that we derive from the original pattern. Our beliefs are only symbols. We see the present as representing all the experiences of people in the past manifesting as now. We derive our literature, art, technology, sciences, etc., from those previous recordings. The dreams, visions and hallucinations, however stimulated, are but shadows for the unconscious to enlighten. Through deep thinking and self-analysis, it is possible for each of us to probe our unconscious and pull back what has been the past and what will be the future.

Life is but an ongoing process where consciousness is always becoming more aware of itself. It is always slipping in and out of time: dreaming, sleeping, awaking, imagining and experiencing copies of its original patterns. The persons and things that served us in the past become our ideals for the present. We are always reinventing what has been before, from a wagon wheel to a satellite, from a witch doctor to a saint. We are always raising the status of those symbols. The contents of the natural world pass through us in much the same way as the sunlight does. As thinkers and doers, we are always working off one another. Patterns are magnets attracting relevant thinkers and doers. When the pattern has sufficient strength and supporting experience within the individual's awareness, the thinker imagines the pattern and the doer creates the form. Whether it is the energy of an atom or the infrastructure of a society, we realize the ideal or idea through our thinking and doing.

We etch the patterns built from living experiences on rays of light in much the same way the camera captures its image on film. However, those etchings are so small that they pass through the eye of most humans unnoticed. Nonetheless, some people have the psychic ability to see those small patterns. Since we do not accept this type of viewing collectively, we often view intuitive abilities with skepticism. The uninformed believe they are daydreaming or seeing spirits and ghosts. In reality what they are seeing are the various archetypes of human existence and experience. Whether the patterns are spiritual or psychological, the truth of such matters rests in the collective unconscious.

Patterns work their way from the unconscious to the conscious just as the entertainment industry dramatizes the behavior patterns reflected in hero myths. On the inner side of life, our personal dreams are as significant because they are insights to our Inner growth. Both the inner and outer perceptions are a part of ourselves for they show what we are attracted to, how we can solve problems, what we hope for, as well as our potential. Since the unconscious cannot talk to us when awake, these dreams can help us stabilize our needs and desires in our patterns of being.

As we conceive the models of history in our minds, it is not difficult to see that the physiology of the human body imitates the workings of the rhythms of earth.

### *Irritability*

The moment we place our feet on the floor after sleeping, the arousal process begins and provokes interest, enthusiasm, or excitement. Thus, our reaction begins to whatever will unfold in this day. This stimulation takes many forms when reacting with persons, places, and things. Irritability may manifest in both the physiological and behavioral stimuli responses that occur in situations that incite the mind and emotions. It would be foolish to say we can live life without becoming upset and touchy. All of us are chemical machines, hormonal factories, secreting hormones for our glands and cells. Our thoughts, feelings and actions are the energy sources for the production of those hormones. Often our deep-seated desires can become unbalanced or unmet which can result in relying on others to help us meet those needs. The way in which we use our emotions determines how we will respond to such a situation. When we unduly depend on information provided by others, we are setting ourselves up for disappointment. Before we undertake any situation that involves another person, we should initiate a plan as to how we want that interaction to occur. Spontaneous action can become over stimulating, especially when ideas clash. To offset irritability, we must be personally responsible for the choices we make with little attention to what others do or do not do. When responding, we must treat others the same way we would want to be treated.

Only by stilling the turbulence within the emotions through patience can we eliminate the irritants flowing through us. Each person must discover for oneself the means for being tolerant. Then, he/she must impose on the personal life a new rhythm of interacting with the dual energies of life. Without the tension of the will, it is difficult to change something from one state to another. No matter how hard we try, sometimes we cannot communicate or understand life outside of the self. This can be annoying in the presence of someone else. Each of us is on our own life wave. Often others misconstrue the separateness of that way as avoidance. Sharing is important, but when we come into someone else's space prematurely, our irritations can surface and we can lose communication. Remember this: relationships require sharing the load, even one's space and time. If there are irritants in sharing, look for the patterns, so we can understand them. Accept the twist and turns that come up. At the end of the day, be kind, generous and forgiving. It is far better to be passive when observing things and events; this allows us to acknowledge them without being annoyed. In time, we begin to see other persons as similar profiles of ourselves. When we hurt someone else, we lose our innocence. We waste energy on negative interactions when we could spend our time on inner serenity, peaceful sharing, understanding compassion, laughter and bright days of fun and enjoyment. When we show sensitivity in our dealings, we use the energies of love/will that can eventually eliminate our habitual irritabilities.

In acknowledging irritability, we are accepting the place we do not want to be by working toward understanding others and ourselves.

## The Never Ending Process

Energy and thought produce conscious awareness, the rising reality of space. This force takes us through all the various realms of existence.

From this vantage point, transfix the eyes on infinite space and marvel at its enormity. Scan the surface of the earth; look into the depth of its oceans with all its diversity moving about. It is impossible not to imagine ourselves linked to some enormous purpose. We come from this vastness and we are always entering back into it. Everything we see around us is the consequence of growth. When we look beyond our little selves, we move outside our limited range of thought or belief about the material world to an existence of Permanency.

When we view life as unending Energy, we are polishing the source of our awareness. We are all travelers seeking ways that will allow us to be of service to this supply of energy. We cannot fully imagine, comprehend, or explain this energy force with the ordinary senses. Logic, rationality and science are restrictive because they are only assumptions.

When we learn from others, we are gathering common and similar senses and intelligence. We gain this through sight, sound, touch, taste and mental abilities to reason and deduce. We gain our view of the world through firsthand knowledge and that experience helps us share knowledge with others. We must learn to use this information to comfort and not to aggravate other people and creatures. Our knowledge leads us into unconditional, unlimited, inclusive affection for all creation. We are then prepared and ready to work in the realm of altruistic service that aids us in absorbing True Knowledge. We cannot find, discover or solve anything unless we reflect on what constitutes knowledge and existence. True Knowledge is like a polished mirror with light shining on it. The mirror reflects everything, does not interpret, or modify anything reflected. The mirror has no emotions, nor is it impatient. It only reflects what is before it. Once we take the object away, it no longer reflects. True knowledge is objective and unbiased. When we polish our thoughts like a mirror, all forms of consciousness becomes equally aware, unmodified by time, space, emotions and senses.

As we pass through this plane of existence, our view of reality does not always match that of others. There is no certain way to find meaning or purpose by analyzing all the various concepts for our existence. If anything, it could obscure the truth that we seek. We know that space is the reality for us in this dimension and what we experience we leave behind for others to follow. Cognitive recognition is the only form of knowing whether other dimensions exist as a fact beyond the three dimensions. Even if there are other dimensions, the reality of them will be in space because space is the generator of them. Matter, or motion, gives purpose to space and we are a part of those ceaseless currents of motion. Space, matter and time are all there is and consciousness is our connection to that trinity. Our essential nature is matter and Spirit. Matter generates the personality that touches forms, and Spirit compels existence.

Love, the Source of true knowledge as matter and Spirit, constitutes the never-ending process.

## *Systemic Consciousness*

Systemic Consciousness is an alert cognitive state in which we are aware of our situations and ourselves. This awareness allows us to relate to the body as a whole as well as to its specific parts. In this cognitive state, our physical system maintains internal groups of small electromagnetic charges that give us momentum. We are always changing in ways that enable each of us to adapt to our individual point of view without completely separating from the quantum subsystems that form patterns in the environmental systems.

Every act and thought are reflected in the world process as atoms, molecules, compounds, cells, tissue, organs, bodies, communities, classes, races, kingdoms, planets, solar systems, mind, memory, power, world, fact, action, duty and individuality, and so on, unending.

Everything is relative in size, degree and characteristics just as everything is conscious to some extent. However, through our minds we become more conscious of the systems through which we are evolving. As we pass through these systems, they are becoming aware as consciousness within our consciousness. This allows for our everyday worldview and the many world systems to gain a broader span within our awareness so that the many possible universes can interact on a larger degree with systems existing on all levels of the universal space.

There is no collapse in Systemic Consciousness because it regenerates, assembles and radiates in the operation of a full spectrum universe that is useful to us as we operate within our individual universe. The only constraint to theses forces is our lack of inclusiveness. Our minds, a form of life, are evolving systems of electrical currents connected to the universal electric energy of the cosmos that is strictly for the benefit of giving awareness to and for the development of the universe: our next great step in consciousness.

Systemic Consciousness gives us a view of multiplicity as we live and connect to all the parts we interact with in time, place, and space. These experiences give vitality to the nerve force or senses that bring various parts of the organic mechanism into union. Our perceptions and ideas have their origin in our sensations, the things we experience. All manifested ideas eventually absorb again into new improved ideas. These ideas are the dynamic characteristics of the forces producing manifestation. Concerning the human system, its psychology, environment, and unity Systemic Consciousness uses flexibility and cooperation in fitting the individual process together with the world process. When a fully integrated universal mind is used, we understand better the various systems of persons, places, and things. In universal consciousness, we equally share in our participation.

Each of us is a world in miniature, rearranging ourselves in a world process that evolves with the cosmic processes.

## Explanation of things

It is our duty in life to be good and to discover what is explainable to the senses. When we hold onto the good, we are clarifying things to ourselves. It is through the senses that we gain experience in the material world. We can explain the concepts of other worlds as to their nature and probability. However, until we are there mindful of the makeup of those worlds, we must take their reality on faith. Just because we are unable to experience such phenomenon does not mean it does not exist. It is for each of us to understand such things and if the explanation is through teachings, then it is up to us to test those teachings and draw our own conclusions. We can gain much from the mature thought of another mind even though those thoughts are imported and are not from our own Inner Voice. We can learn much if we honestly seek to understand those thoughts.

Understanding will not come unless we do the inquiring. The Inner nature is timeless and through our will, judgment and intuition, the doors will open and the explanation of things will multiply for the betterment of the inquirer. We are a universe within ourselves and what we see on the outside is but a reflection of that Inner space. The makeup and content of the outer world are but copies of the power and source of life itself encoded on light. As a result, we download those codes into our minds and frame by frame, we project our interpretation outward as to persons, places, and things so that material life can be lived and understood. We cannot solely accept Life on the faith of others. Rather we should test and explain life by the internal fires of one's own mind and heart. When we better ourselves, we are improving the universe also. The operation of the universe expresses itself through each of us. Our minds have the capacity to interpret the essential stuff of the universe (laws) because we are the product, consequence, or effect of the universe. Each of us has latent in us all the faculties and powers of the universe. We have the essential organs with which to understand the universe, as well as the ability to perceive and explain the meaning behind the hidden veils of our nature.

When we look within, we are building our understanding. The outward life is to provide us with a body so our internal organs can feed and nurture us with the warmth of blood that fuels our minds with light or electrical fire. The manifesting Inner Light is the core of each of us. The real purpose of the mind is so that we can grow in self-consciousness. Societies and their ways evolve primarily so we can build the body/ physicality with the neural pathways of truth. Those pathways hold the key to all the portals of the universe. When we reach inside our hearts and minds, we move toward the awe-inspiring beauty and truth of the Universal life. Directed by the forces of life, we have nothing to fear when consciousness flows from within. However, this type of explanation is a work in progress and awareness does not come overnight.

We can accelerate the explanation of things when we place all discoveries impersonally upon the platform of reverent Truth.

## Self-Identification

Without identifying with another person or thing, consciousness would be static and unchanging. When we recognize someone or something we are able to form awareness as to who or what he, she, or it is. Thus, we are forming our individual identity, the notion of self, a mental model of ourselves. An important part of our identity is gender related which is significant because it allows an individual to view oneself both as a person and in relation to other people. Mental and physical ability is important for self-reflection and the awareness of self. Interacting with others is a role behavior, which enables us to gain personal experience, and the means to negotiate with society at large concerning the meaning of our individual identify. How society directs and guides determines the nature of most of our mental content. How we interact with other persons, places, and things, through our beliefs, faith, and hopes, influences each of us. This play of words and life can seem puzzling and confusing if one is lacking in intuition, that knowing which comes directly from the mind rather than being acquired by experience or from external sources. Each of us has a particular quality that is spontaneous and innocent of the influences of others. That characteristic is our inborn intuition that can direct our decisions as to how we go about processing the information related by others. How we align ourselves with this intuitive energy determines our relationship to the mental impressions that we receive.

What we are seeking to know is the truth about our own true nature. We understand this truth in the terms of what we do and remember. We each have a consciousness that is separate from our thinking conscience; we are either conscious of it or we are not. This is why a stronger consciousness can have great swaying power over a weaker one. Consciousness by itself cannot make thoughts and actions. Our memories of person, places and things allow us to do that. When we come to terms with ourselves, we are using memory and influence wisely to direct outer circumstances. It is through our inner direction that we gain the wisdom to be independent and free from erroneous perceptions directed toward us by groups, institutions, political, religious, etc., who may have ulterior motives for attaining our collective power. In order for our world to run smoothly, our differences must not interfere with our ability to develop the functions that remove the traits that keep us separate from a group, organization, or country. Although our environment and encounters influence our direction, true self-identification is personal. It is up to each of us to decipher the arguments, examples or force of personality and power that someone uses to affect our thinking or actions. The choices and practices that instill self-identification and mental freedom allow us to create our own identity and belief systems. Self-choice that is non-violent and includes every point of view will certainly lead us toward Universal Goodness.

Is it only natural for us to develop our own concepts and pursuits based on our own remembrances and experiences?

## A Guide to Being

Every day that we are aware, we are developing blueprints that will reflect the nature of our individual being. How we chose to conduct ourselves in the past reflects in our present. Our current condition characterizes our lives or events in a particular place, country or society. Choices can influence destiny. They can remove every obstruction, or they can add difficulties. If done intuitively and carefully, our options can instill new patterns in the mind. We forge the quality of our future in the character we now process. All around us, we see patterns of being that others express. How can we select from them? What will be beneficial to each of us as individuals and groups?

We are building the best kind of destiny when we have kinship with others based on appropriate action that will diminish choices that result in suffering and sorrow. No matter where we go in this life or the next, we will carry our patterns with us. If we are striving to be non-violent, caring, altruistic, and self-responsible, we will take those traits into the invisible worlds that lie before us and find there Grace and Peace. Whatever plane we find ourselves on, we will attract those qualities again as time, place and circumstance warrant. In selecting what we use as a guide, individuals have free will. Every day brings with it changes. We are building now what our character will be tomorrow. When a new day arrives, we will be building from our own heredity and character. Therefore, we must be very selective and choose only what strengthens the intuition and the heart.

Diverse patterns fill the world. We form some patterns deliberately as delay tactics while others hinder and block. We use some patterns to form monetary advantage in business and political matters, etc. Good patterns form character, and bad patterns diminish it. Before we form any patterns for our thinking and acting, we should think clearly on the shapes we want to form with persons, places and things. Do not be entangled in or entwined in harmful action. It is easier to clear patterns in the mind than it is to absolve actions from physical creation.

When we regulate the mind rightfully, we vastly improve the plan or model that we produce from the original design. When we charge the mind with moral thoughts, we transform disruptive patterns into therapeutic ones that are good and pleasing without errors, flaws or faults. The life patterns we choose, dark or light, are really of our own making. No doubt, it is difficult to move around in the physical world without some form of disruption. For most of us, all we can do is work on our inner distractions. However, if one is in a position to exercise influence in breaking up disruptive patterns, then it is a service to those who cannot. The building of character and the fruits to bear are not limited to time and space.

The best forms of pattern making are those that bring balance to self and others through rightful action.

## *A View through Heaven's Door*

Many believe that life within the physical universe or the seemingly endless expanse of sky and stars above us are aspects of heaven. We use the term heaven to refer to a plane of existence believed to be a part of our own universe. Our beliefs and hopes in religions and spiritual philosophies characteristically describe this plane as the holiest possible place. Our views on divinity, goodness, piety, etc., justify our beliefs regarding heaven. However, to understand ourselves fully, we first have to understand how the idea of heaven evolved.

Since the dawn of religion and human civilization, the idea of heaven has existed. When we look at that idea impartially how can we but realize that it was and still is a human belief unsubstantiated as a collective physical observation. Since none of us can climb inside of another person's skin and perceive what he/she perceives, we must accept or reject that person's description of what heaven is. Despite all those various beliefs and ideas concerning heaven, we are still incapable of fully experiencing Heaven on earth. Most, if not all, of the reasons for that failure are due to the wide diversity of education, the misuse of power, wealth, lack of opportunity, coercion and the control of public opinion. Most humans are still overly concerned with their own interests, needs and desires rather than demanding that the collective will implement the concepts of Heaven on earth. However, there are other ways!

Every morning that we awaken from our slumber, Heaven's door opens a little wider. Every night that we sleep, we slip out of our physical world and enter into the emotional and mental dream worlds. Because of our attachment to the physical, we are able to perceive through the senses and witness through the emotions to the abstract levels of memory. It is here that we play out and experience our ideas and wishes. When these nighttime visits are clear, we have the ability to retain what we witness. As a result, we can use those impressions as assets in developing our physical life that give us insights into the nature of our being. Upon entering, there are heavens with in heavens containing persons, places and things imprinted on endless time, adaptive to each of our individual characters. In all probability concrete substance, including our physical bodies, will never be able to pass through that door. It is only through the emotions and mind that we are able to enter. It is also unlikely that any of those clear states exist anywhere in the concrete universe. Our physical world is but a shadowy reflection of those higher luminous places. We can use those glimpses to fashion our physical living, but we can never reproduce them fully. Nor is it likely that any two people functioning on the physical plane will accurately describe together the observations in those Inner states. If we are to witness heaven, each of us will need a strong will, a balanced constitution and determination to open its door on our own. Within and around us are the codes that set physical life in motion. Therefore, it makes sense that if things can be fashioned from physicality, they can also be fashioned in the mind.

Through the Purity of the heart, we open Heaven's door within ourselves.

## The Mystery of Being Human

Does consciousness have a beginning and ending? Whatever the circumstance might be at the end of this life, it is a mystery just as the one living it is also a mystery. As humans, we probably will never know the origin of our being or the destiny of the physical atoms that constitute our living matter. Like young eagles that get their momentum while gliding in the wind, we get our force for forward movement from living the experiences that we have just passed through. Yet, we are unable to fully understand or explain this mystery of Being which is older than the enduring mountains and oceans. We are only nurslings of destiny, a set of circumstances, in two immense universes: one consisting of physical matter and the other Spirit or Infinite Being. We stand in this infinitesimal magnitude because of the life springs of our journey. By cleansing our minds of the falseness of the past, we can bring relativity into our experiences and naturally imagine them as we want them to be. On each rising sun, we become a part of the Universal life experience. Through its endless forms and incalculable numbers of manifested beings, we learn to think clearly and imagine rightly. In that Infinite Light as conscious beings, as far as the universe is concerned, we are a small version of something larger.

As conscious beings, we are always infilling space, always moving toward higher means and unlocking the myriad life waves within us. Through careful thought the reflection of other forms of energy take on their true form and meaning. Through the ages of time, this energy is the only thing changing, not as things or beings, but as a perfected form of itself, our consciousness. As we flow with this changing mystery, we will find that it will reveal a depth of being within which leads us on into Eternity, an even greater mystery.

As we expand our minds into the experience of this unknowable mystery, we find the only opening available to us is faith. If we believe in something, we place our trust in it even without logical truth. In doing so, we find that we change because of our loyalty to our belief. When the mystery of being fills us with wonder, it becomes a fresh source for the senses to acquire information about the meaning of existence. However, we must not confuse the mystery of being with religious dogma. For we have in us the capacity to reshape each existence into a combination of different aspects. For example, when we banish from our minds that we are merely physical bodies, we can get in touch with universal laws that will urge us on to produce even finer rarefied vehicles of self-expression. Through life cycles, everything ascend; it flowers into maturity, then falls, giving place to newer forms that in turn develop their own systems of growing upward.

When we look at the bigger picture of destiny and time, we understand more fully the knowledge of the past. Those that lived in ages past are now the children of the mind, heart, and Spirit of the present mystery of being human.

Like a great river that flows on into the Eternal Sea, every life is a Mystery.

## *You Cannot Go Back Home, Only Visit*

When we leave our home, we are like young birds that fly from their nests. As humans, we rarely ever fully return. When we do return home for the first time, most things seem out of place. What we saw as big, seem small on the comeback. The image of familiar faces seems different. When we walk down memory lane persons, places and things are not the same. The nuances of life are now colored by our own choices and through those selections, our view screen has its own tint. Space and time are impassive and have no moral compass with which to measure anything. They simply act as a backdrop.

When we leave our place of origin, we are leaving because we want to grasp our own destiny. We dream about what awaits us. Instead of revolving with the world, we often want to step away from it, to be in our own weightless environment free from the pulls and strains of control and traits of others. When we revisit our past thoughtfully, we can uplift those memories to another level by thinking beyond our immediate wants and needs.

When we journey away from home, we are uncertain at first. For a long time we are forgetful of our actions. Intentionally or unintentionally, we made mistakes in home settings. No matter how hard we try to suppress those incorrect decisions or acts, they influence our thinking in some form or other. On the path of self-responsibility, as if instinctively, we muse over those experiences wanting to give them a different face. When we are in the presence of loved ones, friend or foe, our behavior may be different to us, but often others see only the familiar patterns of what we were accustomed to doing. When it comes to cause and effect, we do not always express self-control, humility, unconditional love, calmness, non–attachment, intuition, self-knowledge, discrimination, happiness, and freedom at the same level of acceptance we want them to be. Because we have awakened to those signs does not necessarily mean others have. We must allow others the grace to see differently, and that they have their own space and time to do so.

We must weigh carefully our motivation to love when we are in the presence of others in their own time and space. All we can do is allow ourselves to empower our individual reality and not to wait for someone else to change for the better. What we can do is make it so for ourselves. When our life folds and our currents change into something else, each of us is individually responsible for our own habits, mistakes and resolutions about going home. Home, never a permanent space, is always moving with us, and remains a part of us always. Though we would like to return to those times and feel what was gathered or missed, even undo the missteps, it is not possible because we are in the moment of now. All we can do is learn from those lessons. When we do revisit home, we must let the humble nature in each of us guide our way.

Nothing stays fixed as it was. Everything gives way and nothing waits; everything flows on.

## *Being True to the Self*

When we leave our thinking to others, family members, religious leaders, politicians, economists, teachers, friends, etc., we can end up with their beliefs and values, not our own. As a collective, they are only extensions of us. When we fail to notice and value our own qualities, we become unable to think for ourselves. In order to think clearly, we must organize and construct our own mental abilities for self-governing in order to distinguish between others and ourselves. When we recognize that everyone has a different style when it comes to thinking, we will understand the concept of unity better. Our imagination and thinking enables each of us to cope effectively with our goals, plans, ends and desires.

It is in time, place and nature that we shape our character and identity. Our awareness is the sum total of the things that have happened to us in the past and make up our thoughts and feelings. We are always in that moment of conditioning. This force is always active and exposes energy through our physical, emotional and mental involvement in persons, places, and events. Through this exposure, we derive the ability to make decisions and judgments concerning the impressions of life. The Self then modifies these shared experiences in order to separate from them. History, titles, names and family relations all continue in the self and function as modifiers. Each of us is an idea, a seed of Spirit planted in matter. The consequence of that planting from which we originated is as indistinguishable as the acorn seed is to the oak tree.

The patterns of self-governing are formed through practical understanding and acceptance of objectivity. Material things exist with those constructed in the subjective mind and all remain as mental film for the self to utilize. Physical life experience provides generous narratives to enhance the genesis of the time or circumstances of something always coming into being. With our mental principles balanced, we identify more intimately with all social virtues. The empathy for sentient life will then be more energetic in proportion to events and circumstance. The formation of the images of the objective world is only possible when we become independently self-conscious. Nevertheless, group solidarity is often necessary and acceptable as long as one does not allow the group conscience to overcome one's own awareness. A group may assist in self-realization, but we still have the responsibility to identify ourselves with our own natural intuition. Through self-responsibility, we pursue a higher understanding of the world around us. We must not be afraid to develop our individual foundation, or we may get lost in someone else's translation because none of us has had the same life patterns.

Our identity is self-induced; it is the physical, emotional and mental 'thinking and doing' part of us.

### Forgotten Memories

Our minds are the storehouses for our memories. The mind/brain organism has the ability to also retain and retrieve information. The brain, that part of the nervous system that includes the higher nervous centers, keeps the physical body moving and acting within its environment. The mind and memory allow us to identify with our surroundings. The mind, the brain and memory work with one another and are co-dependent while awareness is functioning on the physical plane.

Do mind and memory exist independently of the physical body when the body has ceased to be? Ongoing existence, the presence or occurrence of something in a particular place or situation, is only verifiable by the perceiver. It is through our senses that we are aware of things or events and have the ability to obtain information about the physical world. Everything that the world has gone through exists because of our awareness. In time, every material achievement handed down through the ages will return into the microcosm. Nevertheless, some believe that a memory copy of our achievements will exist on a higher level than the material world. The electrical impulses that pass through the grey stuff of the brain contain the same energy of the electrical Fire of the cosmos. As we bring memories to the surface, think about them, and act upon them through the senses, they eventually wear down and we do not recall them anymore. As a result, the electrical nature of the mind dissolves these memories. The waves of biochemically generated energy that once stimulated old memories in the physical brain fuel newer and better memories. Past action equals memory, and we work out these actions until they no longer sway.

We need the ability to recognize and utilize the hidden potential in all things and ourselves. A perfect clarity exists in each of us. However, a lack of focus can hinder us, often the result of forces coming from the outside. Learning comes before wisdom. Mind clarity allows Light to pass through which connects to thoughts that are ethical. These thoughts have little or no interruption or distortion in the perceiver's eye regarding physical existence. This hidden potential brings us success in our inner and outer lives.

When we think with wisdom first, we then see with the eye of mind, the absolute, our own Ultimate Nature. The occurrences in everyday life, in of themselves, are not good or bad, but our lack of clarity makes them seem so. As the mind selects and processes recorded memories, we are compelled to act on their power or strength. As a result, we align ourselves with persons, places and things that have great influence, especially in our particular endeavors. As we reassess these effects, those influences will dissolve and we will no longer remember them. As the core meaning of our hidden potential surfaces, we will recall a higher set of new principles.

All of us are moving toward a greater Perfection in the collection and distribution of memory.

## Self-Security

We can have everything the world and life has to offer: money, possessions, status, and relationships. However, if we do not have peace of mind, we have nothing. Without a sense of inner security, fear, doubt, misery and dissatisfaction can plague our biological needs. When we meet our internal needs for security and fulfillment, our external ones become less demanding and give us greater freedom of choice as to how we lead our lives.

Can one be consciously secure? Consciousness animates the physical and what goes on in the emotional and mental atmosphere of a person guides the physical outer life against danger or injury. How we react to the forces at play around us and the actions we take provide the defensive measures to protect our assets. We can exacerbate anxiety or fear by outer events, especially when our possessions dominate us. However, possessions are not a criterion for Inner security. Since consciousness is not tangible, we cannot assign value to its content.

Tangible forms of expression contribute to the success of someone or something. These concrete forms of matter enhance the physical plane of existence. Physical things are eventually broken down and reabsorbed back into the original elements from which they came. The physical body is just one facet. Self-security rests upon correct thought form making, the activity or process of thinking about ideas that are associated with a particular person, place, time, or group.

Distractions from the outer world divert our attention and lessen our sense of self-security. When we affirm that no matter what is occurring in the outer world, we will not allow it to upset our emotional and mental world, we are moving forward productively. Thus, we are stepping into gainful insights that will unveil new opportunities. These will lead to new learning and growth that will provide us with the knowledge and skill to protect our inner and outer assets in both the good and bad times. A positive reaction gives security; a negative response evokes insecurity. As we perceive our environment, we act on it. The environment reacts on us regardless how we understand or comprehend it. We cannot store up a sense of security in a container, but we can utilize that feeling to develop habits and traits that will allow us to make the right choices in confronting various environmental, political, financial, and spiritual issues in life.

As individuals, we seek what we perceive to be our security. In the learning process, we record in our consciousness the thoughts that will make us secure in ourselves. Over time and through association with persons, places, and things we remove unsafe feelings and insecure conditions when we think positively about our actions. When we practice diligence, faith and patience, we become more secure about our security.

We each light our own candle. Our inner strength keeps the winds of change from blowing it out.

## *The Physical Body: The Receptacle for Light*

Consciousness is the mover of the ether. Ether is the filler of the atmosphere-space and is the carrier of electromagnetic waves as well as the animator for matter of the physical body. Consciousness is the force crystallizing the energies of the ether, mental and emotional bodies. Because of conscious thought, the universe is bursting into life. The physical body, made up of organs and tissues, is a part of the total living being that may also include a spiritual component. The spiritual component rests on faith. The ether holds a blueprint for the structure of the physical body. The main glands and nerve ganglia of the physical body reflect the energy centers (spiritual powers).

The physical body is a mirrored image of the cosmos in objectivity. If we could, through some kind of magic, move back far enough we would see a reflection of ourselves as a conscious entity, a compilation of our thoughts, emotions, opinions and passions. The total density of our thoughts is more than the sum of little grey cells. Matter is the only source through which we can build a physical body. Whereas, consciousness is the only means that allows us to be independent of that form so that we can build and refine it in non-physical experiences. In effect, we are building our way toward Perfection and physical matter is the first step. The energies that surge through the various centers of the body, from the bottom of the feet to the top of the head, are mostly involuntary. Hence, the seemingly chaotic state of human action in nature. However, once we even out the impulses of the nerves, glands and the production of other chemicals flowing in the body, we attain a sense of balance in our habits.

When the time comes for us to evolve without a physical body, its reflection will always remain. Consciousness is ongoing as are the various substances through which we experience. We are but polishing the rock, our First

Light. Our passions, fears and interests originate from the experiences of the Self as it moves through the various forms of expression. Once we move above the distress of the senses, of knowledge, and powers of the physical body, our cravings for person, places and things will come together in their proper place and run smoothly without static influence.

The forces, weight and pressures of the physical body, whether human or the earth, are kept in place by the law of gravity, a natural phenomenon by which all objects with mass attract each other. Even though the Law of Conservation transforms energy from one form to another, the energy of the universe is indestructible and always stays the same. The shadows of the mind, our past memories, exist dimensionally as a level of consciousness or reality.

Consciousness shapes and advances through three sources; (1) in matter as the objective solid plane, (2) in Spirit, the plane of faith and imagination, subjectively subtle and (3) in the 'in-between' plane of the two as liquid and gaseous. No matter is truly solid; it is composed of electrons whirling around a nucleus consisting of protons and neutrons. By contrast, due to space-time-curvatures, all moving objects whether physical, emotional or mental accelerate toward each other becoming conscious of Consciousness. Energy and matter, the velocity of light, are the same. Therefore, when we use this energy as a collective focus for Goodwill, harmony ensues as progressive development. The physical body is similar to a book filled with blank pages. Our experiences animate and fill the pages with conscious life, a quantity and quality that have direction and magnitude. Otherwise, this 'book' (physical mass) has no life of its own.

Our first seeing, touching, hearing, smelling and tasting had their beginning through the body: the mind's first insights into Self-awareness.

### The United States of Now

All people of a particular type, formed by the union of two or more persons or groups, when expressing 'oneness' can be in harmony in the communication of thoughts or feelings with the present environment.

When we are watchful of our actions in the now (which can include the future as well as the past) we can tap into the Wisdom of the ways in which our life functions and influences the judgment and emotions of others. The states of now are in the moment everywhere and in everyone. Whatever the experience, or expression, good or bad, each of us is making use of that proximity of space, time, or relationship. When we are out of that proximity, we are in the moment and away from our past occurrences or future wants and needs. Often these indulgences are not even real possibilities, but are simply how we would have liked things to happen in the past or how we would like them to be in the future. Even with all these wishes, we are unaware that they are often pointless and most likely will never enrich our lives.

However, we can constructively be aware of the past or future while in the state of now; all we need to do is not allow ourselves to be stuck there. We can creatively examine the past and future and imagine how and why something happened. We can think about the possibilities of how our actions now will make the future happen. It is important that we are aware of the reflecting process and not get lost in thought by mystifying reality with fantasy. The united way is to reflect on the cause and effect of our actions. Thus, we realize where we want to go in this experience. Our imaginings can be creative. It can be wonderful to relax the waves of consciousness and permit the unconscious mind to express itself. Nevertheless, it is important to have the conscious mind remain watchful by observing and keeping the creative expressions from turning dark or allowing repetitive hurtful patterns from surfacing. The conscious mind unites and keeps the mental energies in the present, aware and mindful of its actions.

When we are completely involved with our feelings of the moment, we are at one with all states of being. While that state varies from person to person, the general principles are consistent. Young and old, male and female, rich or poor, when the moment occurs each one knows how being in the now feels and how it will enrich their lives. Whatever our goals may be in work or retirement, we are energetic when we are cognizant of that clarity. Our natural process takes over, giving us direct experience of our reality. Thus, we are seeing the truth moment by moment. When a person or group is individually aware of the state of Now, whatever the action, clarity of those events will aid in the overcoming of any dispute. Every life is in a series of never ending moments, moments that keep passing by, and most of the time we are not aware of them. The state of Now gives us the opportunity to grasp those moments without unduly worrying about the past or future.

On every wave, we find there in the moment the Eternal Now.

## *See Things as They Are*

When we take our first breath, we draw into us the power of being. Unconsciously we absorb the vital principles, fragrance, exhalation, odor or perfume of every entity, organic compound, plant, and animal that have breathed, dissolved and moved upon earth. Our individual lives, their essence, are shaped and forged in the first seven years of breath. During these prime years, we choose our life issues from this mixture. Prior to this, the female ova and male gamete formed the physical body. Our conscious behavior is an imitation of that coming together.

Each life, in order to learn and keep its individuality, takes on the appearance and qualities of that inhaling and exhaling: hence, the seeming differences in opinions and life actions within societies and groups. Without air, organic life would not have the capacity to grow and respond to stimuli, reproduce through natural selection, or adapt to the environment in successive generations. Other factors, human and environmental, influence the development of a person to some extent. However, around the age of twenty-one, everyone with a sound mind becomes responsible for the choices made. Whatever those tendencies are, through our own thinking, we can let them control us or we can assume control over them.

We all come into this life with a set of issues that we relate to persons, places and things or we would not be in this present circumstance. How we deal with this condition and how we allow it to affect us is our sole responsibility. Environmental or human, how we interact with others and how we allow those interactions to disturb our serenity is, to some extent, a reflection of what the future will be. Mistakes and failures are unavoidable but when we fail to learn from those failures, we are doomed to repeat them. When we inhale, we are drawing in the pure as well as the impure, but when we exhale, we can choose what we want to keep at that instant. As to the outer world, all any of us can do is see things as they are. However, we derive our Inner world from our own power: the ability to choose correctly.

There is a struggle going on in each of us; one is good and one is negative. The one that will win is the one we feed.

## The Reflection of the Self

We are mirrors onto ourselves reflecting light images of the firmament above: the soul, an ensemble of kindred spirits formed from our experiences, thoughts, aspirations and actions. The names of persons, places and things are not valuable; it is the information we gain from these experiences that is. From a physical life view most of the information coming to us is a result of cause and effect. Our actions reflect mirror images of ourselves as persons, groups, cultures, societies, and races. When we look out across the vast surface of our planet into the blue sky of daylight and the darkness of night, we sense waves of Light and energy particles moving from one place to another.

Where do these energy waves come from and where are they going? This Grand Cosmos is just our Supreme Consciousness stepping itself down into each of us. Our experiences are nothing more than a compass directing us toward that Greatness: a vast path with many turnings. To some it can be a guide to the Inner realm of transformation revealing the hidden side of the Self. To the Will, it is the relationship between the subjective and the objective regarding the feeling and knowledge side of consciousness. The Inner Self, our Ancient Companion, has the possessive power that can lead us to valuable insights, increased clarity and deeper perceptions about physical life that are meaningful to us.

The Reflective Self can take us back into the beginning as well as to the farthest places in the future and all the spaces in-between. It has no other motive than providing a teaching that will aid us regarding everyday life and what we have to master through the elements of the cosmos. Because of reasons not remembered, the Wisdom that lives in each of us has been lost to the conscious mind. We are now at the point where we can rediscover, and through good sense, make wise decisions about the accumulated learning of our visual field. The Reflective Self is the lens that gives us that clarity of mind.

The following are some thoughts to place before the mirrored self. What is my Inner reality now? What is my present situation and what is influencing me strongly? What surrounds me and how should I behave? We must remember to stay open and ready to accept what comes forth, whether they are symbols, dreams or everyday contacts with persons, places and things. These informational clips are the lessons we must learn. Life is a learning process and a period for repayment for an action. To avoid difficulties one must reflect on the true image of the Universal Soul - the power behind creative potential, happiness and satisfactions of life. Surrounding the Reflective Self is the Everlasting Light that we came from and to which we yearn to return. We can never comprehend this Light; we can know it only through manifested ideas. Within this overshadowing there exists undreamed of beauty and completeness. It brings everything to life and vivifies the universe; its best expression is human consciousness.

From the elegant creation of the cosmos, we have the wondrous workings of the mind. As a result, we have the earth as our altar and the sky as its dome, the mind is its garden, and the Heart our true home.

## The Human Species - Things as They Are

The human species struggle against each other in a constant encounter of verbal and physical conflict. The human chain is always clashing between ideas, beliefs, opinions, resources, and territory for the purpose of obtaining, achieving, or maintaining the condition or state of affairs of the human hierarchy. This prolonged conflict saturates and colors the human mind with repeated disorders. How did this madness of war and brutality get started? From mild to intense, there is malevolence in the stages of life. In the human species there are good, pure and true humans functioning along with the bad, impure and false.

On this long journey toward freedom, the human species has been waging war for as long as history has memory. No matter how hard we attempt to rise above this violence of movement, some aspect of society always falls back into its grasp. Persistently, we document and record the brutality of war. However, the descriptiveness of the cruel, harsh, or ruthless reality of its nature has done little to sway the masses toward more gentle alternatives.

In this 21st century, there is no imaginable excuse for war. We have trade, communication, education, and travel on a global scale, never before seen in history; yet we exercise a lack of trust that is more prevalent than any time before. We can only hope that when the human species has worked its way through the pain and toil of conflict, it will settle into a more peaceful approach to human togetherness. Until that day dawns, other than refusing to make war a part of one's thinking, there is little one can do on a personal level to constrain those in power from engaging in war to achieve a political end.

Those who resort to war still have a tribal or national way of thinking/acting. Many believe that anyone who stirs another to an emotional response toward war is a murderer. Regardless of the nature of the grievances, we must settle those complaints by negotiation. It is an unpardonable crime against civilization for any nation to kill other people so those in power can plunder and rule others in order to rob them of their will and resources. When we step away from leaders who are ruled by external self-interest or brute force, we will be governing by the conscious power of rightness and reason from within. Only then will we know enough to select those who are qualified with the knowledge of justice to govern the interests of each of us.

We can no longer afford to hear what our leaders verbalize; we must know what they are thinking. Only then do we know what to do for ourselves. When we allow others to persuade us through thinking, feeling, and speaking, and we act on what they believe to be right, we lose our ability to be politically self-aware. The success or failure of a nation is not the result of what leaders do, it is how we allow them to lead that makes for success or failure. Only when we to take this to heart, will leaders grow out of the need for conflict and its savage state.

No power can make a person be what that person will not make himself to be.

## The Sum of Human Life

Mind or thinking is the sum of human life from the first thinking human to the present. Matter, the platform for the physical universe, is made of electrons. Mind/Spirit and matter/form are all there is. Molded after the unseen Ultimate Mind, electrons and thinking bring the universe to life.

This grand mind, the sum of human life, is unreachable by the research instruments of physical matter.

Each human regardless of his/her status is an electrical current emanating from the Ultimate Mind. Each human is an expression of others who have had an impact on his/her life, plus the intuitive glimpses flowing out from the Soul that impact the human mind. All beings are bound together whether in or out of life. This link is comprised of electricity and electrons in motion registered on the nerves and cells of the mind coming from that Ultimate Mind. Thus, we have the entire creation of humanity expressed as consciousness.

There are two-types of consciousness: physical and emotional/mental. The outer infrastructure of human existence is shaped from earthly elements whereas the inner emotional/mental is forged from thinking and doing. Mind continues while matter eventually decays back into its original state. Latent in the human mind is the means to harness the magnetic force of the rotary magnetic field of galactic space. Eventually, this new type of electro-magnetism will allow the mind to transcend time and space and move unencumbered within the Ultimate Mind. Mind is dual, triple, multiple and infinite in nature, all converging into the sub-conscious mind within; it is the Soul where latent powers and potentialities reside. The Soul is the ruler and director that witnesses, stores and never forgets. The power of words trains the imagination to form a conduit for electrons to receive instructions from the Ultimate Mind field in order to form the mysterious words that allow the use of the magnetic force.

Words are the source for expressing the limitless power of higher thoughts. Eventually scientists will realize that exploring the Inner mind will be more fruitful than exploring the time structure of the universe and its stars because mind is greater than matter. Human induction inaugurated matter into form. All objects of knowledge including the physical universe have no existence except as creations of the mind. We think and see by induction. In physics, a circuit creates electric forces by being in proximity to a magnetic field without physical contact. The human mind is similar to the Ultimate Mind in attributes; the only difference is in degree, power, force or intensity.

The only real power in the universe is the power of mind to think. The only thing able to add to its self is mind, the only architect. Logic cannot upset this rule. When we train the objective and subjective mind to be in harmonic union, the personality can launch into the deep arena of the Soul and sail on toward the Infinite. When the mind learns how to direct electrons so they can rotate as atoms to form bodies of molecules, then the mind is creating in union with the Ultimate Mind. Mind-directed electrons are the workers, the constructors and originators for the elements of matter; they are the impulses behind the evolutionary process: the means of development. Coming in from the outside and directing the objective mind is activity. The movement of electrons, atoms and molecules are the originators of thought. The cell or constructor is the adviser, director and actor for human life. A life is the sum result of all the choices made both consciously and unconsciously through the aspect of the mind.

The Soul is the mediator between the personality and the Ultimate Mind. When we take control of our choices, we take control of our destiny and all the aspects that come from the Sum of human life.

## The Emulator

Who are we and how did we become who we are? Are we just emulators of the ideas of others, imitating their systems of thoughts, words and actions? In the end, are we just the sum of all of this and nothing more? Are there benevolent/malevolent factors of kindness/harm seated at the center of our being? When we are born to this world, most of us follow in the footsteps of other humans and social mores that provide us with the principles out of which we lead our lives. Neither in history nor in the present, are there any recorded instances of an All-Powerful Being that is separate from the world and ourselves in which we can find solace. No doubt, there are friends and loved ones who can sit beside us and give words of comfort during our sadness, grief, or disappointment. However, when we look deeply into the wider aspects of society, our institutions are so profit-oriented that compassion is secondary. Because profits enthrall those who are in charge, they are unwilling to institute laws and customs that are beneficial to all. As a result, the waves of harm and pain flow along with us and we seem uncommitted to stopping those malevolent acts.

Our philosophical and scientific minds have filled libraries with dissertations on the concepts of benevolence. However, it is not politically advantageous for those spoken or written discourses to become a part of the debate for governing; it is more profitable to keep them housed away. Unfortunately, true independent thinking is not often encouraged by government.

The idea of comfort and ease being continuously and simultaneously present throughout society is fragmented and kept exclusively for those in positions of power. Power and authority are more profitable in the hands of the few and not the many. The world is always showing that good does not always prevail, that people can be so captivated that malice can be recognized and modernized as change. A Supernatural Being will become apparent only when individuals or groups find a common ground for action and work toward manifesting it. As long as we attach ourselves to the norms of society, our spiritual aspect cannot grow out of it. If this is difficult to accept, then we have to recognize harmfulness as a part of our system and not let its effects trouble us. Is there a true, lasting meaning to anything? If there is, each of us will create it through a legacy of knowledge, sharing and kindness.

It is in our interactions with and contemplation of each other as Souls that we find meaning in our physical existence.

## The New and Last Moments

Every person, place and thing has its last moments from the air we breathe to the feelings of the senses. Mind and matter fade and move into a different place or condition: that mysterious something only the witness perceives. At the moment of our first mouthful of air, the life force of nature plants itself and oxygenates the blood stream with its vitality. This allows the body to live and move with the rhythms of the earth. Without this vital air current physical human existence could not occur. As the earth passes through its series of actions, we can see the mutually beneficial relationship between minerals, plants, animals, and ourselves. However, science is now in the process of disrupting those natural occurrences. In some cases, entire species are becoming extinct as the fragile ecosystem of the earth becomes unbalanced. Consequently, we are seeing the last moments of some of nature's organisms on which the environment depends. Regardless, since we are all part of nature, we are all in this moment together. We may not be fully conscious of that moment, but our Inner being is.

In the last moments of a dying day when the sun slips under the horizon and the forest of trees and hills turns dark, each of us is alone in the changing seasons of time and dreams. With a free Soul, the conscious mind never forgets what has passed before it. When each of us perceives that he/she is now a body and mind in motion with the stars and earth, one innately knows something has touched the Soul with its living breath. How can we not realize that everything is a part of the universe?

We are like the butterfly: a changeling, a fragment of dust from the stars and earth, a friend of fire, aspiration and Light. The mysterious awareness of which we are a part (matter/Spirit) translates into sensations, guides and directs, exerts itself with our chemical and physical forces and never disconnects from the Light of earth. Everything belongs to this realm of Spirit/matter, consciousness, and in a circular motion has an endless series of endings and beginnings where one meets the other. Memory and affection are not limited to matter-manifested forms of here and now. When time and space align with understanding the association of person, places and things of a wider Spiritual nature, a larger ethereal existence will manifest.

When we link up with the sub-conscious mind (the individual Soul) then we will reestablish the missing link in humans. All life is contained within the time continuum. Thus, a new life begins by a reproductive event that eventually becomes the Essence of life. Therefore, we can see the significance of recognizing the union of cells, electrons, atoms and molecules as the Essence of life: the sustainable continuum of life and mind. This wondrous reproductive current lifts the human phase of being into higher states above the ordinary life as new and last moments.

As everything has a last moment, everything has a first moment, also.

## The Wise Use of Love

We can never fully define love. It changes as the seasons do, but we can use it wisely in defining our relations with persons, places and things. Love can be a strong positive emotion regarding feelings toward someone or something. We can express love toward family, work, play, pleasures, sexual desire, or the adoration for an unseen deity. In birth, living and dying, every language has different views on the meaning of love. Do we love because of the morality expected from it and because of what others believe it to be? If we were free of negative connotations in defining characteristics, would love remain expressive? Perhaps it is necessary that the opposite of affection be a part of our observations and actions in order that we may advance beyond human consciousness. Whatever the case, this duality of liking/disliking is as ancient as we are, and our social norms reflect it.

Regardless of our outlook, humanism is a product of our thoughts, and we could even say the world is a product of that mind stuff which has formed the histories of human behavior. This much we know; thoughts belong to humans, humans belong to the earth and all things are connected: minerals, plants, and animals to the blood flowing in our veins. Therefore, thoughts keep us mentally and emotionally alive as the blood keeps the body alive. Electromagnetism carries information, the brain is the repository for that electric current and the mind is the distributor of it. Once we create a thought, it remains throughout time-space unless it has been demagnetized.

A shift in the critical mass will occur when humanity collectively makes equal sharing a definition of love. Until that happens, its opposite will remain as a disruptive influence. When we use thoughts that keep people or things apart from each other, love disconnects from the collective heart. This mind-set of selfish separateness is the root cause of hate throughout the world and may even cause natural disasters across the planet. When we attune our thoughts to healthy attitudes and attributes, love will become an electrical field in the mind, and the wise use of love will prevail.

Love and hate are rationalizations that result in our direction, purpose, makeup, force or belief. Like tools, these assertions are neither good nor bad. Our use of them brings us harmony or conflict. Whether we use love or hate to justify our present, it is certain these emotions will be in our future. On the other hand, if we listen to that Inner Voice of reason we can prepare ourselves to demagnetize and close those recesses of hate that have long endured in our consciousness. Sensitivity, caring and sharing can erase those negative implants, purifying the blood and nerves so that the vital electrical currents act positively on the mind thoughts. When these progressive thoughts become fixed, stored and permanent we are charging our character with harmony and our erroneous thoughts give way to the wise use of Love.

When we observe our environment carefully, we can see Love expressed by degree in all living beings and all of nature.

## The Struggle for Conscious Identity

Emotions, mind and form have a life and governing personality of their own. The form and its personality do not easily submit to the will of the Soul. The wishes of the body and the demands of the personality are often at odds with the reflected Light of the Soul. Thus, the Soul and personality are constantly struggling to overcome the other. However, the Soul, not subjected to decaying time as the personality is, only absorbs the higher qualities of the personality. The personality, saturated by decaying matter, eventually becomes weary of its repeated battles with pain and suffering and embraces the mental illumination of its higher self, the Soul.

The conditions of the outer world are the reflected attributes of the many minds that make up the collective actions of society. Consequently, each person, as seen outside of another person, exhibits the good/bad qualities of that physical reality. The images, thoughts and feelings experienced while sleeping, daydreaming or imagining can become glimpses of the ongoing struggle in the mind and may throw understanding on how to put something right. No matter how hard we try, we cannot eliminate wrongdoing from another. However, through choice we can refuse to commit an offense against a person, place or thing that will entangle us in a repetitive cause and effect cycle.

A detailed mental examination of our feelings, thoughts, and motives can be beneficial. With a fixed determination, we must set the mind right and escape the negative habits that cause pain and suffering. Instead, we must dwell on equilibrium: a dynamic state in which all forces are in balance and there are no negative occurrences happening. When we take on a higher mindset, the Soul transmits its influence over the lower mind.

The effects of the lower mind result in pain. It exists because of wrongdoing and it is useless to try to find its origin. Nevertheless, we can uncover the effect. The knowledge for our recovery rests in understanding what has been wrongly committed and then stopping its causes. When a person makes something happen, various degrees of causes always exist. Therefore, it is important to understand the reasons that make those actions occur. Are they malevolent or benevolent? When we know how to wisely choose between the two and understand the consequences of that choice, we are in a condition of rightness.

We will always be in two currents of thought, the past and present. The past is latent while the present flows on as awareness. Both are mysteries left to the probing mind to open and access. The entry to these two realms is in feeling, desiring and thinking: the imaginings of the mind. Life is impossible to explain fully. We could say that we all are making it up as we go along. We can struggle with the ingredients or we can develop a recipe and follow it.

### Conversion of the Heart

It is through the eyes of the Soul that the heart changes into something wondrous. In the entrance hall the Soul awaits the reflection of the lower self which deposits there all of the attributes of form life. In this reception area of the lower mind, the higher mind studies and polishes the peculiar habits, mannerisms, and aspects of character until they become assets for the Soul. When this happens, an awareness of clarity enters the mind. Therefore, we must never let go of this awareness because it is similar to the sun that first gave sight to the eyes. This coming together has switched on the Light of Harmony. This observation is not to punish or scold. Rather, it is the starting point so that self-reflection can begin.

There are grades of personalities in the soul-life beyond the form life that the Soul needs to examine closely and carefully in order to resolve cause and effect. This correction is codependent upon heart and mind so that a searchlight can illumine the path that lights the way of the Soul. This conversion of the heart by the sub-conscious becomes a union of spiritual thoughts of the mind with the feelings of the heart: the core of Spirit and Truth for the Soul.

Once the initial encounter occurs, there comes a yearning to make this imprint ongoing through endless beginnings and understandings within the creative process. The fulfillment that we ascribe to now is vastly different from those satisfactions before the encounter. We are now influencing the Self to rethink the ways of the heart and mind in its actions in order that they can be conceived and reborn as something vastly wiser and different. This world of Infinite Light is more illuminating and startling than words can describe; it is a beginning and an entrance into the world of Spirit above form. With careful reflection, it can become something indescribably different from our earthly experiences of the senses. When the heart and mind are in Harmony, any feeling of shame or regret vanishes. We are in a heart that is unbreakable, animated by high and mental/emotional impulses that correspond to the Soul. This place of reflection refines the negativity of the mind. Here the mind beholds nature as an image of all that is beautiful and serene.

The long submerged wisdom of the Soul has reappeared as a more modern form of thinking and feeling. It is a new expression of creation where every part and particle relates to awareness, attitude, acceptance and action. Our own individual uniqueness paints this new portrait as we open to the larger reality around us. We no longer see that reality as jagged but as rounded. The Soul descends into a vestibule of matter and lifts a fragment of its experience into a brighter hallway. The Soul makes an expression of itself into the heart/mind of the wandering personality and converts it into something greater and newer, a mental bond between itself and the Universal Creator.

Walk with the mind's eye turned inward: the direction that leads to the Home of the Heart.

## Conscious Words for an Inner Life

Creator of Heaven and earth, and all things visible and Invisible in the Sacred words of life, lift the Veil from our eyes that we may see and do the things you do. Let us keep things secret that are secret in the Mysteries of your treasures so that we may use them without your offense. Watch over our kind and us and show us how to lead them in ways that are in accord with your wishes. Teach us what is profitable and what is not, and what we are to avoid, and what we are to embrace. Turn over to us the meaning of those words and insights that concern the meaning of night and day, of past, present and future, so that the words of your Eternity may bless us. Let your messengers of Spirit be ready in their nature to minister unto our minds all things that have your name. When we speak, let it be serious, thoughtful, and respectful. Let our confidence originate from your Wisdom and strengthen our hearts. Therefore, all life as yours fills all that is Good and Just. Vanquish the tribulations of the mind that life may honor, not onto us, but onto you. The things distributed as offices, powers and treasures are your ordained virtues that are refined in nature, and come forth unto action by your permission. Truly, each of your creatures is fated for some profitable end in human nature, as your Essence and experience do testify. Whatsoever you give unto us we will fix in mind and regenerate it gracefully. When trouble comes our way, we will hear your words of Comfort for your Wisdom is our foundation, as your Omnipotence directs and nurtures the workings of nature and the creatures that serve life. From their obedience onto you, their wisdom and place become secure, and your secrets revealed onto our kind.

Creator of Heaven and earth, through your Compassion instruct us in the desires that are gifts from your Heart that you gave unto your First Cause that we may work together in all things that make up Paradise. In your belief, true faith comes as the certainty of your truth casts out doubt. For in you we know on whom to trust. In all things which live, you live and have being, and in our Souls who receive your power, we know the true strength and nature of things, unseen and seen. Through your virtues and secrets, Light into darkness that is nature's power in action and word, the Spirits of your Light appear. Whatsoever our Souls desire, wanting is useless unless it is necessary for you. In earnest, we wish to know the Arts of this life and the things that are necessary for it, but darkness and infinite human misunderstandings overwhelm us. Because of this, we can attain no knowledge in them of our own power. Therefore, grant us one of your Spirits who may teach those things, which you would have us know and learn for the profit of Kindred fellowship and Love. Let our Hearts be teachable and apt that we may easily understand and bring forth out of your Inexhaustible treasures these teachings and put them to necessary use. Give us Grace that we may use those treasures wisely and humbly. Let all the righteous Spirits that inhabit the firmament, and in the stars of the firmament, and in the offices of these Spirits, bring forth their fatal charms and render evil harmless by your Limitless Power. You are the Maker of all things, and all that is Celestial and worldly are obedient to your Will.

With the right use of words, all things attain a happy and desired end.

## The Mixing of Human Characteristics

Person, places and things are never identical with thoughts and feelings. Various modifiers affect the meaning of communication and interaction. Even the facts or events in nature adjust for changes. Change occurs because of the alteration in human thinking. We understand the laws of nature through human thinking and action. We identify those laws by reason and observation. However, when it comes to human interaction, the laws of nature that relate to the expressions of societies or cultures are vastly different from country to country.

Are they the same in China as they are in Seattle and are the styles and degree of doing the same? Are the expressions of olden Rome the same as the ones in modern times? If we realistically look at life, the laws of nature are elastic terms similar to the idea of Divinity or consciousness that we can only substantiate while being conscious of Consciousness. When observing our modern day events and circumstances, the interactions of societies seem at most nothing more than savage customs. Whether in politics, science or religion we are constantly working against each other by competing for a piece of the world that is observable only by thinking. Therefore it is probable that the entire history of the human species is nothing more than suppositions that may not be anymore meritorious than that of the dinosaurs.

The means of nature of which we are its expression is beyond the grasp of anyone. Perhaps if we started thinking with a collective consciousness, our dysfunctional attitudes would not be so disruptive or confusing in our interactions with each other. Is it possible that nature is saying to every one of us that we are an independent and unique universe in a vaster universe and as long as we fail to grasp our self-governance, the elements of our personal reality will remain hidden from the elements of that vaster communal universe? The faces and things that make up our earthly existence are like puzzle pieces that we can fit together to give a clearer and more perfect picture of ourselves.

When putting this puzzle together, we must realize that no process is flawless. To think that we can be instantaneously spotless will just create frustration. Nature moves us forward through periods of duality of doing and thinking which are individualistic in consciousness. Nevertheless, since our bodies are constructs of nature's elements, a solid mass of stardust and light formed from the clay of earth, it is foolish not to think in terms of collectivity.

Any image formed upon the retina of the mind is a visual mixture of thinking and feeling of all humanity past and present. Collective reality is an arrangement of parts that show how they are interconnected in sets of circumstances that encourage the growth of atoms, molecules, cells, and forms whether human or cosmic. There are many faces and each face is different, but when all of those features or qualities join through collective Harmony, we are completing ourselves. The world is a body of myths that belong to a particular people or culture. It is a story of ancestors, heroes and Deity's of history, and vast majorities of us revere those myths. In our memories, we are always returning to those happy or unpleasant times in our thoughts and dreams. Nature is just the foundation for us to build our consciousness. As we need a plan to build a house, we need a plan to build consciousness. Humanism is the first step; it supplies us with the needed tools of persons, places and things to shape our consciousness.

The human story we are telling is not a story unto the earth itself with a single character.

## Looking out the Window

As I look out the windows of my den, I can see the tree-lined hills beyond the swaying coniferous treetops of the state park. The sun is shining overhead. Gliding with the wind, an occasional sea gull crosses the horizon as it heads out over the roar of coastal waves. It is tranquil here by the sea; but elsewhere in the world, the forces of nature and political tension or strife resulting from discord are tearing its pieces and places apart. Could this lack of harmony between people be the cause of nature's destructive storms? Are we out of alignment with the very forces that give us life?

In our pursuit of material things we are forgetting about the quality of the air we breathe, our kinship with the minerals, plants and animals and the very nuances of nature that give our form life meaning. As our fellowship with minerals, plants, animals and humans diminishes, so does our partnership with nature. Before our minds gained an awareness of nature's acts, we had no fear of it, anymore than a fetus does while in the womb of its mother. However, once separated from nature's latent qualities, as a species we slowly developed the characteristics for living outside of the womb. As our recorded history attests, we instill violence as a means to resolve our disputes.

As individuals, we no longer have the powerful feeling of union with nature that we once experienced. At that point in time, there was nothing separating us from that awareness. Once we are born to the world, we first strive for the affections of the father/mother. As we acquire gender, we form some type of desire attachments to persons, places and things and we begin to question, unconsciously, those primitive latent physical sensations that were prominent before separation occurred. Hence, we still have not fully realized the difference between the earth/mother/father/self which makeup humankind.

As the mind struggles to assert itself from the confines of matter, it rebels against the gravity of earth. Instead of gradually loosening the ties of dependency and intimacy through fellowship and harmony, we use the process of struggle. Therefore, competition expressed in our social, scientific, religious, political and educational processes has replaced those primitive jealousies that we inherited. These social practices are in denial that there is a collective relationship between the earth and its forms. What each culture is effectively saying is, 'You must be like me -you may not be like others'. The separation seen in our social relationships emphasizes this hostility. Consequently, the earth and its inhabitants, as nations, remain separated, and the storms of nature remain indifferent.

As I feel the soft wind blow through the open widow and touch my face, I feel the wonder of nature's Innocence.

## The Art of Altruistic Living

Altruistic living is evident when, as a collective, we have attitudes and ways of behaving that give every person a belief in his/her own humanity with principles founded on Rightness and Goodness that benefit others.

The more we advance thinking in the direction of rightness, the more selfishness withdraws. The uncivilized become civilized and society attains its higher social goals and skills. These cooperative behaviors lead to positive social interactions that result in mutual understanding, helping and sharing. Altruism is a latent aspect of the personality that only the Soul can awaken. This connection between the Ultimate Mind/Soul/personality, when utilized as Goodness, lifts human nature into a more rarefied existence that exceeds the ordinary levels of social life.

The overriding motive of Creation is fellowship for all humanity, which will eventually touch all hearts with Compassion to do well and be good, a caring that expects nothing in return. When the world gives up its selfish ways and embraces the Spirit of collectivism, justice and fair dealing between all races and nations will arise. As individuals, we will answer the call of nature with new steps toward a good life coming from our hearts, our Souls, our strength, our minds, and Compassion for our neighbors as ourselves.

The art of living altruistically is a day-by-day, morning until night, and merciful attitude toward all. It has no immediate or visible reward except a faith in a future happiness that is beyond intellectual materialism. Altruism reveals that there is something within that is Immeasurable, Infinite and Constant that is uplifting and beyond consequences.

The art of altruism is a quest for absolute Freedom. When we as individuals have freed ourselves from the many levels of our history, we seek then to free ourselves from the limitations of our own erroneous perceptions. Our human world is but one perception based on theories, discoveries and technologies. We have come to know a great deal about our physical world through science. We have expanded our senses through the microscopes and telescopes that peered into the quantum world. As individuals, we can only know our physical reality through our five senses and the thinking mind.

However, there is a growing part of us that feels there is something more in us that is Hidden and when we are true to ourselves, each of us will eventually find our own 'measure of vibration'. It is this desire to know our Truth and the forces imperceptible to our senses that give us knowledge, wisdom and existence. When we are acting for the benefit of others, we are creating a better reality beyond the range of our five senses: a Spiritual world beyond our own bodies. The outer world is but a reflection of our inner thoughts and aspirations. When we use the sixth sense, mind, we are void of time, space and motion. When we feel only endless streams of Love energy, a point of Light within a greater Light, we are approaching a different life and reality. Through living life altruistically, we interpret and appreciate the outer world and gain broader, wider powers of observation and unselfish growth.

When we live in such a way that others view our actions as unselfish, we are making the world a better place for having lived in it.

## The Declaration of Leadership

Sent forth by our Mothers and Fathers, we the chosen, elected, and appointed by the People do hereby swear to uphold the Laws and Principles set forth in the Constitution of our land. Furthermore, we pledge not to work for our benefit, but for the benefi t of those we serve that we will work in earnest to fill the chalice of Government with legislative laws that are expressive of the Will of the People. Moreover, in matters of State we will put the interests, health, education and well-being of our children first in order that we may develop a Perfect Union that upholds the Welfare of the People. We give our word to honor the freedom of speech, self-expression, and promise not to rescind any law that guarantees the freedom to choose and worship, that which is of body, mind, and heart. We further pledge to promote policies that will assure freedom from want and fear.

In our council chambers, we vow to decree that the elements of our land, our minerals, plants and animals will develop in ways that will dictate their safety and sustainability for future generations. In fellowship with other nations and principalities beyond our borders, we will in earnest effort and statesmanship do all we can to promote Cooperation and Goodwill in the sharing of resources, ideas, and cultural traits that will provide understanding so that we may live in Peace together for the benefit of all our Descendants.

In matters of national security, we affirm that our armed forces will remain strong, not out of fear of an enemy, but as a source for character development and group unity and as a response to events that may arise from accidents and disturbances of nature. With forthright insight, we do not know what awaits us in space and time. We further guarantee not to militarize space or install weapons systems that have a military nature, except those approved internationally that would be needed to neutralize space objects that are about to enter the atmosphere. In addition, we agree not to use dispiriting words or gestures in our negotiations with other nations, or posture our strength and resources that would give an indication of the stronger over the weaker. In the Branches of Government, we promise to uphold the Rule of Law in dealing with belligerent parties and that the court systems of the world will bring those parties into compliance with more peaceful courses of action. In addition, we promise to do all that is necessary to make war the last option.

Additionally, we pledge to modify our monetary system in ways that will allow the free market system to ensure that the right to work is a non-negotiable guarantee and that work, according to one's skill and talents, is an Inalienable right: a hallmark toward Happiness. Lastly, as a remembrance to those who have lived by the Rule of Law and have now entered the History of our nation, we promise to do all we can scientifically, philosophically and creatively to honor their passing. We pledge that this world of nations, of Fathers, Mothers, Sons and Daughters, will remain clear and bright for all future generations to live, move and have being in Perpetuity, so help us.

## *Whatever Has Been, Be Grateful*

We do not arrive at an attitude of Gratitude by Will or from the accomplishment of some action that has provided fulfillment in life. Neither do we arrive at it overnight. Gratitude appears when life has evolved into accepting 'what is' as the criterion for living. When we can look retrospectively at the scope, length, and extent of what we have passed through in the crucible of living, we finally know the meaning of Gratitude. No two people can fully grasp the significance of that appreciation in the same way. It is through our circumstances that we are able to view our place in the world. We view this realization of gratitude, not because of some denial; rather, we see those circumstances to better our place in time. We have learned to appreciate the flavors of our moral and immoral habits, not from a need to do, or produce an experience again, but from knowing 'what to do and what not to do'. We come to see the significance of the new Light that arises from passing through those preoccupations. We are now grateful for our soundness and for a newer mind and heart that is yet to manifest. We can now tune our attention and bring into reality a better state of consciousness motivated by selfless thought. We learn to be finely tuned receivers of the Higher Self and step into its reality. This opens the energy circuits and allows for a new set of patterns to form in our awareness, producing a vastly different view screen. As we peer into this new screen, we must imagine ourselves relying more on our own instinctive natures. Whatever we truly desire will come because this new view will create a greater sense of Gratitude for what we already have.

This new concept of Gratitude helps us focus on healing ourselves so that we can see others in a different and better Light of understanding. It is the beginning processes of converting ill thinking into healthy thinking. What we have perceived as being hopeless and inappropriate has shifted into a higher level of consciousness so that the old patterns no longer sway us. No particles that surround us can separate from us, whether they are in us, in space, or in our world. However, with this new sense of Gratefulness we can learn to develop the ability to extend a new type of radiance around ourselves that will regulate our actions and enhance the particles that makeup our being.

We cannot express life, as we know it without a dual reality of things coming together or repelling. Our conventional reality of personality-to-personality, the cause and effects of everyday life, eventually compel us to be thankful for what has been. Without this Gratitude, we could not actualize our Essence. It is difficult to describe with any certainty this core of being but when we give thanks for just being a part of it, we are expressing its fundamental nature that is our humanity. We learn to appreciate that others may not always welcome, feel or see the real meaning of our Spirit. When we recognize the value of each other's Essence, we love unconditionally, whatever has been!

Once Gratitude has seeped into our veins, the Love/suffer syndrome can only arise in the personality to the level of Essence we have come to know.

## A Sense of Serenity with What Is

When we have a feeling or knowing that we are Timeless, we are beyond the boundaries of everyday reality. We can then become completely involved in the here and now; our state of being is neither anxious nor boring and it becomes a model for our existence. When we are unrehearsed in our thinking, we can exist above and apart from the material world while still being active in it. The senses and surroundings become clearer. The substance of persons, places and things in the world reality is the Essence of man/woman, our humanity. Hence, our sense of being is the substance of our awareness. The substance of Being is what keeps us going. We are compelled to act upon the environment in which we each find ourselves. In order to be free from those constraints or duty-bound impressions that have long endured throughout history, a reshaping of mind and heart with perceived reality is required if we are ever going to sense what is Real. Realness can only come when we have a unique sense or relation with being. It is an understanding that speaks to each of us, "I am uniquely me!" The things of the world in a material sense are not lasting. Nevertheless, persons, places and things are an outgrowth of our knowing. When we finally accept our place in 'what is' we are becoming a part of being in the Good side of the present; both life and awareness are about being and becoming.

We determine our future by the choices we make out of our being. Our conscious awareness of being is either real or unreal. We are free to choose what level on which we want to remain. The quality of our awareness determines the strength of Will that we use to pull ourselves out of mistaken beliefs or ideas. Will is useless if we are not conscious of the impulsive influences of the forces in our being. When we exercise positive qualities in the present, we will move into the positive qualities of the future.

It is important that we do not become overly enraptured in current events so that they do not negatively influence our emotional, mental and Spiritual qualities, thus diminishing our conscious awareness of Truth. Remember, world affairs do not have the power to affect our free will unless we allow them to influence us. It is in the frames of the mind that we witness the pictures of the world gushing down as rain drops from the sky splattering images for us to see. The chief debate that underlies the nature of being is rationality versus impulsiveness. It is simply humanity's inherent relations between Good and ignorance. The trappings of people and their character show up in behavior, either in truth or in distortion, in order to gain favor in their social positions. We are in 'True Being' when we see the venues of earth as shadows passing before the bright sunlight. The patches of dark and Light that pass through the mind are but aspects of fiction and truth in all human beings. It is up to each of us to select the scenes that motivate our truth of being with what is. A metaphor for True Being is the Heart. It is here that we can feel and know the Essence of Goodness, thus vanquishing our mistaken beliefs. When we look at being as both impulsive and rational we can best understand our place in it. Without that dualism, we would remain unchanging with little or no awareness at all. Through Light and shadow, we experience the nature of our diverse being and gain a sense of Serenity with what is.

We each attend to our way of doing things; thus, we create the type of universe we will ultimately inhabit.

## The Universe and its Dual Relations

Humanism requires having two parts, functions or aspects that are of a similar kind. For example, a relationship occurs when two or more people interact with one another. Such relationships may be benign, emotional, platonic, physical, or mental in nature. However, there is less consequence or exploitation in role-playing when the relationship is of a Kindred Kind. When we take up a relationship with others, it influences many important aspects of life. What influences or power (forces of personality) do others exhibit in their thinking or actions that could be contrary to one's growth?

It is important to differentiate when choosing relationships because another's fate could be similar or not. Work, career, power, position, marriage, wealth, poverty, situations, finances and personal abilities are some of the aspects to consider when going into a committed relationship. When there is an instant feeling of familiarity, there is a sense of connection stemming from a previous positive experience with persons, places and things.

The places, objects and persons will not be a full reproduction of what was before, but we will feel the vibrations, nuances and familiarities. The Fire, warmth and glow of relationships constitute the apex of human thinking. From remote households of our ancient ancestors, the lowly and exalted shrines and buildings remain as a part of our Essence. The slight difference in meaning, feeling, tone or color of the mysteries of our past permeates our awareness now and fills our minds with knowledge. The experiences and connections that happen in life do so to develop the qualities and characteristics needed for understanding dualism. We pattern these experiences in our relationships such as abuse, abandonment, love, manipulation, power struggles, rejection and intimacy. Whether in families, groups, communities, or nations, similar relationships draw us back when we fail to learn from our failures or when we do not share power equally.

The mental and emotional qualities of humanism outlast the mixture of atoms and molecules that make up the tangible body and its outward infrastructure of crystallized thought. The observable universe and all that it comprises within it is a balancing act for our development and growth. Regardless of society's view of the Origin of the Universe, whether scientific or philosophical, the continuation of the universe is dependent on an individual's state of awareness.

Perhaps because we are aware of the universe it has consciousness through us. When we die, does it die or are we just a low-level expression of it? As one expands, so does the other. Fundamentally, each of us must be aware of our contacts as well as the guidance and influence we desire. Our instincts win out in the end. They fuel our creativity, thinking and emotional responses that give us self-awareness. Therefore, our observations and relationships allow each of us to sense our place 'where the earth meets the sky'. Our relationship with duality gives us awareness about ourselves and of our space within another person's place.

Nature is repetitious and diverse, a mixture of multiplicity: relationships, combinations, mixtures and complexities that become more than just one process.

## Live and Let Live

As I came out of sleep, I noticed the clock hands were two-minutes from midnight. I pulled my body up in an 'L' angle. Sitting there, I could see the moon silently hovering out over the sound of a surfing ocean breaking on the seashore. I got out of bed and walked outside into the crisp air and silver pale light of a full moon. Off to my right a single deer pranced up the street in front of me unperturbed by my presence. I looked into the vast star-moon lit night of a revolving living universe. Everything seemed to be in a state of 'live and let live'. Most of life just wants to sleep at night, but alternating states of restlessness and calmness are nature's way of arousing the living process.

As we move through life, we are better off if we remain untroubled by the thoughts, actions, beliefs and behaviors of others. However, can we really 'live and let live' when it comes to the core issues of life? Can any of us live a complete life without disturbing another's place or thing in it? Dogma and creeds have saturated human thinking throughout history. Myths and legends, hero worship and savior rescue stories fill our imaginations. Much of humanity believes such stories will actualize and become a part of life.

When it comes to foolishness or wisdom, no one is responsible for another's interpretation of it. Just like the moon, sun and stars, awareness is Fixed and Immutable: falling asleep and awakening. The one holding that awareness, once aware of it, is its sole arbitrator. Live and let live is historically non-existent. Just glance at the coercion in the pages of history and the intolerance imbedded within its pages and one cannot help but see the impositions placed on life. Thought and action makeup life just as energy and force constitute the workings of the universe. Mutually supporting these two natures cannot exist without the other. However, when we overcome the dictates of others through self-discrimination, 'live and let live' becomes a spontaneous non-aggressive co-operative behavior that unifies the objective constraints of the world.

The two-parts of life, our senses and our thoughts, exercise our awareness. One informs us about the outer nature of the world and the other penetrates our Inner nature. These two aspects define our experiences. When perception and cognition align, our individual awareness is void of dualism and perceives life in a way that does not cause worry, concern or distress. Being at odds with another is out of the question. It is when we obey our bodily instincts or conventional demands without using empathy, we become unbalanced toward our fellow human beings. Each of us must experience life in our own way, and if others desire to live a different way, let them be.

Two aspects reside in us. One concerns the Heart, the other the mind. To loosen the grip of the world each splits off from the other to raise itself in its own Inheritance.

## The Politics of Being

When attitudes toward death change, they will alter the political landscape to win the consent of the people! As we move into that part of life where the physical part of us is immovable, our fate, our character and appearance will become an unknown future. Our words, our associations, the familiar faces, love and all the other various avenues of our being will become our imaginings. We will find our awareness is in a place that does not seem to fit, or be appropriate to, the context of what was our past being. The politics of being is concerned with the absorption of that which is material, including the expressions of human beings. When we view a being, regardless of its expressions, as not final, but rather as a new beginning from the old, our thoughts, our consciousness, our true selves journey into the memories of what was the past. What we have attached to and shared ourselves with will come with us. The body of corruptible politics does not exist in that state of being.

The world, a seemingly possessive place, thrives on profit by association. In connotation, death and politics are synonymous. Do governments arise because of the necessity for property and the preservation of it? Taxation of property and people create the wealth of governments. Politics can be generalized as 'who gets what, when, why, and how'. All around the four corners of earth our loved ones are dying, defending power and property. It seems those who hate each other's way of life will gladly die defending their way of life. Those in power will justify the cause as righteous; thus, those who died did not die pointlessly. A leader will rise and say, 'Be comforted by their bravery'. Death in the natural way can be a fair-weather friend. However, the political persuader who plays with death with an entrepreneurial 'can do attitude' is behaving recklessly with being.

The politics of being must become an art of governing where leaders organize opposing views into a higher level of holistic understanding. Presently transforming the political culture is not a part of Main Street nor is Spiritual transformation. One is internal and the other is external. World politics can become a state of being that changes the world from the inside out. Moral accountability is more than a private one. True political being is about stated principles of Harmony and Kindness toward one another regardless of political persuasion. This new way of 'being political' must be more about human health and growth than venture capitalism. Most of us believe that in some way death will recreate us. Why wait to understand our deeper causes behind our problems?

When we heal our collective ills now, the tomorrows will be brighter in both the here and the Hereafter.

## Fallen Leaves

Fall is the season when leaves fade on trees. In the crisp air, the coastal mountains are vibrant with the colors of fall. Under the influence of gravity, amber/red leaves drop from tree branches to the ground. Some of the leaves are carried off in the breeze to other places and there lapse onto the soil to be absorbed back into the earth as an inheritance of nature. As conscious beings, our thoughts are similar to leaves. Our intentions and actions are always falling away to be replaced by other ways of thinking. We can remember our old feelings but rarely can we ever fully return to them as leaves do on trees at springtime. Perceptual experience, bodily sensations, mental imagery, emotional experience and thought processes make up our mental reasoning and provide the means to understand the objective world of nature.

The whole phenomenon of life is an absorption process. Thoughts and feelings are to the mind what the soil is to fallen leaves that nurture the roots of trees. Each is a gathering and a returning. The vitality of the Inner world and the outer world are important to each other while we are aware in this condition of being. We can rationalize that the structures and functions of the world gave us a physical body, but those processes are not enough to explain how we became conscious. Perhaps we have always been conscious in a rudimentary way, we just do not remember. Consciousness is no longer subordinate to the body but gravitates toward another something, just as the leaf does to return to the earth. What that something is could be termed 'the pull of life'. We can only know of it when we are in it.

Life is a complex series of events and circumstances involving energy, force and matter pulling on one another. The core of that interplay is what feeds awareness. That single leaf that falls from the branch of a tree, though similar in texture and color to all other leaves, will return as another leaf only after the soil reabsorbs it. Can we truly say we are any different from the tree and leaf? Are we not in a symbiotic relationship with earth? Without this cooperative, mutually beneficial relationship, mind as we now think would be void of a body. Earth, plants, animals and humans are co-dependent. Therefore, the natural world contains something more than the physical world. It is conceivable that the earth is conscious as we are, except we are not yet aware of its energy states. As we awaken more to those states, it is likely we will remember as fallen leaves.

We all have a time of harvest that is vigorous and complete where we gather in our memories the things we have sown, just before they fall away.

## *Infusion of Consciousness*

Space, matter, Spirit, visibility, Invisibility, consciousness, and thoughts are some of the words that form ideas that infuse this Something called Life with Awareness. It is widely believed that the universe started thirteen-billion years ago because of an extremely dense and incredibly hot initial state. Could it be that this penetrating volatile energy Light force has not reached its peak experience with dark matter thus far? Perhaps the Big Bang is yet to occur, or may never occur? No doubt, scientific evidence and observation supports this model of the cosmological universe. Nevertheless, do we truly know what finite time is and how it interplays with nature and Consciousness as a whole?

When we look at nature and all its various forms, animate and inanimate, we can see the forces of attraction and repulsion going on in the world of cells, molecules and atoms all the way down to the immeasurable neutrino. Does any scientific theory say with certainty that any singular, exceptional or unusual quality has occurred that will give us an accurate definition of the Cause of life? The only definition that gives plausibility to life is the acronym, 'I think, therefore, I am'. Because we exist, think and have being in creating and destroying persons, places and things, we somehow believe that we have scientifically gathered the evidence that says a Big Bang occurred. As long as we have an awareness of Consciousness, we will never stop theorizing about our Origin of being. Realistically, as thinking human beings we are standing in the center of the grandest wonder of all: Life as we see it now. When the light goes out of the eyes and darkness comes upon the thinking mind that is in each of us, will our theories hold up? Until each of us is there, it remains uncertain for the now. Unless we have an awareness of this place called earth and those we have left behind, scientific theory will be mute. The plausible explanations for the continuation of science are: 1) after death we enter this life dimension again and start over where we left off 2) there are other universes constituted of the same elemental structures, and memories of life go on after death. To exist there has to be an awareness of existence within existences.

Science is only a part of that gathering which benefits the now and our intelligence capabilities. In terms of space, length, width and height, and time we are a continuum spreading outward penetrating matter. Feasibly, when the life Light fades out, we enter the cosmic womb and infuse ourselves with the Greater Light, on and on, repeatedly in the space-time continuum. Perhaps, the super-novas and other explosions we observe in space happen each time a human life fades out. None of us knows for certain 'whither we come from or where we are going'.

A good theory is worth a thousand words. Who knows where it might take us? Whatever we meet on the road, whether it is science, philosophy, religion or anything else, we must be grateful for what it provides us. If this knowing has merit, grasp it. We are not mythical beings made out of super powers. We are narrative beings creating a life on earth and for the universe, and we pass that story on in the infrastructure of being: a conscious being orientated toward Life. Each day that we see the sun rising and setting, the smile on another person's face, the changes of the seasons, the kindness of a caring person, a warm embrace, or the laughing innocence of children, we are witnessing the infusion of Consciousness.

The encounters of reality are nothing more than what we have encountered before in fantasy.

## *Imagining the Unity of All Things*

Consciousness, body, mind, and brain are structured and unified as one. Once consciousness is, it always manifests. All the parts are required to maintain the systems of awareness. Each part of total awareness is mutually dependent, constantly reabsorbing and refining one another. If we refute any one single part, the whole system is defeated. The ingredients of a single life, its thoughts, feelings, aspirations, longings, cravings, talents, etc., are never in cessation from its original Unity. The tiny particles that hold up each life give space its meaning. Body, mind and awareness compose that Unlimited expanse where everything is located. This space in-between helps us measure our place in existence.

Most of us observe the same thing every day. For example, when the sun sets we observe twilight for a while. Although the sun is below the horizon, it shines upon the upper layers of the atmosphere and reflects sunlight. Each of us is a reflected light particle, a ray of Light. Centered between the shoulder blades within the area of the spleen is a miniature orb similar to the sun. It is the combination of light particles that make up the earth and its chemistry of living.

Every life form on earth is imbued with this smallest of Light particles. As the body and brain cease, either through disease, accident, or old age, the atoms, cells and molecules, the chemistry of earth life, comes apart. As the components of the body dissolve and separate back into the elements of earth, this tiny orb passes out into its total Essence and there re-evaluates its experiences. There is no feeling of separation in this Essence. Even in the reevaluating process, this sense of unity becomes a knowing that All is well. When it is time to reweave a new experience, previous selected memories reconstitute the cause and effects of the circumstances of the past and all that is worthwhile is set in motion once again. The how, when, where and what are only known to the knower and those who choose to play a part.

We have learned that these particles have not been in the wrong place, we have merely put them there so that we can learn to be brighter and more generous toward each other. Without the multifaceted orbs there would be no dawn, no twilight, we would not know our part in the glorious sunlight of knowable persons, places and things. Without Light, shadow and darkness, these sunset glows would be absent, below our horizon and our life would be in darkness: no twilight, no afterglow, none of the Songs of eventide. With Light the finer and better particles of other beings will remain in our layers of consciousness to be manifested with different glows, different names, different places of togetherness that are for a new world to see. The whole of creation is so eye-catching that all any of us can do is Wonder in its phenomenon. If we observe carefully, we can see glowing influences orbiting one another as the earth circles the sun and the sun circles a greater sun that is below the horizon, but is not yet visible.

Imagination invades knowledge and makes it something more than what we already know. Thinking directs us toward what we have yet to discover and create.

## *The Benevolent and Malevolent Forces of the Imagination*

The most volatile creation of human grasping has been the concept of a deity in the image of our desires and expectations. Individuals, groups, societies and nations have copied themselves in this imagined creation. Each in their own creation has striven for superiority in this imagining of someone or something, then proceeds to compete endlessly in the shaping of its wisdom and power. In our striving to bring to fruition this benevolent imagining, we have also created a malevolent nimbus over ourselves. Presently all we have to show for this mixed imagining is a world often filled with worry, conflict, and anxiety.

In this mixed caldron of mind and feelings, we have embodied our nature with both fearfulness and wonderment. Human imagination has carved stone, painted the walls of caves, carved totem poles, and built grand cathedrals to give vision to this imagining of the mind and feelings. We have created shadowy stories of creatures with hoofs, tails and horns, and saintly figures of halos and robes so we can choose which ones we will imbue ourselves with and to which ones we will relinquish our fate. What we have commanded with the imagination we feel we must obey, and so we set out to follow its course hoping it will lead to our own path. If we are not careful, we will fall victim to the mass movements of irrationality and our own wishful imagining. We must be wary of anyone who wants to change us into angels and equally so to anyone who wants to turn us into dancing dolls; both are spoilers of human nature. We do not need to clamor to leadership in order to take responsibility for ourselves.

We are of this earth; it is our duty to unravel its Mystery. Extreme power and extreme faith lead to exploitation. It is in the Self that we rise above those reactions. When we inhale our own realized faith and turn it into individual awareness, our imaginations become our wellsprings. Only through our unique character can any of us hope to survive. In order for each of us to realize ourselves, it seems that we need a nemesis to overcome. Once we have seen into the void of our intentions where beauty and ugliness, truth and error are always passing into one another, we can make our own dreams into golden ones. When we establish patterns that are good and work for us, we are rising above the primitive, superstitious mentality of others. When obstacles come up, we must learn how to turn them into opportunities. The trivialities of life can become our chief source of imagination. At some point in the past, not all of our manufacturing necessities were essential; they were merely playthings that eventually became inventions. Example, the wheel was a plaything before it became a wheel for a cart.

Fancies and luxuries will always fill our imaginations, whether it is a well-formed body, the well-planned infrastructure of a city or government, a deity or friend. It is when we look for a relationship between our power and conquest that we become ignorant of the creative process in the world of the imagination. As humans, we are alive in the things we create. Out of the predictability of nature, we have introduced a semblance of order in society. However, a harmonious society is still at work in the imagination and is not yet visible. Somewhere, sometime in the realms of the imagination Compassion will separate the good from the bad impulses that are still at work within us, and our weak natures will submit to the strength of our 'All-Embracing Care'.

Through the common underlying principles of imagination and awareness, the personal order of persons, places, and things are but different expressions of the Universal order.

## Beauty and Ugliness, Truth and Error

Most of us want to surround ourselves with persons, places, and things that are beautiful. We want to give our perceptual experience aesthetic meaning. However, when the opposite of beauty approaches us, often there is a loathing, a tendency to turn away because it does not give pleasure to the senses. We tend to think of ugliness as immoral or wicked. Presently, as a cultural creation, there is no commercialized value to ugliness. Often, beauty is the basis for the central part of our lives. Is it necessary to see our artistic and visual perception as two distinct views? Is it mentally healthy to see another person's human anatomy as something less than our own?

Philosophers have been pondering for ages how to define beauty and ugliness. When we see life as inclusive, our acts, assertions or functions no longer deviate from what is true. Philosophically, life's reflections are only attributes of our Inner truth. It is safer to see those attributes as being separate from ourselves. When our childhood years encourage a sense of self-worth and appreciation, we become more tolerant of the physical attributes of others. The health and wholeness of the body, mind and emotions will dominate. Good eating habits, sound learning, exercise and a positive outlook on life will decree what is in the eye of the beholder. Happiness is the effective treatment. It soothes the stresses and wrinkles of our Inner person, and puts our thoughts and visions in order. Thus, we see all persons with a sound and nonjudgmental mental picture.

Perceived reality consists of images, ideals or patterns of persons, places and things that have existed in previous experiences and serve as models for our acuity. The objects of our perception are reflections or examples imprinted or recorded on memory. Often we are merely seeing what we have failed to come to grips with in ourselves. When we learn to see with equanimity, we will have learned the truth of our errors. Anything that we can take in, confirm, and substantiate can become a truth. Whatever we are seeing and feeling, whether a human body or tree, we are witnessing it through the language of the mind which affects human character and the social order.

When we view ugly things, we are having a hard time seeing with our words. We are using violence against the senses and our faculty to think thus separating life into two divisions that differ widely from each other. In the end, this division becomes a testimony for the lack of nobility in our character. We often equate beauty, ugliness, truth, and error to morality and religion. Some examples of this are: beauty is on the true and good side, ugliness is on the side of the false and bad, and beauty equals balance and ugliness-imbalance. To a certain extent, this dichotomy is a constant menace to the world. If we stopped making distinctions between beauty, ugliness, perfection, imperfection, Spiritual and sensuous, it would be far better for human happiness. When we look to the faults of others without first measuring our own, we are wandering away from our human essence, the commonality of the human condition. The solutions to our human condition are not dependent on the sum of our aesthetics, but on the acceptance of individual uniqueness.

Light, shade and perspective are how we evaluate something. If we see the form of that view as Perfect, it becomes a Miracle of creation.

## Energy, Force and Consciousness

Here by the seaside where the mountain meets the ocean, the sun's energy is always rising and setting as the earth orbits the circumference of the sun. This occurrence is predictable in the narrow range of the human eye. The force that sustains this everyday observation is an ongoing performance. We are constantly manipulating the elements of the earth in an attempt to measure the ability of one object to change the state of another object. What we ultimately observe in our everyday consciousness is an unending interaction between objects, the earth, the mind, and the objectified universe. The results of such observations are, in actuality, nothing more than a mind-set of the beholder. Energy, force, consciousness are the fundamentals of the universe and we are but expressions of that electromagnetism and gravity. The mind is constantly at work equating itself to force, i.e. knowledge.

All of us are constantly devouring the present before our eyes, subordinating our Inner essence, its substance, and creativity to the objects we rearrange for our enjoyment, amusement, displeasure and, sometimes, ill will. In all this force and energy, does Consciousness have the ability to predict a final outcome? Consciousness is always working and has the capacity to move matter against an opposing force. Consciousness expands when there is movement: the eyes move, thus observing, the hands work, thus gathering, and the mind forms.

Force and energy are just physical definitions that help us understand the world around us. It is a relationship of matter, time, and space where mass and energy are equivalent. Mass, length and time change with velocity. It is where the speed of light in a vacuum is constant and everything is relative in the universe. However, if we are not aware of being conscious, we are mute of the electric and magnetic field of Light that surrounds us.

All of us are energy components of matter that are smaller than an atom and this is the fun part; we are traveling at the speed of light and are not even feeling it. When we have the capacity to feel this magnetism, we will also have the ability to be co-creators with this magnetic power. However, here on the physical plane unregulated power can unduly influence a person. This diminishes self-power and results in eras of repetition. When we instill in ourselves that we are each single atoms echoing memory in space/time as energy, we are living within a mass that is beyond our means to express it fully. Only by degrees can we gather the understanding to work within its living, moving being. Energy, force, and consciousness are in some degree a search and gathering of something wholly new. It is a voyage of discovery and exploration always birthing new suns, planets, galaxies and solar systems of human consciousness. This voyage is the sum of the events and circumstances in which we are located.

Here by the sea where the sun, wind and rain come up over the mountains and fall into the ocean, one cannot help but witness energy and force through Consciousness.

If it would be possible for the universe to run out of energy, in some form or other, Consciousness would rearrange its liveliness.

## We Cannot Get Where We are Going by Talking

Talking is great for finding out directions, gathering information, asking questions and communicating with one another. However, when we have to get something done, being somewhere in time and space, we have to move our muscles to get our bodies there. The real art of talking is when we silently listen to what others say, think about what the words communicate, and then respond accordingly. Words are just mental expressions, thinking aloud, of ideas that we have gathered from other sources. All of us should do a lot of talking to ourselves by thinking, and then have a conversation with ourselves. When we can say something that is truly from our own uniqueness, we are saying something worthwhile.

Most people in society are open to persuasion so they can take action. We see a lot of this in the courtrooms, political rallies, religious gatherings, etc. No doubt talking is an important social etiquette; it defines us to others. We must be careful though not to be overly introverted, or we could create a psychological condition that could take us away from everyday reality. We can have a 'beautiful mind', an imaginary world within the self, which is safe only when we are selective with whom we share it. If we look to this Invisible part of ourselves as a solace to our loneliness, imaginary meditations can still our thought processes. Meditation/affirmation can be a friend to the mind. One example of a powerful affirmation states, "I am a thinker of the past, present, and future. Having these remarkable qualities I am Infinitely vast as a beautiful thought wave upon the horizon of my mind".

On the social scene, there is another side to talking, a side that can be deceptive, alluring and intoxicating to the uninformed. We often use descriptive words to soothe and appease public opinion. The governing of a nation, the administration and control of its internal and external affairs, can only be fruitful if it is the result of positive words and actions. Only when we look at our words in a self-governed manner can we overcome the influence of others by using language as a self-analysis. Art, literature, religion, politics, economics, all sway our infrastructure, our outer as well as our inner one, and while we are in the present, we cannot get away from those influences. All any of us can really do is to be selective about the words we want to stick to the inside of our mouths and minds. As with eating which gives us energy, our words give us the means for interacting with others and the effects that will follow.

When we charge our wordplay with rightness, we are taking advantage of the meaning of the action before we participate.

# The Commonality Factor

At all times, and in all places we must have respect for what our eyes see, for none so carefully watch where we go as they do. We develop human reason, infinite in matter and diversity, in the same way we form our opinions and manners. We create conflict not by nature, but by custom and in that tradition we abuse others and ourselves. Society's laws are customs formed from manners and opinions established by one's own people, not the innocence of nature. We derive power from struggle that overwhelms and traps us to the things it imposes. To undo power's grip is to come to ourselves by understanding the conditioning of society. In order to learn, we must study ourselves the same way we study a good book. In our own manner, we each come into this world to discover our own authority without looking to other forms of power that are contrary to our natural conduct. Often, people who are accustomed to authority are complex and go against naturalness, constantly creating the same difficulties.

Through nature, we are born, and in nature, we will return, but not everyone is content where he or she is born. We are constantly moving through the customs of other nations and their people. When everyone views customs without questioning, it masks the true aspects of things. Through nature, we infuse both normal and abnormal actions and allures of life. However, can our customs and morals define with accuracy what is in nature's heart? Does nature abstain from any of its characteristics on moral grounds? Is there a wholesome, tender face to nature?

In truth, such questions are complex. To answer them according to nature would be subjecting one to wild opinions. When we unlock the aggressive injustices of customs, we are discarding the ancient influences bound in domestic affairs. The natural world is one character but its features are many. Nature and man are two different things: one is neutral the other divisive. The impartial is fruitful, the divisive stirs up competition and injustice. When it comes to our actions, our labor, our fortunes and our lives, commonality connects us to society. However, our natural intuition reveals that society has nothing to do with our thoughts and the place where each of us lives.

When it comes to vices, none can be worse than those vices committed against nature or the self. We defend our common nature when we free our true selves from the unprincipled conduct of humanity, its blindness and injustice of customs. It is difficult to focus fully on our true essence because we have given so much of our blood and spontaneity to the progress, issues and laws of society. The laws of nature have given us much Goodness as in the regulation of the seasons. However, nature has also spawned humans, who often disrespect nature and institute laws that go against the environment. Carefully and attentively, nature watches, molds, and edges us on slowly with pains and pleasures. Inside our minds, nature stamps us with amazing ideas and marvels that are yet unseen.

Nature by law is our commonality factor and is Incorruptible; human kind is not.

## Think 'Everything is OK'

As we unfold in this experience, the diversity of life can at times seem overwhelming. Nearly all of the fundamentals of living confine or restrain us. In most cases, we have to develop our own efforts to seize our essentials of growth, understanding and maturity. The things of nature by law are comprehensive and inclusive. We are all gatherers, builders and creators in the soil of commonality. Trees do not shove away what is standing in their shade. Water does not gush up and drown the drinker, and soil does not discriminate which plants will grow. The only animal that goes against this commonality is the human one.

Through division, the survival instinct of the strong over the weak has fragmented the naturalness of the earth. Through our pursuit of individual material cravings, we have not correctly conformed to what is just and necessary for our survival. In the general sense, we have interfered with nature's capacity to meet life's everyday demands. The variables of nature are becoming increasingly unstable as evidenced by disrupted weather patterns and waste products that contaminate the soil. These waste products also soil the air and water, along with the ozone: a form of oxygen found in the stratosphere that filters out much of the sun's ultraviolet radiation. Because of these unstable variables, we need to utilize material things longer and more wisely. Otherwise, the total energy of the earth will become disturbed and unequally distributed. When we do not adequately monitor and maintain the inter-relation between heat, function, and internal energy of a system, whether that system is a person or a planet, it develops a fever. We must conserve and direct the energy of the human body/earth thus cooling down molecular activity.

The microscopic systems of matter and energy of the earth are always exchanging. Once the exchange process starts, it cannot return to the same energy state because disorder and terminality occur and everything in time returns to its Cause. This disorder is perpetually occurring throughout the entire universal creation. Just because disorder exists does not necessarily mean we will be an active part of that process. The choices we make influence our mental outlook and what will come to be.

When we think, "All is ok", the energy that created everything and put it in motion is in charge. This energy becomes more than what it was before. Each of us is an active part of the process of earth and what we learn from it constitutes our own awareness. However, it is the misuse of thinking, not the earth, which causes human turmoil. The desire of personal power over the control of others, fame and pride are the causes of most human problems. When we embrace all life as an aspect of energy/force that began movement, and that every person is a worthy participant in the process, the measure of currently hidden energy will become more apparent and there will be less strife in its utilization.

Because of new Beginnings, in the end everything is OK.

## The Most Minutely Exquisite Images

In the confines of the heart, the most minutely exquisite images that make up life are those of the children: the treasures of our future. They are marvelous, and by degree, are our fortunes. Many avenues define the characteristics of a child. The genes of the parents, the interactions and well-being of the family, ethnic customs, environmental opportunities within the community and the economic sources of the nation each play a part. Some children have their beginnings in low conditions while others evolve in higher settings. From birth to adolescence, those early conditions form the physical, intellectual, social and emotional changes that occur in a child. Those in charge form most of the child's attributes of learning, language, thinking, reasoning, socializing and self-awareness.

All these factors play a part in what a child will inherit for its future. As a result, many abilities and characteristics formed in those formative years last a lifetime.

All children are similar in behavior and thought around the world. The effects and difficulties that children face are not always predictable at birth. A teacher, parent, community, and a nation must act as guides to the child. With proper oversight a child should be able to discern and choose wisely, thus opening the way for self-invention. Socrates made his students speak before he spoke to them. He thought it best that his pupils judge their own learning and pace so they could develop self-confidence in meeting the challenges of life.

The success of any nation rests upon the quality of the fabric used to quilt a child's cover. We reward both the family and nation when we instruct every child with the same lessons and measure of direction even though those children may have different and unequal capacities. When we show a pupil or child how to examine the nature of being, the knowledge instilled will be a testimony to memory and life itself. The child will have learned many subjects and forms that will accommodate the natural pace for vigor, freedom and success.

Minds work best when we fill them with trust in the self. The authority of another does not need to captivate one's mind, nor does it need to follow the appetite of someone else's fancy. Guidance, whether it is in the form of a family, a teacher, or the Constitution of a nation, works best when it comes from the shared aims of others. As a result, the diversity of opinions and self-choice become evident. According to Plato, truth and reason are common to everyone, and they are, "No more his who spoke them first, then they who speak them after".

Judgment, instruction, labor and study of oneself are only beneficial when we use them for the shared aims of everyone, especially our children.

## The Conundrum of What Is

Like sunrays that pass before our eyes when the sun is bright, the images of this great world are many. There are multitudes of species in the animal and plant kingdoms, but only one is able to differentiate and that is the human being. We mirror ourselves with one another and we behold ourselves as a study in progress. Many judgments, opinions, laws and customs teach what we presume to be correct. Yet, each of us must discover and understand our imperfections and natural weaknesses. Upon the light of our journey, we leave impressions of the many mutations, kingdoms and revolutions of chance, realizing that no permanent wonder of our own is everlasting.

In this Book of Time, place and circumstance, so many names, successes, and defeats are swallowed into oblivion that our only option is to derive from memory our better nature that is imbedded in that ruination. Presently we are a species often filled with pride, arrogance and traditional ways. We try to win influence or approval through flattery and attentiveness just to behold the luster of our own stateliness. The many similarities buried before us resemble what we aspire to make better. In books, poetry, and art we ponder our demise in love, story and dance, just to be spectators of the lives of others, so we can regulate and judge our own perceived natures.

In the absence of all this, on what source do we draw our beliefs? Are we mere puppets dancing at the end of strings attached to the hands of society? Is there a sign from which we can know and contain our contentment? We are both ignorant and wise. What should be our end of study is often just the beginning. Aspirations, materialism, power, weakness, lack of control or liberty, even disgrace are only comprehended when we are outside of the human circle and in our own center of self-knowing.

Nevertheless, there are secret springs from which we can quench the thirst of our agitations and anxieties that keep us from making decisions; we should only concern ourselves with what is true and what has real utility. Truth and value teach us how to know ourselves, how to live well, and how to discern the attitudes we have when we depart this life. Only the Self knows the secrets of life that are outside of the boundaries of society; the universe and its systems originate in the Self. The continuation of life is dependent on the strengthening of the Self. However, the races of humanity have weakened the roles of individuals. Once the Self is aware of its continuum and the concept of Love, it gains control over the outward and inward forces of the universe. Then one understands that cruelty and wastefulness from nature shape and perfect the beauty of the Spiritual self.

The flame is not aware of the moth anymore than the moth is aware of the flame. Fire can warm or burn us. The flames of the past Light the way for the future.

## *The Futuristic Journey of Hope and Enthusiasm*

The events and circumstances of life help to shape futuristic goals based on a belief in hope. Hope is a conviction that implies a certain amount of perseverance where the outcome is positive even while there is evidence to the contrary. The aim of enthusiasm is to give others a feeling of excitement, an interest in a movement, idea, or program of which they can become a growing part. We all build our goals for life from a belief that we each have purpose and in most cases, we look to others for guidance in forming those achievements. Another's enthusiasm has the ability to become a mirror that can take on a life of its own, for both the deliverer and the receiver. When the individual utilizes the strength of hope, the desire to enrich life with new ways of being and doing for society takes on a new meaning. Since the dawn of human life, the eye and ear direct the way, and the brain and hand work through thought, imagination, feeling, memory and understanding. Without enthusiasm, we would win few of life's struggles. The message of hope is to preserve life for the future. When the heart and mind are open to truth, new ideas for change replace old standards.

The ability to facilitate a movement stimulates feeling and leads to action. Feeling produces energy, and energy becomes productive power. Everyday life is an expression of that strength. As long as hope remains a source of strength, it can turn a person, place or thing that is seemingly of no value, into one with value. When viewed by the majority, life's energy is a force, a virtue, or a malice, which urges the many on. Whatever the secrets that unite hope with the future, it is a possibility of mind and feeling, a physical and sensory blending that leads to a greater liberation of force.

Through enthusiasm, we have a yearning for the unknown. This yearning creates an act or movement toward something new. We all have an eagerness to be a part of something that is bigger and more powerful than we are because power when alone is powerless. However, when one becomes superior to the other, apathy sets in. We are either followers or leaders; to curb one and develop the other shows selfishness. We are stronger as a whole when we recognize the strength of togetherness. Hope and enthusiasm excite energy and release strength. It has helped control the primitive sides of most, settles the primal nature, and drives us onward toward greater fulfillments. The principle motive for enthusiasm is excitement because it helps people harness action and the reactions caused by their actions.

Reality, dreams and hope are states of mind becoming better than before.

## The Art of Thoughtful Wishing

The visions that we place in our minds through the power of imagining can captivate us to the extent that they can become a part of our life. We can see what others do not see. When we disengage our thoughts from the effects of everyday occurrences, we can enter the true and natural state of the Inner self. The love of the Self illumines this place, and the dust from which we have physical form does not contaminate it. This type of imagination results in enhanced pleasure and happiness in the Joy of Being.

When we employ thoughtful wishing our nature is radiant and healthy. In this sanctuary of Self, we no longer feel guilt and all is in accordance to what we imagine. This domain of the imagination belongs only to the one that sets it in motion. In this imaginary world of the mind, emotions form pictures that have shape and color more vivid and real than colors on earth and there is no cause and effect. On earth, elements create our necessities. However, in the imagining of the emotions, we can attain desires that seem unattainable in real life. Here, we can freely explore exotic feelings for they are derivatives of the Self.

At first, these images can be distorting, even intimidating. However, with clarity and focused-mind painting, they will become as alluring, stable, and enjoyable as any person, place or thing on the physical plane. The customs, laws, principles and rules of society control the glamour of physical life. We learn to hold back desires because of guilt and fear, especially those desires relating to the physical needs of the body. These needs often contrast with the material interpretations of spiritual or intellectual conceptions of life.

Institutional behavior is self-serving, usually for the few, rather than the many.

In the domain of the freethinking mind, there are few restraints. If restraints do surface, it is because the mind has not loosened itself from the enthrallment of the world. When motivated by imagination, we can feel the power of fancy as we do in clear dreams. Our amorous desires are natural for they emanate from the Self. We try various ways that can lead us to this Self but the world's confining principles often hinder its free expressions. Through imagination, we employ the art of thoughtful wishing without the interpretation of others. We enjoy!

We create images solely for pleasure and they have no lasting principle as things of necessity do on earth. In emotional and mental wishing, any forms the mind creates will dissolve like clouds in the wind. They do not remain behind as physical artifacts once the creator of the image has vanished. In the realm of thoughtful imagining, we have more liberty to do things while in the body. The art of thoughtful wishing is just a tool for self-awareness and expression for the inner life. We should never use thoughtful wishing to diminish the responsibility of physical living. This type of wishing can prepare the translucent nature of being, the mind, to be its own creator within the greater creation once it is no longer associated with the physical.

When we wish, we become the masters of our destiny.

## The Translucency of Physical Life

Memory transparency is physical life imbedded in Light as memory. Those images are no longer visible from the solid side of life. Once we relinquish the physical body, the remembrance of that life becomes active in the memory field. None of us knows how big our memory field is. It is conceivable that every thought acted upon and produced in physical reality expands that field. The objective world sets memory in motion. Our interaction with matter and its forces enables us to create memories through experience. We know that there are massive amounts of energy spread throughout creation. We can only ascertain how that energy reacts to the memory transparency field by the emotional and mental awareness of the one entering it.

Another factor relating to memory transparency is the concept of time. We have only a finite conception of time, of how it works, and of how it passes. Most likely time is irrelevant to our memory field. It is fundamental that we believe we exist in this vast expanse of memory, space-time, matter and energy. Each of us brings memory alive in our imagination, and once that occurs, it is infinite. Memory is the body of the universe and we are always entering it in some fashion or other. The persons, places and things that we share in the physical phase of memory are either fleeing from us or joining with us. Either way, memories breathe music into life's concreteness. Translucent light is refined and colorful in its nature. That which has died becomes more vivid in its light. The images there are more alluring, more comforting for the heart. Whatever has dwelled there remains, strengthening the imagination.

Our goal in creation should be to acquaint ourselves by means of energy, space, and time with that Limitless Source and center that is our deepest emotional and mental life. We are forever journeying from yesterday on to tomorrow in the company of the Self. In the presence of our memories, we see the Light of the effulgent face of the Self in the Fire, and take back what we have put in our hearts, to be a mirror for today and tomorrow, one memory losing its being in another. In its totality, memory represents the Life of the universe and all that is contained within it. Memory is the caretaker of Light, and from it, we supervise the universe.

Translucent light is the vital power and will of the Self that unites and brings together all forms relating to memory. Thus, the life force of the Self connects the thoughts of matter. Memory in its first phase is a living force created by humanistic actions. In its second phase, memory becomes vital electrical currents collected for the Personal Self. The purpose of this vitality is to unite physical memory with subjective thinking and to bind the energies of creation with the unseen and seen. Life is constantly evolving from one level of experience to another; every memory is an aspect of being just as a sunbeam is for the earth. The translucent nature of feeling and thinking embodies the re-manifestation of those memories. Memory occurs because of manifestation and differentiation, and light is its recorder. Memory binds again, what was scattered and guides us to recreate what was a past cause.

# The Movement of Energetic Consciousness

Energetic movement is energy under transformation: from the quantum level to the biosphere and cosmos. These streams are vigorous, purposeful and full of energy, enthusiasm, and keep awareness alive. The intensity of the First Principle (Creative Mind) did not originate from external sources; it was solely a brilliant gleaming point that broke dark matter up into its various parts at the start of things obvious and manifest. Magnetic properties of things ascribed to nature are dependent on the four elements: air, fire, water and earth. Air carries thought; fire fuels desire. Water saturates the emotions and the earth provides stability. The more we attune and compare ourselves to creation, the more we learn about the uniqueness of individuality as it relates to mind.

Consciousness is not something that suddenly had a beginning. In its existence, there is no justification for a beginning or an end. Consciousness always has been and always will be aware of Consciousness. Whether we are awake or dreaming our minds constantly receive waves of light signals according to where and what we are attuned to at the moment. While in the body, we have an objective material awareness. While thinking abstractly we attune to our inner mind, which is not always relating to concrete objects. Whatever level we gravitate toward, it must be a gradual process so that our hidden virtues can be opened and adapt to the gleaming brilliance out of which each of us comes and returns.

Similar to the sun that lights our physical being, a miniature sun also heats and lights the Inner mind. This particle of light is smaller than the atomic element known to physicists and physical means does not detect it. The miniscule indestructible light of the self is responsible for recording sensory images. This permanent mind source is the recording apparatus for the association of images and experiences that pass through the physical brain and remain there as memory. Physical consciousness, the brain, registers the meaningful experiences of feeling and imagining through the senses. When the body is asleep or the mind is daydreaming, it relies on memory to evoke meaning to the Self's awareness.

Once consciousness or mind has vacated the body permanently, its Essence remains in the self-atom and moves out into the greater memory field. The

Self motivates us to act because it is the mover of mind and consciousness. The Self is the aspect of awareness that regenerates balance by changing our feelings to match what is in the mind as desire. The ongoing movement of awareness is guided by the Self's internal control system that guards against deception and judgment errors once memory has vacated the physical brain. The unconscious motives of the personality body do not trouble the Self once fully back on its home turf. The Self is constantly balancing and checking future action before it executes a decision conveyed into the brain and its different compartments. The brain/mind/body has motives that it carries out in physical plane living, independent of the Self during its lifetime. The systems of desires that we gravitate to while in physicality often quell or dim the Light that the Self is trying to communicate to us and we end up making erroneous decisions in shaping the magnetic properties of life, quality and appearance.

The powerful feeling of physical desire is the source for corporal existence that causes voluntary action and induces involuntary ones.

## *Obsessive Entertainment*

The world is an entertainment zone where all types of people come together to enjoy themselves and be entertained by others. We use all kinds of methods to pursue attention from other persons. For example, the erotic nature of form, audio/video/radio/television, performing arts, literature, music, and dance are methods of amusement to satisfy our needs. However, is it possible the influences of the creativity of others and their artistic powers diminish our ability to call forth our own aspirations? Thus, are we depriving ourselves of the real satisfaction of the creative process? Diminished creativeness often allows boredom to sway mental and emotional perception. In an attempt to avoid boredom, we embrace those who provide us with distraction: the cornerstone of the entertainment industry. Sadly, this boredom has no age limitation. Children grow up wanting to aspire toward another's creative talent, even mimicking their forte. Overlooking of the Self's own ingenuity and replacing it with that of other persons, if not adequately balanced, has the potential for evolutionary stagnation. Is it fruitful for our inner being to saturate itself constantly with the digital electronic commentaries that blur our own view of the matters of self, community, country and world? Viewing this data excess leaves little time for personal inner reflection. To a degree, by not relying on the innate nature of the self we copy the inclinations of the entertainer.

We tend to gravitate to the creativeness of others instead of relying on our own creativity that the Self is eager to express once we have weaned ourselves away from the enthrallment of others. It is far better mentally to influence our own ways that bring us leisure and enjoyment than to be over stimulated by the expressions of others. When we copy the mannerisms of others, we are diminishing our own progressive development. Once we become less obsessed with being entertained, the more we will be free of boredom. The pursuit of obsessive entertainment is not a sustainable enterprise. We can never get away from moments of activity and inactivity. However, the need for others to stimulate us out of our boredom with their style of entertainment will only intensify our involvement with material life.

Our own Innate ways deserve their own sun-splashed attention and celebration.

## The Art of What Is

The art of what is encapsulates beautiful thought-provoking perceptions on which one can build the moment. Nature in and of itself is grand and wondrous, but only the human imagination has the capacity to color the moment with its own creation. We can explain the 'art of what is' as a state of readiness that accepts new first encounters, new associations with different things, and new emotional or mental responses that arouse the imagination. The outer world is a mixture of different life pictures that reflect everyday experiences. Because of the attracting and repelling principles of the human biosphere, life is a series of varied emotional expressions. If we do not know how to view these expressions as passing clouds, we often pass them on to others. Just as a baby needs practice to learn how to walk, the human mind needs affirmations to counter its upsets. Human existence is a game of endless dynamics, vigorous movements that counteract one another, often with negative consequences. When we are not acting positively, those actions can become opiates for our frustrations. Regardless of the situation, if we create positive mental images, they will enhance our reasoning power and allow us to move about freely.

When we step back from our daily situations that govern life and see them with open minds, we can attune to the moment. No doubt, it is healthy for us to see the future in a positive manner. Whatever the state of being, it cannot become more than what is happening at this very moment. There is a probability that the similarities of today will arrive with tomorrow, but none among us can say with certainty what each of us will be experiencing. The more information we allow to enter our minds about what others think and do, but do not use our own individual discrimination to determine what we should retain, the less we know of our real selves.

Any movement that gives society power over individual will is not sustainable, just as the body is not permanently sustainable in objective reality. Only the autonomous Self can ascertain the real state of things as they exist through a combination of mental concepts extending into the physical biosphere. Contrary to society there is another area in the imagination called the phenomenological visual sphere; it is a much broader and more personal level, the private experiences of wonder, study and choice. This visual sphere is a reality uniquely individual and may never be experienced or agreed upon by anyone else. To the one experiencing it, it is phenomenally real. This individual perception results from choices that allow one to see or believe what one perceives as truth.

Society has produced many things through science. However, to be beneficial to the individual's physical reality, more than one person must see and experience it, whereas one must view phenomenal reality singularly. No one can go there except the self and its visions; this is why objective reality is by nature collective knowledge and subjective reality is personal knowledge. In the art of what is, the most important aspect is to understand both realities through nonviolence and non-judgment.

We create our existence by believing in something that has yet to exist.

## Don't Look Back

The guiding light for living a balanced social life is a mirror response to the behavior of others. This type of action gives something back that is equivalent to what someone receives. These acts are positive or negative responses toward the actions of others that stem from justice, gratitude, mutuality, or morality/malice. Reciprocity is the mechanism for the evolution of cooperation in the phenomenon of existence. There will be many pop-up signs that warn travelers what they should or should not do. However, many of us will continue without noticing the signs. The personality of others enthralls us and we pay little attention to the Inner self. We succumb to their whims and charismatic appeal instead of relying on our better judgments. This is similar to the mythical biblical story of Lot's wife who looked back longingly at the city she desired and instantly became a pillar of salt.

Life is a two-way roadway. One direction is for those coming into being; the other one is for those who are leaving it. When we pull the plank from our eyes, we can see that there are many signs along the way to direct our choices that can aid or worsen the conditions in the navigation of that two-way roadway. The persons, places and things that we encounter either assist or hinder us in meeting certain parameters. The nature of that meeting usually determines what we can alter or leave as is.

The end is always meeting the beginning or the opposite. Reciprocal acts keep the life waves coming and going. When we are with others, either one-on-one or in a group, we are in an 'interactive event'. What occurs is a reciprocal exchange of ideas and experience, especially when touch and vocal expressions are used. Reciprocal actions can be positive or negative depending on the makeup and demeanor of the participants. The focus of this interaction should not be for attention but on shared experience; it is not about control over what is happening. To remain practical the occasion must remain democratic, otherwise repressive traits surface and prevent a give-and-take environment. We do not have to look back when we act with equanimity. For example when we are with friend(s) be supportive, with partner or co-workers share authority, with parents, honor them, with teachers, master their teachings, at work, perform well and in matters of community be lawful and nurture goodness. The roadway we are paving now will be similar to the one on which we will be leaving. We cannot achieve inner social stability and security through disruptive demands posed by a competitive mind, but only by the renunciation of self-interest and the development of a sincere concern for the welfare and holistic feelings for others.

Life is decision based and it is part of time. When times are hard, we still have to make decisions regarding what we will do and not do. At times like this, all any of us can do is just let go and move on. We must choose a new direction, but before we do, we must think about the possibilities and the ramifications that will carry us toward a new dawning. In all the learning and gathering that will be encountered, only by knowing ourselves will the decisions that we make be the right choices. As we journey on this two-way roadway, remain positive step by step, day by day, and know that there is another tomorrow on the road. Its landscape will be comforted with our kin and kind.

Remember, do not look back, we are not going that way.

## *Waves of Light*

The evolution of existence manifests on waves of Light, the supporter and upholder of being. This essential energy is bisexual in nature and is all-powerful. By definition male/female are expressive of its nature, therefore there is nothing that exists that this duality cannot make or destroy. The totality of the light field is unidentifiable and indestructible. As persons, places and things, all life is in its grasp and all we can do is be. We believe that we have reign over its undulations, which is why be behave the way we do. No two people react the same way to this energy field. No matter what we say or do in the wakefulness of it, it passes into other actions. We go on thinking that we are separate from the cosmic picture that the mind forms; but nothing can be further from the truth. This state of mind we conceive is only a fragmented part of the whole that is dreaming dreams within dreams. Chaos cannot put order back as it was before; it transforms it into something else. Haphazardly we toss about, sometimes seeing as if through a haze; other times we see systematically with clarity. Neither lasts so we pass into new mirages that appear on the horizon and once again, they sweep us away.

Whether we want to believe it, we are like moths flying into a flame, unaware. We create myths and legends to give us hope that one day we will be free of the conflagration. We pull from the firmament particles to shape our landscape only to have them come apart as we move from one state to another. This constant state of construction enraptures us. When something comes apart, we strive to rebuild it, only better. This 'something' is what we call knowledge! Knowledge is a gathering and passing on of what existed in the past. Knowledge on its own has no feeling. For example, if someone speaks of love, at first it may seem sincere. It is only when we interact through knowledge and put ourselves in that person's place can we gather the true meaning of love. Unconditional sharing is more than words. It consists of ideas, motivations and dreams that shape our essential energy field.

This living breathing process we term life is composed of opposites: negative/positive, male/female relationships. As awareness, one is conscious, the other is sub-conscious. The experiences and reflections that each of us witness are only attributes of that inner part of us. Some religions touch on this awareness, but they often become institutional knowledge based, and wind up feuding over their own importance. The 'Marriage Song of the Heavens' is the closest phrase that represents the evolution of two conscious beings. However, outside attractions are often greater than the inner ones and the waves of Light in the heart dim until we work through these enticements.

Therefore, we must be honest and true to the Self. If someone should come along that cares about the Inner self and wants to share that intimacy, we should embrace it. In all probability, it is our singular Light Wave. When we know we are in the world and not of it, the rose will bloom infinitely. We should not waste light on the impulses of others. When the light of the eyes go out, the Inner Light of the one we love most will be the one that guides us on in the Infinite Sea of Illumination. The old troubling forms of knowledge will vanish. When the Master was tempted in the wilderness, it was his task to put the false things of the world behind him. In turn, each of us by choice builds from the present what will be our future.

If we are to be free from sorrow and strife, we must be certain with whom we share the present.

## The Rising and Setting of the Self

The world that we live in, move in, and of which we have awareness, comes from the understanding of our behavior as we interact with nature. We are constantly describing what we see and experience with the Self being the go-between in that process of body and world. Many related abilities create the property of the mind and academia is just one of them. Often the type of education we receive will indicate how we will shape the present and our ability to comprehend and profit from experience.

One does not necessarily need to pass through the academic circles to be intelligently aware. However, if one's desires focus only on scientific material, understanding the academic world is very important. The nature of intelligence results from an innate quality as well as interacting with the environment. It is in combination of these two aspects that we are able to learn, reason and problem solve. The living process is self-motivated. Each of us in our own way makes the decisions that allow us to move ahead in life. We can never return to what was before, except in our memory. The Self is always identifying with objects outside of itself, therefore it is always manifesting from its imagination and desires. Regardless of the methods used to fill our minds with information, it is lasting only when we are aware of ourselves outside of that knowledge. When acquired knowledge is logically consistent in its use, the world as a whole benefits; but when it is used for contradictory purposes the world, the body and the Self become unbalanced either within itself or in relation to others. Thus, the history of human activity, up to the present, has been often argumentative and inconsistent.

The True self, that dynamic part of nature, is peaceable and always moves in that direction. It is self-discriminatory in its observations and has the ability to move freely around in the circles of manifested life. On the other hand, it can disengage from these circles to the periphery for a self-contained look at what will best serve its interests. The Self is similar to the sun that rises and sets distilling darkness on the surface of the earth. Each rising brings a new day for stirring and each setting provides repose. As the earth is clothed in the sun, so is the body. We absorb its outward streams and by its touch, we shape the faces we will become through birth, life, passing, living and being. When we are in tune with the Inner self, we impart harmony to the world.

When a state of confusion or uncertainty occurs regarding persons or institutions, a system of unchecked power is often the result. In this state, places and things can become industrial teasers where commodities and assets rise and set, thus promoting fear which is the ultimate source of control for those less prominent. When we do not allow others to control or sway us, we are self-aware and are in control of our own decisions. We can witness and avoid the unwholesome atmosphere of others in the gaining of experience. The personality can corrupt when fame and vanity override the worth of others, especially if it shuts out the altruistic light of the Self. If we stare at the sun too long, it can blind. The same is true if the magnetism of others mesmerizes us.

We are opening the gates of Truth when we see the Source of our existence; this Source is the same in everyone, as the diamond is to coal.

## In Praise of the Moment

As thinking human beings, we are very selective as to how we perceive nature, reality and events. To understand ourselves we are constantly extracting images, descriptions and similes. We are praising the Moment when we are aware of our connection to everything else. Thus, we view all systems of that linkage as a whole and not of separate pieces. We pride ourselves as individuals, but in our self-importance, we can become lost in our own processes. As a result, we find ourselves in situations that have two aspects that are complementary or opposed to each other. Consequentially, we are relating to energy and matter under different conditions. We easily fall out of favor with one another, which is a loss of fellowship with the moment. Thus, we face the conundrum of good and bad, or life and death. The moment is formed by our perceptions, whether it is space, a planetary or human body, and by the concepts that give meaning to our awareness of differentiation or unity. Impressions form connections. Connections are aspects of consciousness, originality and imagination of which the human body is a Spirit. When we are forming the moment, this Spiritual presence within the body can be felt intuitively and we become immersed in our 'unthinking'. The mental manifestations of our ideas vanish and we are beyond thought.

When we are in the moment, do we have a future or is it just an expectation? The moment defines events and circumstances such as the origin of the world, our place in it and our relation to it. In the past, we have experienced persons, places and things, but we will base the time to come on expected or projected states that may or may not happen. The future will be, but not necessarily, as we expect it to be. We cannot be as aware of things to come as we are of them in the moment. Everything that we do not create by thinking, we leave to the generative power of nature.

Therefore, there is the likelihood that the future is occurring now, similar to what we are experiencing in the moment. The hypothesis of a future is seductive and attractive. For that reason, it is to our advantage to take pleasure in it without worrying whether it will come. We can take solace in the knowing that we are part of a dynamic design where past, present, and future are relative as to space and time. We are in its silence! In this moment of worthiness, pure potentiality, we touch our Spiritual intellect. While in that universality we gain the strength to return to the process of forming conceptual connections of ideas in concrete substance. When we are awake in the moment, we have subdued the wind of our restlessness, and rebuked the turbulent sea of choices. In that Silence, we feel our equanimity, the acknowledgment and grace of forgiveness with all that lives and moves. Free from distractions we see ourselves as grains of sand on a quiet beach, or as a lake of placid blue water, reflecting a tranquil blue sky.

Whatever comes into being in the present moment will always end and dissolve back into its Essence.

## The Stamping of Life

Can we be certain of our finality? Is our awareness a never-ending, boundless arena of energy and space? If so, what is our full capability? Starting in early childhood, parents and society imprint in us very deep and thorough ideas about life. We spend the first quarter of our lives in that upload and the final three-quarters trying to understand it. If we look at the growth of life, as we know it, which is through material perception, it is not difficult to see that it is a transferable process from one generation to the next. Instead of fostering idealism, picturing persons, places and things as holistic and ongoing, we have been impressed to accept that when the body dies, so does our connection to the life just lived. This is because we do not have the ability to maintain sense contact, the faculty by which we perceive outside stimuli, with the person whose life has passed. A more balanced and integrated stamp for early childhood would be picturing life as existing within a force and Intelligence that overlooks life and all that is in it. This would allow children to picture themselves as being a part of this force and intelligence. Irrevocably, we are all in this energy spiral; otherwise, there would be no conscious life.

As the earth, and all its forms, animate or inanimate, are in commonality to Light, as light is to the sun, there is one consistency to all persons, places and things that passes through us, our thoughts, born from our minds as humanity. We are individual rays living in that essentiality. As we live and relate to that vital framework, we are all making it what it is. The traditional method of stamping life casts it as an unknowable mystery, and when it has run its course all that is left is belief.

Conviction is as important as the elements that we fashion ourselves from, but it does not substantiate, or prove how our next experience will unfold. As self-aware individuals, if we choose to look back over our lives, open mindedly, we can see that it was our thoughts and those of others that helped us shape our minds to perform the actions we chose to undertake. There are advantages in this process, such as the heaviness of form that keeps awareness anchored in matter while in the physical state. Also, this thought process forces us to look inward as the cells in the body break down. This introduces us to the concept of pain and its effect on our minds and emotions. Pain eventually teaches us to control feelings and body movements, instinctual behavior, and the natural stimuli associated with living.

Nature did not create pain, human thinking did. Our actions and our attitudes toward one another induce pain. If we change our emotions and our thoughts, we can eliminate the vexing actions stemming from the mind. The more sensitive we are to pain the more aware we become and in this wakefulness, we see the cause of it. Once we familiarize ourselves with the causes of pain, we can begin to eradicate it through our educational and scientific living process. We are all in this together and as a result, we are a part of each other's pains and the creators of those hurts. Physical, emotional and mental aspects fashion our essentiality and those qualities create our existence in various places, as persons and things. We reach our full potential when we master that essentiality one plan and one plane at a time.

From existence to existence, we pass; there are many phases in the screening and correcting of what is.

## Masking the Mask, Twisting & Tweaking What Is

The events of the world and the characters that act them out are not always reflecting the true concept of what is occurring or what has happened. Those in power conceal the truth of those observations and obstruct the true view of the world. This masking is not limited to one nation; it is worldwide. However, like the ivory towers built on false foundations, this concealment results in various problems in society. In order for human life to take off this mask of disguises, it will need to have a global awakening to the causes of this planned misrepresentation. Often the occurrences of the world are the vocal half-truths, the twisting of events and circumstances, as well as the tweaking of historical facts so that much of the current generation lives in fear and uncertainty. With all our force, we should condemn this false ruse of hierarchical importance. It is immature to go on acting as if this screening of facts is not occurring. It is far worse defending or ignoring a wrong instead of correcting and replacing it with cooperation.

Public opinion has been used to sway much of society to believe they are a product of wrong doing, these transgressions are self-induced and go against the laws of organized institutions; thus society is supposed to follow the rules of a few powerful hierophants. The peace that these interpreters so often speak of is always on the horizon or in some distant paradise. However, nothing could be further from the truth. Instead, we have created a memory field of depersonalized marginalization and disruption that is historical in nature. This organizational manipulation focuses on the people, not the ruling parties. As it has often been the task of historical writers, it has also been the role of current media outlets to make sure this ruse continues.

We do not view hunger, ignorance, aggression and disease as terrorism, but dissent is, especially if it goes against the strong. We often label those who arbitrate for the poor as agitators and their causes have very little limelight. The ruling parties see the downtrodden as draining their coffers and refer to them as the unfortunates. Currently human sympathy and understanding are not a part of the equation in solving the woes of nations and races. History has shown when the elites make enormous blunders in leadership and guardianship, very little accountability is forth coming.

To avoid blowback the powerful players invoke 'plausible deniability', the denial of blame. When illegal or otherwise disreputable and unpopular activities become public, high-ranking officials may deny any awareness of such act or any connection to the agents used to carry out such acts. We often mask avaricious activity as an oversight. What we have percolating throughout the world is structured hypocrisy. The words, platforms, and actions of those in charge must match; otherwise, those actions are not authentic or positive. Guardianship is most effective when it takes into account the feelings of those in its custody; it is not only concerned with the big picture but with the small one also.

We are hearing the truth of the underlying reality when we 'listen' to action. Then we are effectively unmasking the words that influence and flood our minds.

## The Originator of Space, Air, Fire, Water, and Earth

This living moving, breathing consciousness that is life does not distinguish between this or that and has no partiality to any particular person, place or thing. It has only one purpose: to expand awareness. Once this connection is brought to fruition and the substance of its gathering has been taken into account, life/consciousness either continues to progress on a material level or it dissolves back into the firmament. Consciousness is always redressing itself and Essence is the provider for that redress. Regardless of the circumstance, this primordial core is inherent in every person and is the guarantee of progress. Individuality has many stripes and each person is always choosing what type of background he/she wants to develop. We gather the fundamentals of experience from one or a combination of three aspects: creating, preserving, and destroying. Each of these aspects is a facet or phase of the whole from which they originated and constitutes the viewpoints of life as witnessed by the participant or observer. Regardless of which of the three we find ourselves immersed, we create and choose it. Therefore, we should look at these experiences wisely and, through our feelings, mentally work them through. Gathering is the chalice for thinking and learning for our structure of being. We must understand the place in which we find ourselves. Once we realize this, we can freely move within the Essence.

The movement of pure Essence, as distinguished from the four elements of our physical nature, fills the region of the universe above the earth. This Essence is invisible to the human eye. Its continuum is not dependant on human form but on mind. This universal Essence, mind, is simultaneously present throughout the whole of creation. Once it becomes a model for our thinking self, it goes with us wherever we go. Just as air, argon, and atoms never change, Essence/mind is always around and in us and never dies. The same elements that were in our ancient ancestors and prehistoric animals are in us today. Those same atoms will also be around forever as air for earthly forms to breathe. Creation is constantly renewing and restoring itself through each of us as awareness.

As we look out across the horizon of our daily experiences, we can sense this archetypal energy in us the same way we feel the breath of air moving through us and across the skin. This space of consciousness is the breath of creation that pulsates through the earth into each of us as our Source of permanence. Though most humans are not aware of this Essence as their own, nevertheless Consciousness is the originator of their dreams, hopes and expectations. Science postulates that space represents the primordial matrix from which all the other elements come into existence, including us. Always filling us with its sustenance, this Stuff of life fills our being, empowering us from the moment of birth until our last inhalation where something new aspires to reawaken the best of what was.

With the mind, there is the potential of re-connecting to the Original Harmony that existed in the universe. When we depart, we leave behind a part of ourselves, which is why we die to one life before we can enter another one.

## Imagine How It Will Be

The compelling preconditions of life are all around us as atoms, cells, and molecules. Physical life as we know it has characteristics of organisms, which exhibit homeostasis, organization, metabolism, growth, adaptation, response to stimuli and reproduction. An entity with these properties is considered be a life form. Every person contains these attributes. We respond to changes in our environment and inside ourselves in ways that promote our own continuation, hence the cause of our physicality. When we look wisely at the requirements we cannot but ask ourselves, "What was the Cause?" The only logical answer is Consciousness: a state of mind and thought, of being awake and aware of what one perceives. The physical processes, subatomic, chemical interactions, qualities, and properties work together to form a mutually beneficial relationship between matter and Essence.

However, we do not need contact with those processes to be conscious of Consciousness because they are part of the power of the subconscious: our Invisible guide and guardian. When we utilize this power of consciousness for betterment, the subconscious motivates the mind to imagine how it will be. As co-creators, we expose our hidden purpose and we become more intuitive regarding our better nature. We are then on the journey of realizing our potential ideals. We create our own reality by expanding the perception of the world, thus becoming something more. As we further our understanding by resolving the imbalances of the mind, we focus on the nature of reality. We strive to do the best so we can leave every situation better than when we entered it. Consequently, we see Beauty in all of nature's forms by loving something bigger, greater, and beyond ourselves. It is intangibility made Sacred by our very belief in it. Only good can come to us when we endow this unseen power with Love.

When we imagine ourselves as part of this Power, or necessity of life, we cannot help but define our place within it. It is crucial to our continuation. When we imagine, we have the means to represent something that we do not see now. We utilize imagination by building upon what we see. The observable is important to the independence of the mind because it helps us understand our acts and situations; thus, we can imagine the possibilities of our current circumstance. Imagination also gives us the ability to visualize what we do not see: for example, the atoms, cells and molecules in our bodies. We know of them only by learning, thus, that which is not present by sight provides us with momentum to act and do. Therefore, that which is present also gives us the possibilities to co-create with what is not present becoming the medium for feeling, knowing and willing. Imagination does not always produce but it does open the space from which we can understand ourselves as a combination of different ideas, influences, or objects into a new whole. In order for good to prosper, we must imagine deep and wide. We must exchange places with others. We must be aware of their pains and pleasures as we would our own. It is through the imagination of doing right that the power of our own nature can be appealing to others. Imagine how it will be!

Reason and Imagination work together: first in the body, then in the mind.

## *The Power of Coercion*

Power is the ability of an individual or group to carry out actions that influence the behavior of others in order to get them to do what the challenger wants rather than what the opposition wants. Coercion is a system of threats, manipulation, and intimidation of the behavior of a person or group forcing them to behave in an involuntary way, actively or inactively, by some form of pressure or force. A leader in authority implements power by using human resources in the form of people who work and give assistance, support, skills and knowledge. There are also psychological and ideological habits and attitudes toward obedience and submission that are absent of a common faith or sense of mission. As a form of control, a leader can use material resources to hold back wealth, property, natural resources, communication and transportation. A leader may also use retaliation or punishment against her/his constituents and/or adversaries.

When we look at the behavior of humanity and the present actions of world leaders today, it is not difficult to see that the power of coercion is in full force. What the present day leaders attempt to do is deal with the underlying 'mindset' problems within society and not its symptoms. Resistance and failure occur when we act without positively dealing with attitudes and thinking styles among the various cultures in their efforts to change structures. There can be no true stable culture when coercion is used. History has proven this as a fact. So what are we to do when leaders or governments have ulterior motives?

Governments and/or leaders acting for their own benefit, and not for the people of the world, do not have the willingness or the ability to draw forth a vision that maintains a balanced state of action socially or environmentally. Open-minded leaders nurture and encourage their people to be open, creative, and innovative in achieving objectives with other people and nations. This type of guidance is not forced. It is an ownership vision belonging to the people's observations and not of a political party or organization. Progressive thinking instills self-choice where every person is an intangible asset, trusted and respected, and not just a cog in the bureaucratic process. When the focus is more on community and world service to people and a better way of life, power through coercion will have no authority. Thus, leaders will use positivism to influence and help people align their personal values and goals with those of others. Liberty of conscience is the right of every person and every culture should legally guarantee it. It is a right vested in every person to be free of another's unwarranted power of coercion from any authority, civil or otherwise. No authority should have the right to punish or suppress anyone from being open or from manifesting and declaring any of their ideas by either word, or voice, regardless of race or sex as long as they are non-violent. When leaders allow free room for discussion without duress, no authority will dare resist the truth and trust of another to express his/her self. When someone acts against his or her will due to the force of the political order, public opinion or law, justice and human rights become fragmented. Leaders can never foster justice and legitimate rights when they use force and coercion to uphold the rights of some while disregarding those of others.

Politics, international or domestic, is a struggle for power.

## *A Wide, Wide Look at Life*

As humans, we customarily judge persons, places and things by their manifestation instead of by their meaning. However, time and human imagination will allow us to discover the hidden meaning of those revelations and we will view everything as organized with a plan and purpose. Dichotomies can fill human existence where separation occurs through two divisions that differ widely from or contradict each other. If we are to make any sense of the present, we must look forward with a wider vision and imagine how we want our place in the sun to be. The world of today is an extension of the world of yesterday. From this two-fold mindset, we have a humanity extricating itself from a vast arena of discord and strife. This graveyard of memories fills our streets and byways with both the good and bad forms of living.

When we begin to look at the symptoms of 'why this?' we will start to see clearly the causes of the manifestation which are the result of our own choices. Only by unlocking our sense of Compassion can we ever develop the sensitivity to look beneath those masks to those of our pure aspirations. As a society, we can allow every new generation to become isolated toward one another, or we can find ways to look wider with clear thought and common sense. When we use language wisely, there is a natural connection between it and the higher reasoning faculty. The derogatory and hypocritical ways in which we disclose information through the shaping of public opinion only widens the divisions.

Language is the key to meaning and is the mover of our strength, verbally and mentally. To think we visualize with words. Through words, we act and create. Our words can give us a positive or negative outlook that creates a reaction in others. Language makes the world what it is and produces some kind of cause and effect. Languages reveal the histories of bygone eras. We often judge cultures and races by their language. As a result, word mistranslations frequently lead to misunderstandings. With the advent of modern visual technology, we can interpret language and body gestures more easily. This new form of technology enables the brain to understand better what is going on both inside our bodies and in the world around us. Emotionally, mentally and physically, reactions to words can increase or decrease our vitality to persons, places and things and can have a ripple effect in our lives and those around us. Sensory perceptions, when activated by positivism, enhance the input of our sensory organs; these perceptions also enhance the processing of information in the brain. Changes in outlook and environmental practices will enhance our production and processing abilities. Individuals, groups, nations, cultures, and the politics of governments everywhere must self-regulate their demands if they are to manage wisely their responses to the manifestations that are in front of them. When extreme responses interfere with everyday life, over responsiveness can worsen the situation.

We are constantly mispronouncing life.

## Critical Thinking

Each of us must reflect on the knowledge we gain. After we obtain information, we must not blindly accept it. Rather, what we need to do is use our level-headedness by polishing the gathered facts or theories before we accept them as truth. Knowledge can be factual or fictional, as something assumed true. The presenter of information often uses charisma to inspire enthusiasm and interest when discussing a topic. We must carefully analyze the subject and presenter(s) before taking in that source as a belief or working model. It is easy to fall victim to a false 'authority syndrome' where someone thinks they know more about a subject or person than they actually do. Expertise in a particular field does not always correspond to actual truth. Often speakers use shrewdness through impassioned appeals to the prejudices and emotions of others. Because of that shrewdness, a speaker creates opposition in order to fuse a desired result or solution. There would be no problem if an informed unbiased citizenry would take on the self-responsibility to uphold the separation of powers (by limiting them) and recognize that unalienable rights protect all people from the coercion of authority.

Information presenters are skilled in the psychology of the comfort zone. They know how to apply the right amount of appeal without creating a sense of risk in others. These presenters have established an alliance or association between two or more people, organizations, or countries that are their centers of influence. Once that particular center forms, they shower those in it with rewards and praise. This action keeps their base in that zone of mental conditioning. Because of the lack of mass commonality, those mental boundaries are not permanent, nor are they real. Only when people feel secure with new experiences will they step outside of that comfort zone and experience different responses within the environment. Therefore, most people choose a worldview that gives them comfort. Even when there is evidence that contradicts that view, people will often ignore it; they believe that if they overlook a conflict, it will resolve on its own or disappear. None of us wants to feel deceived or that we have been mislead. Critical thinking is most effective when it involves independence, insight, fairness, and exploration of thoughts and feelings. Thus, critical thinking creates a sense of humility, mental courage and integrity in analyzing or evaluating arguments, interpretation, beliefs, or theories.

For freedom and government to become self-evident, we must educate our children and ourselves to be critical thinkers.

## Mother, Why Did I Do This?

The world is no longer isolated. Humanity is experiencing a wide disparity in feelings, ideas and interests that we have never seen before. Brought on by international travel, the internet and its dissemination of information, this rift will only widen if we cannot reach a commonality of purpose through international relations and problem-solving diplomacy. At no other time in world history are skills and tact in dealing with other people, cultures, and their interests so important. As the people everywhere in the world see what the more affluent nations have in terms of prosperity and opportunity, they are wondering how they can achieve the same results. We have opened the crevice and there is no closing it.

However, there are solutions to this pandemic wanting. Stronger nations can no longer insist that weaker nation's leaders limit their own production of technology because others perceive them as a threat to a stronger nation's sovereignty and security. This oppressive approach reeks of a dinosaur mentality in dealing with other nations. The disadvantaged have hopes and dreams even though they may be living under the yoke of a tyrant. When pressed, the underprivileged often support the interests of their ruler because they have no choice or resources to compete for the protection of their well-being.

The criterion of stronger nations should not be about expanding their own influence through force. Rather, it should be about world Goodwill and human betterment void of 'manifest destiny': the belief that promotes and defends democracy throughout the world. The virtues, mission and destiny of every nation are different. No person or nation has the right to interfere in the sovereignty of another unless that nation invites an intervention. Military annexation should be a violation of International law when imposed by coercion or force. Conflict resolution requires astute mental leadership, a nonviolent approach that builds community through diplomacy and mediation.

The young soldiers who fight the conflicts of nations are innocent and bendable to the influences of comradeship and protection among themselves. Often leaders regard them as expendable in conflict situations. In any conflict, it is most often the civilians and infrastructure of a nation that withstand the worst of an assault. In addition to human suffering, the monetary expenses of war are staggering. For example, the United States alone has spent trillions on its wars!

Imagine if nations throughout history had utilized power and the monetary economic infrastructure wisely for the commonality and well-being of people; disease, starvation, poverty and social class divisions would be mute. The world is at a crucial stage and nature is saying, "Things cannot continue as usual". New types of leaders must come to the front. Leaders must understand that progressive changes will lead to a united human culture, where belief systems are not divisive but reflect human uniqueness that instills interconnectedness.

Responsible individualism is a social contract with other citizens and takes the form of world citizenship, the real focus of a nation.

## A New Time

A new time has come upon the worlds that rotate around one another in the infinity of space. The long-endured thinking of man/woman, used to shape the worldview that we thought placed us at the center of life, no longer holds true. We are now compelled to move away from that center of little consciousness and place ourselves in the greater Consciousness that requires individual accountability and responsibility to the Whole of life. The controlling factors so strongly held by a few are no longer appropriate with the new rays emanating from the abstract mind. All suns build a system of worlds in which Consciousness is to evolve. The earth, the source for human consciousness, can no longer remain a child connected to the hip of its parent to gain experience. As material ambitions fade, the natural human environment will expand to meet the broader Universal environment. As such, loftier ambitions will take root in the old desert sands of dead habits and the mind will take control instead of the body. Those dead habits will fall into a sleep hold and will not awaken again if the Light is strong enough to rouse our righteousness.

In this process of re-birth, we undertake a new path. In this knowledge, no one will evoke feelings of anger, hostility, or animosity toward another's heart and Soul. It is a course marked out by individual approaches to rationality and not those relying on doctrine and dogma. From this force, each individual will awaken to his/her own nature and not that of others as defined by creeds. This self-directed way of relating to the natural order of persons, places and things is elemental. It will cause seeds to sprout, grow and bloom in the magnetism of space and Light. This hidden power that is independent of physical existence lives in varying degrees in all things. It will be recognizable and put to use in the formation of thoughts that will be transferable through mental cognition and sensory perception. We are now only the thoughts of yesterday and what we are thinking today builds our life of tomorrow: Mind becomes our creation.

Do space, time and awareness need a Consciousness to exist? In time, we will view all objects in the universe as aspects of everything else. We will realize that the worlds of space and time are only what one believes them to be. Does a person's awareness always need to be awake as Consciousness so that other persons, places, and things exist? We cannot measure, see or give form to Ultimate awareness. To do so would mean a cessation of things existing as an underlying reality. An awareness of this magnitude depends on cognition. Wakefulness defines conscience. Without objectives, we could not acquire social principles. Mind and existence vary according to one's state of mind. Thought processes either intensify or weaken depending on the awareness of the sub-levels of being that encompass the overall state of physical systems. Through reasoning, Intuition, or perception we acquire the knowledge to unbind all things, giving them life. Therefore, creation is an expression of Consciousness that takes on all forms.

As we awaken through the right selection of ideas, we will come to realize that on-going change is a basic feature of our most effective teacher: the Energy of the Universe.

## The Beautiful Stuff about Us

Currently as we look around the world and compute the everyday occurrences, it is easy to get befuddled and numb to the events and circumstances that are enveloping the world. It seems as if every family is being impacted one way or another and most feel powerless to do anything about the big picture. Harmony and balance seem to be lost in the desolate sands of consumption and self-concern. The consensus of what is best for the world and its inhabitants has taken a back seat in the political life of nations. In our interactions, are we losing our everyday language that allows us to mentally connect and guide one another? As we map out our way on this earthly journey, are we abnegating our self-responsibility and our physical and psychological well-being in the pursuit of a 'momentary consumption fix'? If we choose to recognize it, regardless of race, culture or sex, there is a commonality waiting in us, to change us into something better if we but look to one another as equals. How can anyone doubt that we are something Sacred as we view the pictures taken of earth from space? When we look excessively at the disparities that exist between people without any means to do something about it, we are allowing our own self-control to wither.

There are controlling factors in life that we cannot escape, but they need not diminish our Inner reality. The only way we can help the world is for each of us to stand up, take control of our actions, and not slide into competitive inducements. The best way to do this is by respecting the Beautiful Stuff that is within. Regardless of the color of Spirit, we should not be fixated about the glamour's of life. Most are out of reach anyway, but the beauty of the Self is not. It is around and in us no matter where we are or what we are doing. The more we focus on the opinions of others and the ways of the world, the less we will be concerned about the Self. There are no misgivings about our place in the world. It could not exist without each of us being on it, and this is true about our place in the universe.

The actions any of us take are to a large degree induced by our relationships with persons, places and things. How we perceive truth, logic and the laws of nature rationally and how we relate them to others, define the course of action we will take in meeting our goals and expectations. An integrated communication system defines the functioning of order in life and the infrastructures of society. Without that coherency an incidental condition or illness can occur thus creating an unbalance in a person, group or culture that inevitably leads to acts of violence.

When actions are not fruitful, meaning and purpose lose their power, random acts of violence plague societies, and the coherent natural process called Conscious life becomes irrational. It is important that the 'central command post' which governs the workings of society fits well into the overall picture and general functioning so that laws, logic and truth are mutually coordinated and beneficial to the Goodwill of everyone in their work and play. It is through mutually cooperating laws, truths, and values, that our conscious life brings forth the Beautiful Stuff about us.

We are exercising the energies of the Soul through the mind, emotion and body when we use imagination and memory to guide our hands in work and play. Not only will our own thoughts guide us, but also thoughts of those from past ages will assist us in forming the human race we want to create. When we work this way, we cannot help but see the Beauty that is in us.

## Across the Divide

Life is a series of two's. Before we commit ourselves to anything, we should create an opposite to see if the action is the right thing to do. For example, are the parts and the source from which the parts came from the same? John is guilty of breaking the law, is society guilty of the same since John came from it? Is one person's weakness another person's strength? To gauge truth from the standpoint of laws that society has currently ordained may be contrary to what we revere as truth in the future. Therefore, how do we evaluate something so we can form a judgment of another's behavior, feeling, or abilities? Whether we want to accept it or not, there are many kinds of truth.

We can accept truth as fixed, absolute, or comparative. There is truth of the Heart and mind in both smallness and greatness. Some of us will fall and some of us will stand tall in this dichotomy of life but in the end, we come back together again in the whole, because in one way or other we are all the Begetters of one another. In the grandness of differences that exist in the singleness of life, in a person or universe, there is actuality in it all. None of us happened by our own doing but through others whose actions we inherit. While the actions of others have built the edifices of law and infrastructure to meet the needs of their time, we ought to personalize these structures according to who we are now. Each one of us has an identity that is uniquely our own. For that reason, complex structures, organizations, monuments, etc., must be expressive of the aspirations and hopes of all who live, work and exist within their sphere of influence.

Reaching back into recorded history, governments, politicians and civic leadership have neglected the Welfare and happiness of their constituents.

This neglect has been the fundamental cause behind the ills of society and the violence that leads to warfare. To close this ill-begotten clash of ideas, we each need to walk across that divide by using our own discriminative power. It can profit society when we allow extreme points of view and expressions. When we censor or wash over such expressions, they fill the divide with danger. Accepting and judging extreme views without demeaning criticism shows that we are not afraid of social equality. It shows we are confident that an agreed upon idea is better than one that is deemed bad without consensus. When we look carefully, we can expose an idea that reflects avarice and extreme odium for all to see. When a good idea comes along that is expressive of the Will of the people, it can ignite a storm of energy that will sweep through the population bringing change with it. When ideas are engaging, they effectively give more freedom that will ensure the health of a free society. When we begin to interpret ideas correctly, especially those that aspire toward human happiness, we can mend and repair the fault lines between individuals and civilizations. Global politics will no longer be misconstrued or manipulated for political or ideological ends. Circumstances change, ideas do also, but words bathed in Hope spring things Eternal and remain permanently in the mind.

We do our duty best when we work toward bringing a non-violent society into expression. We must lift our Hearts and minds to see across the chasms that divide to a world without want and fear.

## *Long Ago and Now*

From long ago when the forests were ripe with the ancestry of human tribes, the sun and the sounds of the woodland birds and insects measured the passage of the time of day. They saw time as so many suns, moons, the positions of stars and the digits of hands and feet. At this dawn, there was no writing. They communicated by miming, the use of music, the sound of the drum and the wooden pipes. There were rules of land tenure and property for the planting, harvesting and hunting of food. Each tribe had their space, their own supernatural beliefs and superstitions, their evil and good spirits to give directions. Their capacity to observe and think was no less than our own now. Though different in degree and necessity, they developed and used the soil of the land as we do today with our modern methods.

Heredity seeded those early times in our minds. Though we choose not to recognize those ancient pathways of the mind, they are nevertheless a part of our insight. We are what we are today because of the way they were then. Are we any different because we view our world now through the lenses of dogma, philosophy and science? How will the human race view us in the far off future? What parts of our journey will turn out to be true and what parts will turn out to be false? These questions are just part of the dichotomy of life and each time period will develop because of its own features, events or personalities.

There are yet undiscovered ways of seeing the Mysteries of life and nature in our everyday experiences; all we need to do is develop the Insight to see them. As the sun holds the earth in space, we hold life in the memory of mind. Human action, Consciousness and the mind mold nature (matter). The pictures of the world that are in the mind appear outwardly stable. The living universe and the sun, its flow of energy, work in unison with nature and magnetize the mind that in turn responds to life and its conscious needs.

The modern human mind has created so many negatives in its pursuit of shaping the world in its image through technology, that nature has become unbalanced and is now beginning to reassert itself. In the end nature dominates. Humanism is not the arbitrator, nature is. The ancients recognized this. The more we assert with material and mind power, the more nature will rebel and its destructions become bigger and bigger. Greed and consumption have caused us to renege on our sustainable contract with nature and on the strings that bind us with the way we were long ago. Modernism can become sustainable; all we need do is lessen our use of it. Inventions need a longer life span, and we need to use them longer. Families need to be smaller and governments less intrusive and less dominant in the affairs of others.

This age of experience, along with the experiences passed from the ancient knowledge systems, can give us insight in developing commonality with nature and the energy of the universe. When we retain what we create longer, in terms of energy/time cycles, we will relinquish the causes that upset nature. Thus, the broken aspects of cellular and atomic life will be intact and compatible. This will result in a multitude of cells and atoms that will divide to form a holistic living process in the ecosystems of nature and the universe.

As we view ourselves as living beings, we should view our earth as a living, breathing Being and see it as belonging in and of us, long ago and now.

## Possibilities

Through the phenomena of the mind and the laws of nature, the human story is an amazing complex of personality/sub-mind interacting with the elements of earth. Man/woman is a being so complex and intricate that the imagination is seemingly perplexed about itself. Hence, we question the concept of being a part of something outside ourselves, esoteric or exoteric. Life is a study in cosmic change. Beginning globally, it synchronizes a complex network of electrons, atoms and mental neurons that brings about a progressive unfolding of Consciousness demonstrated as Rightness that extends into all parts as life.

It is certain we are life forms now. With this knowledge, it is important to enter tomorrow prepared to meet its conditions, to be alert and not to alienate our positive sub-conscious minds with uncertainty but prepare for any eventuality. We can never be sure of the conditions or quality of possibilities, but they are Unlimited. The potential for successful future prospects are in us if we but work on our own nature. Everything in the universe is constantly recurring and will go on doing so in a similar form for an infinite number of repetitions. Time somehow repeats itself in the reality of wakefulness that is the universe: hence the necessity for self-reflection. Being in the now makes Eternal return a likely possibility. Simply put, we are evolving in an Infinite circle where time is a circular experience that repeats itself after a set period has past. As rational beings, our Consciousness experiences time as a straight-line progression of events fixed in our relationship with cause and effect. Anything that has occurred in the past is the Cause of current effects.

In order to operate in the arena of persons, places and things, Consciousness must be aware of itself through experience. Time, cause and effect exist within the mind where the end always meets the beginning at a loop point. The type of reoccurrence would depend on one's thoughts. They could be exact as before and repeated, or if we maintain the ability to make choices from the previous trip, we could take a different set of actions for the sake of improving the experiences. Thus, when we improve ourselves, the Universe improves as exponential effects farther along in the system of creation. When we transform ourselves to be more powerful, more aware, and more active in knowing life positively, our Eternal return is more balanced and beneficial.

Each of these possibilities begets new experiences that are similar but never quite the same. If we view these experiences from a positive light, everything in life, including a moment of time, is a work of art in itself that justifies our being. When we analyze the past, we cannot help but create a favorable outcome. We must ask ourselves repeatedly, "Do I want to experience this existence once more and immeasurably many times more?" If not, we must each weigh our actions with the greatest of care. Whether it is by Intuition or by inference it is up to each of us to understand our place among persons and things as they appear to us, outside ourselves as well as inwardly. There is a universe of multiplicity of realities underlying the phenomena we call the life of the Self as it appears to us at various times. It is this Something that is beyond the tangible world that allows us to gather our possibilities.

Within performance, there is the potentiality of Infinite possibilities.

## The End of Physical Being

It seems there is equality in living and dying; one person dies and another is born. When a person has just passed away and physical communication has stopped, is that the end of physical being for that person? Does that person exist as awareness elsewhere? Physical science has its means of clinically defining death. Since we have lost communication with the deceased, there is no sure way of establishing the continuation of the departed for those left behind; this leaves us with a profound Mystery. Nevertheless, we can do much in our physical being to keep ourselves awake beyond the door of physicality. We are all irreducible components of human society; and we 'will' a part of ourselves to it through our values and expressions within the culture in which we are born. Our physical being is lived as shared traditions such as genetic traits, religious values, and other collective aspects of memory that constitute the common life.

In large degree, the content of our present awareness is the result of how we allow those traditions to influence us. Everything in life originated from an idea, beginning with the wheel up to our present techno-skills. The present period of physical being reflects the belief in a non-religious doctrine of human rights. From the moment of birth, we must instill the idea of Universality, along with the idea that birth and death are synonymous. Without this approach, the mind will remain imbued with its view of national sovereignty and power politics that make struggle an ongoing necessity. This mindset creates a disjuncture between one's Inner self and external social practices.

From the cradle onward, we have control over our ending process; all we need to do is believe it. The cessation of form is just the renewing of a New Beginning at the end of physical being. When we believe in the Self, the Inner observer, as the arbitrator of experience, then we awaken in death as we do from a dream in physical being. Each of us has the capacity to validate our personal continuum in Permanency since we independently pass out of the sphere of objective existence.

Conundrums, the play of words induced by others that are often puzzling, pervade the world. Only we, on our own accord, can free ourselves from such arbitrariness. Personality traits, such as anger, skew one's true identity by preventing it from spiraling into something grander and loftier. Shared life principles should build trust and enhance our continuum of persons, places and things beyond our present boundaries of existence. Each of us needs to live in a place that continuously develops interactions with others that take us beyond those stilted boundaries of physical being to that of Unending Consciousness.

The end of physical being is just another stage of becoming something new, something more that is Accepting, Forgiving and Loving toward the Self and others; it is designed to fit us to our internal definitions of who and what we have been and what we will be after physical existence.

## *Decisions Made*

We should consider whatever we experience in life, so that we can assess the thoughtfulness of that undertaking! When we make a decision that includes others, we must be aware of the differences that others may have toward those decisions and the circumstances that they may have on life. However, if the choices we make pertain only to an individual action, these decisions will not affect others and the strength of will is self-realized. Sound judgment should be absent of a sentiment or emotion which clouds level-headedness. If we base a decision on the right use of mental energy, mental strength stamps out selfish personal activities by replacing them with integrated and inclusive ideas.

When we consider all the varying possibilities and ways that life expresses itself in time and space, a central Universal energy becomes apparent. When we make a decision from this central perspective, we should involve the strength of this energy since we are all a part of its matter, whether coarse or refined. The state of one's consciousness determines the decision-making process and its garnished fruit. The more Light we throw on decisions by thinking them through, the more consciousness will expand in our cycles of living.

When we assess our actions, we mirror the effects of those actions in our relations with persons, places and things. We must first remember that decisions, made singularly or in groups, form the basis for everything created in the world. We fashion that interplay from the energy coming from our minds. Right and wrong activity is due simply to right or wrong direction of consciousness and not to the energy and force currents inherent in being.

Each of us is only an atom, energy, light and force. The thought energy utilized in our decision-making process holds our existence together. As a result, the choices made help us fashion our Inner and outer awareness. The disordered occurrences of physical life are due to obstructions in humanity's thinking and the failure to imagine inclusively. It is feasible that we could avoid incorrect judgments at any level through mobilized Goodwill.

There are many lines of force crossing human relations, merging and mixing in the thought processes that characterize our ongoing material reality. This plays upon matter forcing it to assume certain shapes, to respond to certain vibrations, and to build visible forms and relationships in the material world. These forms of matter are derivatives of the mineral, vegetable, animal, human and Higher forms that we do not see with our eyes.

From stage to stage, we show signs of the decisions made and we are but reflections of those choices. Decisions made help us explore all the avenues of right and wrong knowledge. From these decisions, we descend into the valleys of despair and up to the mountaintop of hope and joy. Decisions can swing us beyond the thought of space-time and self-interest to a focused centralism. When we function with clarity of choice, we gradually form the strength of our Inner being. It is a place where all forms are veils of sound, color and shape. From here, our Souls watch, assisting us to think with reason and rightness. When we spread our thoughts wisely for others to use correctly, we are quickening the right use of energy. seeding our motives. Our thoughts, speech and actions sprout with worthiness and strength of the decisions made.

We all have an Inner knowing and when we are attentive to it, this Intuition guides our decisions and helps us avoid errors.

## *Accepting What Is*

Regardless of our place in life, there is no freedom from wishing. There is a constant internal conflict between accepting what is versus what we want to be. The desire for something that is beyond our reach is our momentum for moving forward even though we may never arrive there consciously. If we are not careful, wanting life to be different according to our wishes can place us in a self-imposed conundrum. Nevertheless, we must keep moving on. On the front line of life, we are productive when we strive to do what is proper and right in our actions. When we are positive, we fashion things to believe in that bring a specific meaning to our desires. Hence, we endure patiently in that belief. In our own Sanctuary, we rationalize those meanings and feelings as normal and suitable. In the garden of our fate, there is no right or wrong way to express a desire or for wishes to come to fulfillment. The outcome is positive as long as we do not enter someone else's place without an invitation. When we are welcomed, we should do our best to honor the wishes of those who have invited us in to see what they wish upon.

Because of the attracting and repelling nature of atoms and molecules, our physical place may not always be able to manifest our wishes. Thus, we create our own wishes to occupy ourselves with what is. When we accept these wishes as harmless imagination, we can free ourselves from guilt and stop wasting energy on unnecessary desires. Thus, we accumulate the life energy of the Soul's fire. Wishes are mind stuff that we can neutralize by thinking. When we accept what is, we build up our own self-esteem about life by not allowing others to determine the future. We are always passing through events and whether those past events are good or bad, we cannot fully change them.

No matter what our state we have to clean up our own undertakings. Others can help and guide us as to how we should go about it. However, we have to honor the knowledge and accept the gain or loss of the situation. Resistance to what has happened in the past is in most cases futile. The currents and trends of life are always flowing. Being perceptive regarding what to accept and when to move on can be a challenge or an opportunity when we apply the concept of accepting what is.

When our hearts and minds are in the right place, we can turn the unpleasant into something enjoyable. When we calmly outline our current reality, whatever it may be, and accept responsibility for it, the difficulties of things and events will be resolved. Significant to the universe and beyond our imagination, each of us is an important part of the currents that sustain life. Just as fog dissolves by the heat of the sun, our wishes and fixations are 'passing clouds' in a dream body of flesh and the light of the self guides us through them. We must move beyond defining ourselves through exterior factors to those within. The tiny choices we make number in the thousands throughout each day, and each plays a part in molding our individual and collective character that shapes the world and ourselves. When we give up attaching ourselves to the outcome of what is to be, we are free of the choices that others make in accepting what is.

Understandable or not, things are what they are!

### I just do not know!

Often when we ask others to give an opinion on what happens after we depart this life or what is in the future, they say, "I just do not know". Do we really want to admit that we do not know who we are? Perhaps, it is because we are busy with the 'now' experience and do not want to bother inquiring. There probably are as many reasons for wanting not to know as there are people wanting to know. However, can we truly say there is no such a thing as the unknown? It is just a word without meaning; the unknown is simply the lack of experience. The more we know the less 'unknown' we become. Fear, a learned behavior, also plays a part in not knowing. Our habits, mannerisms, upbringing and culture instill opinions and beliefs that we cannot always substantiate. Therefore, it is often safer to say we do not know than to understand or recognize what we cannot be aware of with our senses. In terms of death, it would be more optimistic to expand our awareness with the thought, "What is there to fear? Since I am 'consciousness' now, I will remain so in another experience." Throughout our lives we can reinforce this belief with the thought, "Since I exist now, there cannot be any unknowns to my continuation; I exist now and I will exist in the future." The unknown is a vital part of the enticement to discover. Unwittingly, the unknown keeps us moving forward whether or not we are aware of this movement; it is a part of our survival. When we say, "I just do not know" this attitude of uncertainty could actually further alienate us from examining our lives. Our instinct is to explore and fear is a paradigm that keeps us aware, but we do not have to panic when we know this fear is just a nervous response.

In trying to grasp the unknown, if we are not thoughtful, we can create hurtful experiences. We do many things that go against our better nature and we know how to do them well. We smoke, we drink and drive and fail to wear safety devises because they makes us un-cool. We kill each other, we lie, we cheat, and we steal and rape other humans and nature. We build armies and defense systems because we are afraid of the unknown. Often, we lack commonality with others beliefs and cultures because we are too busy to get to know them. When we do not explore the 'when, why, where and how' of our being, we probably will truly never know. Fear and not knowing the Self keep the mirror of clarity unpolished. When we consciously say, "I just do not know" are we being safer than we are certain?

Our actions and individual choices form the basis of what we consciously seek to know or not to know. We fear the unknown because we have already experienced past events that have caused pain, injury, loss, ridicule, rejection, etc. Humanism has created theories and imagined solutions for the unknowns of the universe. We begin to fear these theories when the explanations are not familiar to the known. When we embrace the unknown as limitless possibilities, we reduce the causes of fear from our past and embrace a leap of faith that can take us into the knowable.

It is impossible to attain awareness without confronting, recognizing knowing and not knowing, as knowledge.

## The Final Illusion

As we tread along the path of our final years, let us look at what reality has been: the noise, images, words, thoughts, memories, fantasies, sensations, people and pleasures, good and bad feelings that we have encountered. We must directly look at all the thinking, doing, listening, running, talking and whatever else we have been and there see the reality of it. Our past, our traditions, our searching, wanting, controlling, needing, doubting, praying, fasting, keeping, dreaming, desiring, manipulating, forcing, grasping, fearing, using, wasting, lying, seeking, moving, believing, holding, imagining and thinking and even our DNA have conditioned us to follow this reality. Society has made grave mistakes in separating itself from the hearts that reside in it. When we do this reality check, Stillness will dawn upon the Heart and in that sunrise, we will know everything is 'ok'.

In our own way, each of us has strived to be successful and prosperous. We allow our egos to gloat, "Look at me, I am better, I am famous, I am special, I am powerful!" However, in the final moments of mirrored reflection, we see how the ego created the effect. In that moment of Quietness, we are the reflected face of humanity's embodiment. In this final breath, we become the Pure Silence of quintessential Love. We know that no matter what we have been in life, we are that Essence.

The natural laws and formulas have their rise from matter and energy. Atoms, molecules and chemicals constitute our physical awareness. In this moment of physical wakefulness while interacting on this Universal dance floor, we sometimes dance chaotically and sometimes calmly. It is in the final breath that the illusions of living rush in and fade into pure nothingness. In our final years, we should not focus primarily on necessities. Rather we should use them to understand there is nothing more to realize, nothing to learn, nothing to experience, no enlightenment, no salvation, no heaven or hell, just this subtle awareness of Gentleness and Love of what is. It has always been there whether it has been work, play, creativity, or the arms of a loved one. Once we accept and feel this subtle awareness, that there is nothing more to learn or know, the remaining years will be lived well and we will meet anything that arises in Silence and Peace. It is no longer a time of learning, but seeing.

Look at nature, there is peace there, even in turmoil, for it regroups. Are we any different from the flowers blossoming and dying? The forms of nature differ, but they follow a natural course and we are a part of it. When we realize that we are all what we see, we are at peace. When we understand that greedy thoughts are a form of obsessive thinking and doing that disturbs the natural Silent state within our minds, we start letting go of the noise. When fresh flowing water stops, it stagnates into a dead pool with no oxygen to sustain life. Greed is a misuse of matter and energy culminating into obtrusive noise. Truth and Silence flow through each of us according to our own uniqueness. No person or group holds a patent on truth or purity because mere form cannot conquer these attributes. The final illusion is the form, for it cannot triumph over or change that which has always been the Source of our being. Only in Silence can we realize our Permanence. Our final years can be a magnificent time of tranquil moments when we allow the Inner nature to surround us with its generous love, a Love so unique that we need not look anywhere to understand it.

No person or group has the Ultimate Truth. Only in our quiet moments do we become sensitive to the revelations of the Soul.

## The Speed of Light and Life

The beginning of the story says, "Let there be Light." This narrative of Light and life has been going around for an indefinite time. Without Light, the story of life would not exist. Light allows us to go back only as far as we can see and time is based on speed. However, the story goes on! Scientists have hypothesized that light travels at 186,000 mps and, regardless where we may find ourselves in space, its speed is constant. The relativity of matter, time, and space guards and guides every particle in the known universe. This show of Light reminds us of the fact that mass, length, and time change with velocity. We base this awareness on the assumption that the speed of light in a vacuum is constant, and that physical laws have the same mathematical form throughout the universe. We are in effect electrical currents interacting with mechanical forces.

The actions of the universe and those of our bodies are mostly involuntary. Much goes on without and within us without our awareness. Light is the quintessential Fire that animates life. We think of light as bright, clear, and shining. Light is associated with the sun, moon, and star systems that make up the universe. In addition, we use the term light to explain the coming of truth and knowledge into the mind. Life is what is alive, moving. The uniqueness of human life is its ability to observe, to make its own decisions and perhaps detract from the norm. Light is what occurs in and of phenomena; it is a potential or manifestation of an inherent quality of nature! Every subject undertaken is about life, religion, philosophy, science, art, and so forth. Light is alive animating our bodies. In youth, light fills and stimulates the imagination. In old age, light slows down and cells of the body decay; we depart back into the Light of the Self.

The more we communicate on a subject, the better we form words to understand the differences in life. Light and life, knowledge and wisdom are the language of Light and an animating force. We are waves of Light that live in each of us through our thoughts. It is by believing in the intrinsic nature of the Self that we awaken again beyond the body of form to a body of Light. We can stabilize consciousness only on one plane of laws at a time. We do not yet know if Consciousness is able to function on all planes of life, objective or subjective. Nevertheless, it is a probability as Light and life penetrate and gain a greater revelation of one another.

Like passing clouds, we pass through this earth as rays of Light colored by our wants and wishes. If we are wise, we will let go of the lesser light and attach ourselves to the greater. Day by day and moment by moment, we can explore the temporary beauties and glories of this moment in earth, or we can at the same time reach for the more Permanent blissful origin that is in each of us. We are particles of Light in a Greater Light, the Universe. The two, the person and the universal, are interrelated within and without as matter and Spirit. Regardless of all the seeming limitations of physicality, Light is the source of our transcendence into a fuller Eternal self-existing life. When we communicate selflessly, words unfold the mysteries of earth, life and Light. We contain the whole living system of Life, all that has been the past, all that is present and all that will be the future.

We had our starting point in Light and the presentiment of things to come implies that life will begin again in Light.

## *The End of Separation*

Are we separate from energy? Do we need the concept of a universe to exist? Through direct observation, we have the potential to see space so absolute, so perfect and so radiant that we do not need to know of our Origin. In our laboratories, observatories, recording methods, microscopes and telescopes, we can glimpse the Story of Creation in the world. However, we know from our mortality that this form of information gathering does not last. So what is the purpose of this scientific knowing if there is no provable continuation of the learner? When physical life ends, assumptions begin about Immortality for those left behind. Until we scientifically gather, formulate and pose questions and hypothesize about the end as actively as we do about the Beginning, can we ever expect the same result about the continued existence of the inhabitants of form.

The vast community of life resigns the nature of death to belief. We do not have the zeal or wisdom to see our Essence in the same way we do that of atomization. We know that the fundamental laws of physics hold that we cannot create or destroy energy, only change it. In a nuclear reaction, the destruction of matter is impossible. The energy released is the result of a sustained release from the reaction similar to the sun. The unit of matter in a nuclear reaction still exists in a net system; the amount of the energy, mass and change is constant. As a thinking form made of the same substance, our energy must be releasing and existing as well, even in the death experience.

Life on earth is organic and is composed of organic molecules that are simply the compounds of carbon. The brain, the reservoir of the mind, or consciousness/thinking, is an electrical and chemical machine made of cells, primarily neurons. A neuron is similar to an on/off switch that is either resting or sending messages. These neurons send messages to other parts of the brain. We live in an electrical-watery filled space of blood and plasma. There are plasma, blood cells and platelets that flow through the body to the heart. Blood carries oxygen. Then there is plasma of the fourth state of matter beyond solid, liquid and gas, in which electrons split away from atoms leaving behind a highly electrified collection of nuclei and free electrons. The particles in plasma can self-organize as electronic charges shaping themselves into helical strands that attach to each other in a counterintuitive way in which like can attract like. They can divide to form two copies of the original structure inducing changes as the less stable ones break down, leaving behind the fittest structures.

Form or formless, life is a web of electrical circuitry connecting and unifying nature. This Light is in our bodies and is constantly organizing our better natures. To an intuitive mind, there is no end in an electrical universe. From one vibration to another and in all states of matter, we live and move in the electromagnetic space of the visible and invisible. The work of life is awe-inspiring. We can only see and know what is on the horizon by working our way up from the bottom to the summit. We can be full and empty at the same time. We are Rarified Light. When we are aware of this light just as we are aware of our bodies, we have finished our manifestations. Once we are fully born in light, there will be no need to return to the womb of matter, the end of separation has begun.

Eternity is existence: behold it! There is no end of time when we know we are expressions of its energy.

## *Let It Be*

As the author writes this page, life here in America is experiencing a downturn. For the first time in its history Americas President is a black American. However, he and his Cabinet have inherited challenges never before seen. The economy is at its worse in six decades and our children and their children will inherit a century of debt. Homes are foreclosing and jobs are being lost. The nation's military is fighting wars in two countries and illegal immigrants are inundating its borders heightening the fear of terrorism. The demand is up for the use of illegal drugs causing drug cartels to war against one another for control of the flow of drug money emanating from America and elsewhere. The health of the nation is declining and its infrastructure is eroding daily. The political will of the country is so lacking in bipartisanship that the only way out may be in the complete failure of representation of the two-party system so that as a nation we can look at our unprincipled ways.

There comes a moment in our lives when we fully realize that the world has gone beyond our ability to influence it. It is here that we have to take stock of our own priorities, motives and reflections on existence. Here we strip away the surface elements of culture so we can gain a fuller perspective of what we have done or made of ourselves. When we take control of our personal attitudes, we put aside the influences of society. As such, we manage our own lives and search for our personal treasures and not those of the unscrupulous. We never completely win the battles for this earth.

When we resign the ways of the world to a Greater Purpose, the pressures, conflicts, resistance and fears of humankind will let go. Looking for solutions stirs the fire of debate. Fire by its own accord is not hot. Only when we get too close to it do we bring the heat on ourselves. Pushing the heat of the world away is a difficult task that we cannot master. Heat, the energy of life, of itself is of little moment. However, what we do with it makes it important. The secret of this new thinking is in how we think and how we see which enables us to influence everything that comes into our lives. Being in control governs how we will act upon or have an effect on somebody or something. When we let go of the world and give up control, we are removing its power over us. Truth of the Self is self-evident. Mirrored comments of others lead us to form pictures of what we think we are like. From this, we can form a more accurate picture when we discount the negative and emphasize the positive.

In this new moment, we can merge into an Infinite variety of positive thoughts, feelings and actions that establish self-responsibility in an independent Universal Essence that shapes the properties of our better nature. Out of our remaining time, this new thought stage could enhance life and our image of it within the vaster existence.

Whatever vanity we ascribe to the world, let it be!

## How We Travel In Space

As we live and move on the earth, we are also traveling in space, orbiting the sun. Even the stars and galaxies are traveling around and away from each other. On the human level, the value of experience is how we travel. The knowledge and wisdom we gather from other persons, places and things are stored in our consciousness. Through countless generations of experiences, Consciousness has created a double and memory reflects that duality; it moves parallel to the physical body in a separate world of remembrance.

These two worlds of thought are merely points on the long continuum of Consciousness that originates inward. Through the Inner senses, we evaluate our stored experiences. Gathered experiences form our multidimensional existences that are the result of education or self-discovery. These aims, qualities, or aspects survive and belong to the Inner self, and we utilize them whether or not we are in a body of flesh. When we sum up life, its surroundings and our place in it, it is not difficult for an open-minded person to realize the visible exists because of the conscious knowledge of it, that Consciousness is merely a series of awakenings.

Awareness is due to the activities performed in the waking state. Whatever we are aware of, awareness occurs because of our thinking and doing in relation to persons, places, or things. It took many centuries of thinking and fashioning so that humans could invent the wheel to produce a cart, a wagon, a train, an automobile and air travel. As a result, we have physical transportation to travel around on earth and in space. However, none of these modes could have come about without contemplation. First, we imagine traveling in the mind. Whether the goal is just down the road or the far reaches of space, we first visualize traveling in plans and then put them into objective realism.

Through intense meditation, or dreaming, we can induce ourselves to leave the form body. Concentrated practice done in waking life on a regular basis can lead to spontaneous experiences beyond the form life, and there one will be wakeful, alert and in control of that experience. While in that state, we can gather information that is vital to our continued existence in the continuum. This on-going existence is a link between two things, the formless and form, a continuous series of things that blend into each other so seamlessly that it is impossible to say where one becomes the next.

Controlled meditation and dreaming inspire awe and fascination for improving the world that we inhabit and for ourselves. The traveler that trains his or her mind and increases the ability to concentrate will be able to direct this energy toward a desired state of Consciousness or new form of knowledge. When we are in control of this awareness, it takes away the fear of mortality and gives us a more vivid picture of our place in the cosmos and a continued sense of being a part of the existences of our departed loved ones. Life is traveling, whether in the mind, on land, sea, or through the air and out into space. In wakefulness, in dreams, fantasies and creations our ship or means comes about only because of the journeys of those before us. Through those bygone travelers, we each have enhanced our experiences as to persons, places, and things.

How we travel in space is dependent on a beneficial link with the earth's resources and our intelligent appreciation of the Life of the Universe.

## The Loneliness of Knowing

Unless we are communicating or sharing our awareness with others, we are without companions; we are alone. Loneliness is inevitable at times in every person's life. If our physical, emotional and mental makeup is not balanced, loneliness can trigger certain medical conditions. Realistically, each life, from the nursery to the nursing home, faces complications regardless of our place in it.

The type of loneliness written about on this page is not of the relational type. Rather it is the knower coming face to face with the answers to one's own self-questioning. Answers lead to a personal truth or certainty of something that has not yet seeped into collective knowing in this subjective experience. It is in this place of knowing that the knower realizes that one person's tea may be another person's poison.

This state of aloneness is not a desolate place. More accurately, it disposes life to a definitive knowing that there are no solutions, only choices. As individuals, we have a choice whether we want to be lonely, and how many people we want to have in our lives. Whom we know does not fully define the character of our life. It is how we know that does define it. In the end, it is not only how we choose to relate to persons, places and things that are important, but also how we have come to see and know them as they are. All of us are in our own space of knowing and unless others invite us in to share it, we should not violate their space. If we grab a beautiful rose without seeing its entirety, the thorns on the stem will certainly prick us.

Gravity and time hold everything in space. The same is true in humanism. We love to discuss the idea of the supernatural, but loathe entering that still Singular place that houses it in us. There is a certain place along the path of loneliness where the magic of Solitude can energize us in ways the natural world is unable to do. While in that place, we have the foresight to know that all of us are traveling along two parallels: one harmony, the other discord. The choices we make, the influences of others, and the sources they use to sway our thinking and acting will determine the parallel on which we reside. For each of us the ways of earth hold similar and opposite knowing. Only by attaching ourselves to one or the other fully, can we witness the finality of the loneliness of knowing.

Through loneliness, we observe the secrets of Creation and its laws. Loneliness provides the space and mental clarity to see those Mysteries as true or false. We learn best when we use our body systems inwardly instead of learning from the outside alone. In this system of knowing, the chaotic activities of emotional and mental camaraderie are calmed and new thoughts and images of rightness arise. Thus, we recognize the True state of knowing, the Origin of our manifestation of things.

When we journey inward, the path never ends!

### In Memory's Light

Light is the recorder of life. From the first Light of awareness and through all the life waves of persons, places, and things from the past to the present, all actions, all thoughts are there remixing and animating life in an endless series of events and circumstances. We aspire to gain control over the existing conditions surrounding and affecting events or activities. However, we can determine the outcome only by the choices we make in forging our relations with the existing condition. Because we all live and move in this Light, we are susceptible to its influences as a participant or observer. Our conditioning paradigms, the patterns or models we have used to make choices, the words we form, the thoughts we ascribe to, our emotional, mental and physical well-being, all play a part in guiding our actions in confronting an event.

At the moment of choosing, most rely on an ethical framework, a set of ideas, principles and rules, authority, legitimacy, jurisdiction, etc., to substantiate the action. Nevertheless, what we perceive as just and right for the present can seem unconscionable in the future. When we take the plank out of our eyes and look at the events and circumstances of history, the amount of human suffering let loose by the accepted ethical systems, and the elusive concepts that favor the powerful and the aggressive, it is quite easy to see how the future will unfold.

Whatever is transpiring in our lives presently is because we did not pay full attention to our surroundings that constituted our past actions with persons, places and things. Through a penetrating self-examination of our beliefs and motives, a culture of continuous improvement can become ongoing in Consciousness. By constantly reviewing and improving the process of our past and present actions, we can undo the impacts of suffering and delete negative cause and effect in the ongoing memory of life.

When we step outside of the box, we are on the path of self-consciousness, a state of being aware of one's own being, actions and thought-form making. Electromagnetism is the power source behind Light and Life. Similarities attract in such a way that our mental, emotional and physical events become aspects of one substance called life. Light, Life, and memory constitute the stuff of the universe that ultimately we recall as consciousness. Objectivity is a truth that we discover, not create. When we realize the existence of something without reference to other's impressions or ideas, we are in a place where we can actualize correct mental cause and effect and thus see with clarity our true destiny.

In various ways, we are all searching for the Cause that produced our memory.

## The Inevitability of Life

No matter how hard we try, we cannot avoid or prevent what is to happen because the outcome will be the same. When we look at the patterns of life, what we see is repetition in motion. The seasons follow one another as wakefulness follows sleeping. Most of us go through our days doing pretty much the same thing. Whether we want to accept it or not, we are in the rhythms of nature. No matter what we do, we cannot escape nature's activity, its cycles of night and day and the repeated functions of the body. When the universe, Light, came into being as energy and force, a current state of motion was set in place with fixed immutable laws bound to a chain of two or more variable aspects: the observer and the observed. Even though our thoughts and actions make up the equation, we are each fated to do what is being done.

Free will and that which is certain to happen do not contradict one another. Nor does it diminish one's personal responsibilities. For example, if a person chooses to sit in a room and never leave it for a lifetime, that decision was the determined individual potential. Therefore, free-will and choice resulted in an action. Because the happening occurred, it was predestined in past time; otherwise, the event would not have occurred. The thought process of free-will and choice must have occurred at the beginning of life by inscriptions on atoms, the source of reflective light, and our conscious behavior. Regardless how we label, categorize, departmentalize or socialize achievements, they were the results of the laws of nature. A physical constant is both universal in nature and constant in time. For that reason, what life has set in motion cannot be deviated, only followed.

Intrinsically, we uncover the whole of physical life and its secrets in the pulsations of nature. We come out of it, and our bodies go back to it. The air we breathe contains the same molecules that originated in the First Cause: the Ultimate creative force behind the universe. Are our thoughts any different from the air we breathe? Without either, life would not be possible on earth. The originality of every person was in that moment of singularity. The relationship that exists within us and the very moment of existence make up our being; and every human being owes his/her existence and characteristics to that splitting instant. Encounters are the results of that happening. We cannot get away from the happening but, with the right attitude, we can make it work in our interests.

We cannot change the past or the way people choose to act, or the inevitable, but we can, with a right attitude, live better.

## *Reconstituting Our Makeup*

Bringing memory back into its Original state after it separates from form life is involuntary for most, similar to the functions of the physical body. We do not have to tell the organs of the body to do what they do. The body systems are highly interlinked in complicated ways most of which is beyond current understanding. There are three processes that collectively control the phenomena of human life, (1 unconscious: storage, (2 conscious: judger and (3 subconscious: the internal body manager. The first one is our basis for survival. The second counteracts our instinctive nature with morality. The third consists of an awareness of the world that is essential to the character that makes up the Spirit of the person. This three-fold process is separated by 'a space' or electromagnetic field that exists between the human form and the physical planet. Therefore, an object never makes physical contact with another object: human or otherwise. What we feel or perceive as touch is the electromagnetism of space, the essential stuff of life. When we develop a healthy character that matches reality of perception, we interact with realism and insights that accommodate instincts and desires.

Only through our creative and intuitive minds are we able to be fully conscious of our next creation. For that reason, we are adept at consciously drawing from our experiences, emotions and internal dialogue. Who we really are, and what is to follow when we are out of form, depends on the efforts applied to understanding the here and now. The more we self-analyze our worldly actions while in them, the more accurate the call back of persons, places and things. To move through the Universe of Life consciously we must shift our view from the involuntary state to a revitalized self-renewing state that includes both substance and psychic recall. The real universe is the electrical and magnetic Essence that exists as us.

The insight we gain from the self-analysis of beliefs and motives places us on the path of self-responsibility. Thus, this insight represents a new way of seeing the future with meaningful purpose. From the combined wisdom of memory, reflection and life force, we have the ability to overcome the profound separations that keep character and substance divided. We can awaken ourselves from a state of not knowing to being conscious that we know. With this in mind, at each moment we can recreate the living universe. Without us, there are no views or freestanding existence. Minute by minute we bring the phenomena of life at every level alive. The universe does not exist on its own, only through us does it have a certainty. As long as we are conscious of the universe, we connect to its predetermined growth, and our self-analysis leads us to decipher our reconstitution from our own makeup.

Our Inner nature, and the things we ascribe to by their importance or unimportance, should govern our personal lives.

## *Building a Better Life*

A better life is self-induced. We can have all the riches of life, luxury, fame, money, power, etc., but if we do not know ourselves and our place and importance in life, those treasures can become impediments to our equilibrium. The electrical currents that sustain our patterns of thinking become over-heated, disrupting the movement of electrons. This disruptive process can occur in both the individual and society. The body, the mind that thinks, the house we live in, the necessities that sustain us, animals, plants, even the planet we grew from and the star dust that it formed from, when viewed untainted, emanate our better nature. When we mishandle the currents of our thinking and action, it causes a disruption.

Consequently, in playing this game of self-interest we take steps toward that reality, which is ultimately the reality of ourselves. The earnestness that we display, the balance we maintain, whether in mind or on earth, shows our ability to play fairly in characterizing other persons and things. We imagine life to be germinating from our own unique experience instead of those derived from others. The outside nature is but a reflection of the Inner. When we free our minds of arrogance, which has been either self-induced or contaminated by the presumptions of society, we are beyond the horizon of human experience. We are in the Clarity of self-reason. The solidness of life dissolves in the Essence of our better nature and we are free from life's myths. Though we may still be in the world, its way does not confine us.

Eventually, the laws of life in time and space, economics, politics, morality and physical form dissolve. As we open our better nature, we do not recreate our past missteps, and we are open to the spontaneous impulse of Spirit to identify with something other than tangibility; we are back into the play of children. Such is the attitude that we must develop in bettering our existence, here or hereafter. Regardless of where we are, we must make the best of serving the present hour. All we need to do is assemble or reassemble what we are, and where we are going in our own art of living, then bring it to life as our own, not judging the humanity we are in but seeing humanity as a festival of passing forms.

When we are open to change, the more we will come to know about the Self and the social roles to which we have ascribed. Thus, we become comfortable and self-confident with our actions. The objective of self-knowing brings a sense of ease in balancing the vertical life (mind) with the horizontal life (form) within humanity and the Greater Existence toward which we are moving. Consequently, we cease wandering the halls of erroneous beliefs: looking here and there, desiring and seeking, expecting happiness from circumstances. As we build a better life, let us engrave on our hearts and minds a friendly and thoughtful disposition toward everyone and everything. In all occasions, in all matters of life, great or small, we can strive to meet everything appreciatively and there dissolve our troublesome imaginings.

In building a better Inner life, we come to know that everything is Pure Essence.

## Words of Silence

Words spoken or written tell the story of the needs, well-being, interests and dichotomies that give meaning to the world and human life. Words evolved out of physical perceptions and a need to convey those observations. Words have a personality and appearance. The living experience creates and sustains those vocal and written sounds. The visual landscape of life gives form to words. Our inventions, heritage and history would be lost without words to keep their stories going. Nevertheless, from time to time it is necessary to enter the domain of Silence to understand the vocabulary of life. The elements of living change, they grow and evolve as do the meaning of words. Just as humans pass away and others retain their memories in the mind and in written form, words die out or they continue in idioms, causing them to lose their original meaning. Words give Consciousness a language to inquire into the nature of meaning. They seek to explain what it means to mean something, not only as an individual but also as a collective entity.

When we look at life impartially, we can see that it is still an incomplete sentence. The intricacies of nature are veiled. We have yet to experience the better qualities of nature instead of those that are solely conventional. A disposition derived in Silence from the outside world will help us form words that replace our dislikes with affection and beauty.

Just as words are important in understanding nature, Silence is an integral part of human nature that enables each of us at moments to be expressive of real nature, not a representation, or simulation of some long past experience. We use Silence to complete ourselves. Therefore, Silence should precede every word we utter, making Silence a part of language. Meaningful words can draw us closer to one another, thereby transforming the misunderstandings we have created with our words. We do not express Silence; we experience it. Proverbially speaking, we should not speak unless we can improve the Silence. Stillness eventually wins over the noise and excitement of a persistent ego; thus, the individual self releases the chattering for the freedom of Solitude.

As the seasons of life pass, the rustle of words end and the need of Silence creeps into the veins, refining the mind's eye. The grandeur of nature comes into bloom in the Sanctity of the human heart. When the shadows of the sun's fire falls on the lush meadows and the loom of the wooded hills molds into the form of the turning earth, unfilled dreams awaken to all things. The firmament of Heaven brightens the stillness. Straining to grasp the whole, endless wafting colors fill the eye with magic, blend, and shift the Eternal harmony of the moving spheres. The vast ambitious arena of thoughts seeks to trace Eternity's face upon the infinity of space. The Maker of all things, knowledge and Truth, touch the great to the small, the wise to the unwise, the bright with the beautiful in order to know from what place the living come and where they go in the words of Silence. Thoughts are like light waves, they travel on and on.

We are our thoughts, and words make us who we are.

## *Life as a Practice*

Every action, from moving from the cradle onto the floor, to talking and interacting with others, requires repeated steps in order to improve our human performance. The more we concentrate on doing our best, the more clearly we see life. When we think outside of the proclamations stated to be for the good of society, we are looking beyond the customary to our own unique views of life through an open mind. Thus, whatever is in front us, good or bad, is personal to our own inclinations. When we practice life with profound honesty as to what we see, think and learn, we can become independent of authors, speakers and principles. Thus, we can clean up mental confusion that will enable others and ourselves to read reality clearly and accurately. Rational thought requires constant practice in order to smash institutional belief systems and political deception. No one is going to rescue us and make our lives great. We each have to free ourselves from the alluring and false notions that affront life from all corners.

Every day in our thoughts and actions, we must strive to improve our individualism, to avoid deception and to foster no illusion about the plain natural things of life that give us value. When we engage in practices that are in accord with nature and its laws, we can eliminate from our psyches the erroneous feelings that hinder happiness. Then our better qualities, that we have longingly cherished, will surface. As we touch our individuality, its inclusive nature will be present to our community and social setting. As long as we are aware, we will always be in kinship with our kind. When we practice the better qualities of our nature, we will not only enliven our personal well-being, but that of our environment too. Our perception of life will become wider and brighter with a sense of concern and happiness for other people. Because of our self-independence, we will become interdependent with all other sentient beings.

Our inner workings are so sophisticated that we often misread the hidden images that surface from time to time, creating false images that can limit our growth, even distorting our wakefulness. Whether awake or in sleep, our daily and nightly interactions with persons, places and things can have an effect on our psyche and cloud our judgments. We can undo our vulnerabilities when we learn to see that behind dark clouds the sun shines. By making that image a part of our daily life practice, negative life experiences will fade into positive ones. When we brace ourselves with optimism, our life process leads to a constant practice of betterment. We have inherited a set of learned tendencies. Undoing them can be difficult but not impossible. We can never attain everything but we can practice being better at it. To let life be motionless would be giving up on moving forward. To a progressive mind, there is only a following of revelations. If we truly seek to understand and profit from the practices of life we must realize that everyone is in some way or other doing the same. We can help light the way by being better in our relationships with others. To get a musical instrument to sound melodious, it takes everyday practice. The more mindful we are of character, the more we need to practice at being better. The more aware we are of life as a practice, the more harmonious our everyday experiences.

When we cause good things to happen, we like ourselves and the people and circumstances we face even better.

## *The Finality of Conflict*

Conflict involving humans has been around since the stone became a plant, the plant an animal, the animal a human and the human a reasoning, thinking entity. From all this differentiation in nature, we have warring parties. Perhaps when we reach our Higher side of Self-Consciousness and full knowledge, nature will cease to use force as a means for progression without human-induced violence.

Without conflict in nature, we would not have any birds, animals or human life. However, nature does not force human life to evolve as it does the lower kingdoms. There is a certain amount of voluntarism and choice in human action in giving up the old for the new. As we become more psychic, the lower aspect with its proclivity for conflict will give way to a higher state of reasoning. The sole purpose of nature on earth is to evolve the human. The sooner we involve ourselves, non-violently, in this process, the sooner we will discover our higher calling to aid humanity and all creatures in their progression to a Higher state.

When minds are of a strong moral constitution, and there is a will to succeed, the quality and conditions of our society could be so developed that conflict will no longer be a part of our impelling personality. Conceivably, the essential elements of group processes could tune to a singleness of purpose, ending the opposing feelings that have endured throughout the history of life. It is difficult to tell where and how life and conflict, so closely woven together, began. Some thinkers believe that life could not have evolved without disagreements or clashes between ideas, principles, or people, and without those conflicting struggles, the human brain would not have developed the survival inputs to move forward.

When we look at the character of the world, its persons, places and things, it is apparent that a combative personality has ruled our judgments. It is also believable that we are at a place in humanism where we can begin to use the power we are developing consciously, so that we no longer need sacrifice, conflict and struggle to secure our advancement. Conflict is an idea that originated in the mind. For conflict to begin or end, thinking has to be properly conditioned. There is credibility in believing that we can achieve better forms of interaction without conflict. The whole process of nature is atomic, molecular and cellular, and as long as there is a relationship with physicality, there will be involuntary struggle. However, since human conflict is self-induced, we can influence the will to overcome the dominance of conflict. Whatever the occasion, we have the power to make action and restraint, speech or silence, fit our progression without harming one another. When we know how to do the right thing, at the right time and place, and in the right way, we possess real power. Without will, power, judgment and self-restraint we are not acting wisely and efficiently in our behavior with others. The secret for eliminating conflict is in self-discipline; it enhances knowledge, widens intelligence, quickens perception and above all else, strengthens the will to avoid being hurtful.

The duty of another may be full of danger, therefore be mindful of your own.

## The End Justifies the Means

What are we striving for as conscious beings? Is it to achieve a better life of equality for all and a sustainable productive life for the world and ourselves? Is it a progressive determination to unlock the secrets of the laws of the universe? No doubt, these are grand visionary goals. However, if we are to get close to these aims we are going to need to merge the ideal with the real in our approaches in time, place and circumstance. We must develop a conscious awareness that future generations need to have a healthy and safe environment to be productive. For the economy to remain prosperous, society must think in co-operative terms based on democracy, openness and participation so that we can restore the biological diversities and ecosystems to ensure a dynamic society. Furthermore, we must create and promote all renewable matter everywhere. For insurance, observers should form a neutral committee, free of political persuasion, to make moral judgments to ensure such standards. These observers should be skilled at grasping the consequences of any action as could reasonably be expected. Their paradigm should be that right action is the action that will bring about the best consequences for future generations. A more knowledgeable society is better able to bring about the reality that what is good for all ensures a better life for the individual. There are two ways of gaining sufficient and reliable information as we observe the happenings within our social settings: 1) reflection on events and 2) intuition that bolts into the mind. For humanism, the mind is the mover of progressive development. Whatever the conditions of the present, we ourselves were the makers through our conduct of the past, and what is ahead largely depends on what we do now in the time and place of our awareness.

The power of living in the present requires observation and concentration. When we attune to the simplicity of our surroundings, and let go of our excess indulgences, we are in touch with the cyclic functions of our bodies and understand the subtle meanings of other persons, places, and things that permeate space. Through introspection of our thoughts and actions, we can connect to our own nature: our own Book of Life. We can only appreciate in others what we know about ourselves. All emotions and ideas that are in others are just revived memories of experiences which are also our own. The deeper we have tested the experiences of others and ourselves, the more responsive we are toward what is happening to other people. Another attribute of living is the ability to accommodate ourselves to involuntary change. Often, fear of what others will think of change and how it will affect circumstances accompanies our security. When we give up our fears, we embrace our true reality: happiness. It is unwise to think of a troubled future, for all we are doing is painting a troubled picture of ourselves.

When we are diligent about our present actions, immediate obligations, and responsibilities, we create a happier and more secure future.

## *Experience Powers Awareness*

Understanding what we encounter, whether it is imaginary as dreams or real, strengthens consciousness and gives us a sense of control in shaping our destiny. We often think the more we have and know, the greater our affluence and influence in the social setting. Quantity can diminish the value of quality thus numbing the appreciation for the experience. When life becomes hectic and crowded, the mind lacks space in which to reflect. Then we go through a sorting out phase much as we do when we remove the worn out items from our home. When it is all gone, and we are grateful for the space, we should be mindful of grasping for too much. Therefore, when we change our perception of experience from quantity to quality we will have a deeper understanding of the happening. As we get older, most of us think about the experiences that gave us pleasure and happiness delegating the unpleasant ones to the unconscious. We are only frustrating our truth of the self when we fill our needs with experiences that we choose to forget about later. It is far better to expose ourselves to events and people that increase and align our thoughts and feelings of the past with our future while in the moment. Persons, places and things do not fill us with joy or sadness; we fill them. It is our sole responsibility to discover our own reality and not that of others. If we have an enemy or friend, we have none other to blame or praise but ourselves. When we recognize the Inner self as our true realism, experience becomes our friend and not our enemy. We are constantly labeling outside experiences, but they are meaningless until we bring them inside and color them with our own descriptions; the inner life is always matching the recorded outer one. When we are in the moment, we do not immediately push away inappropriate thoughts and actions without discriminating. When we separate the positive from the negative thoughts, we are improving the consequences of our future acts.

From birth until the present, we have gathered two kinds of experience, one type that is temporary and made of matter (persons, places and things) and the other is the Permanency of memory and Spirit. The temporary relates to time, space and the past. Memory and mind are made of Spirit Essence. This type of experience is 'sustentative dualism' in which the physical body and Spiritual body, mind/memory develop together and stay together. The only difference is the physical body deteriorates, gets old and passes away, while the mind remains young forever. At death, the conscious mind awakens in the Spiritual body. From here, the events in the mental environment that are outside of time and space connect to the mental senses. Thus, existence continues.

In the physical environment life is a combination of good and bad experiences derived from our personal interpretation of things. From our language and labels, we form meaning from the props and backdrops of our living. The thinking mind (Spirit) and the physical body must act conjointly like couples who love and breathe the same essence. Physical life gives us an impetus to modify our behavior so that we can see the reality of what we are thinking about before we act. For that reason, thinking is a reaction to what we want; it helps us reach a state of higher desire. When we color our experiences with Love, our lives become better physically and our future becomes spiritually brighter. Therefore, while we are experiencing the dualities of life, it is important that we analyze our misunderstood acts along with our positive ones: both power our awareness.

First, there is the experience, followed by the effects of that gathering.

## The Silence of Solitude

The reclusive element in the life of a person is a place of Sacredness that stands alone in the gatherings that constitute a new form of awareness. This part of one's makeup is an identifiable portion of a distinct group within a larger group. It is kindred in nature and may or may not be synchronistic in the same time. Concerning human consciousness, formless awareness, and the overcoming of the ego, there are two parts of the human experience which offer an outside and an inside understanding to one's place in the creative story.

In this sacredness of Inner aloofness, the Soul is indifferent to the complexities of material life, and the personality determines the importance of foibles, addictions, cravings. In order to understand how the personality and Soul differ, it is important to comprehend how solitude enables one to concentrate on character, its approaches to Essence and the makeup of the circumstances it encounters. The conditions of physical life can never be equal and the laws of reciprocity govern it. Only a certain number of beings at any one particular time are on the path of Contemplative Solitude that is non-affiliated physically.

We are in the habit of practicing life so intently that we stamp a part of it on others, often with good intentions. Nevertheless, in some life chapter we will have to deal with those intentions. In busyness, the personality acts like a feeding machine in identifying with persons, places, and things. Eremitism is an opportunity to think optimistically about what has come up in life thus closing the traps of the ego; it guides the reality of human life away from the hazy world of doubt and wild fantasies.

In Contemplative Solitude, one redeems the secrets of the days and nights and suppressed memories in spite of their negative qualities. In the thoughts of Silence, one learns the words of individual truths through the experience of the mind and its dreams. Here the thoughts of the Soul ebb and flow like the murmuring of the sea and the treasures of the Infinite spring up for the eyes to see. Self-knowledge is as uncontainable as the wind.

In solitude, we can become more intimate with the now by being fully in the present with what is. When we are in this state, we become aware not only of what is in our own ego, but also in secret, what is in another's ego. The process of sense gives materiality a personality purpose so that it can create for itself and others. Acts stemming from individual convenience drive human perceptions.

We overcome our lesser natures by confronting the concepts of the ego. This helps us improve human consciousness and gives us a greater purpose in the human experience.

# International Thinking

International thinking is a holistic language that is sensitive to the standards of sovereign communities that instills a deeper sense of society. Its standard discourse is one that prescribes permissible forms of behavior through example rather than dominance. International thinking is a shaping of words that brings about shared values that each community can achieve. To understand the dynamics of any country, a common language must be spoken that will produce activity and change in any relationship of power that exists between people and groups. The purpose of such communication is to extract a sense of positivism in relation to physical happenings and events.

As a living force, this concept of thinking has the possibility of becoming a direct line for the development of humankind in every department of human living. It is widely believed, scientifically, that 'all is energy' in varying states and relationships. Therefore, thinking must be the force behind the universe; otherwise, there would be no awareness or memory of things, past, and present. What is yet to come is but an offshoot of our responses to thinking. The sum total of energy in the universe is constant, as is the nature of thought (existence). The only difference is that we can alter the path of thinking. Like air currents, thoughts are vital and have a force of their own. However, we are unable to control the flow of air yet, but we do have the capacity to control our thoughts and actions. Both of these streams are vital to human life, are co-dependent, and are fundamental in creating new ideas and things.

Through assessment, correct international thinking clarifies thoughts and developments before one institutes projects. Before we communicate with persons and groups, we should achieve a calm concentrated awareness in forming a theme of action. Innovative thinking requires a stable emotional consciousness in order to achieve stable physical conditions. For international relations to be unifying, it requires a purity of motive, not as a council of 'my way', but one of Selfless service in uplifting the human family. There are many ways of thinking through a relationship with another national family so it can develop and clarify its place in the world. We start by looking behind the appearances and by searching for meaning and significance of other streams of thought in order to look for causes, not at effects. The wrongful use of power and influence is the basis for historical anxieties and their effects that often continue. With the right inspiration, those acts can become reflective instead of combative.

The thoughts essential for nation building are similar to building a home. We must be aware of the materials we use, and we must design a beautiful, practical, economic and a 'good-to-live-in' house. International thinking takes in mind similar factors in its communicative skills. The right use of mind in its application of resources does not belong to any one particular nation but to the world of nations. Nature and humans in their sum total are holistic; most humans are not aware of it yet. For the air to circulate, the water to flow and the green things of the earth to grow, nature remains inclusive in its form building. Should not the process be the same for nations? As time flows, the themes will differ as well as points of view, but the means is in inclusive human thinking.

We are all living blossoms born by the human tree.

## *The Kernel: Self-Mastery*

The most essential part of life is awareness. Everything that we notice or realize gives shape and purpose to our being. This predominant Consciousness is the core of our sentient being. It diffuses our existence throughout creation and colors our Spirit with its fragrance. The circumstances that we find ourselves in are there because they have always existed within as a repetition of time and a repetition of fact. When we choose to be awake, away from the conditioning of others, we are in the kernel: the centrality of our own prominence. We know how to do the right thing in time and place and in the right way. Through will, power, judgment and self-restraint we call into view the productive use of our Inner essence. Every day and in every way, we must strive to go beyond the everyday customaries. We must break the patterns that contrive to mask our real outer world. The reality of nature endows us with physical form; this is the first rung on the set of steps that will take us beyond physical appearance. We cannot measure the unfolding of the Self in length and time. Self-mastery does not kill feeling, sentiment, and emotion to a preferred intellectuality. We can be pleased without a release of pent-up emotions. We can appreciate the subtleties of life without a frenzy to devour them. Self-mastery teaches us how to appreciate the appetites of the form without using others. It also teaches that there is no difference between Perfect and the imperfect because the One life, the One intelligence, and One love are present throughout everything. Discernment is the secret of power.

We can never control Consciousness by brutish force: only right action can do that. Each of us, alone, must traverse the foibles of our less-restrained natures. As long as we are in form, we remain connected to the magnetic swaying power of materiality. Only by continually striving to self-reflect on our better side will we arrive at the place where right action leads us to a place dominated by moral sensibility. We are acting wisely when we choose to become better in all circumstances, not only with our own acts, but also in the acts of others with whom we share responsibility. Independent Essentialism (our ideal nature) is uniquely within each of us. How we use it determines the state of conscience we use in dealing with life matters. We are truly ethical when we follow the ideals that aid all life in a non-threatening way. All things have an Essence that reflects in Infinity as mind, the instrument of the self, which acts as a unifying agent in things perceived. 'Isolated Unity' is the stuff of the Self, not that of the mind, and we weave it through silent discrimination. Consciousness and its identifying nature assume many hidden qualities, but only those that are the result of reflection are free of impulses. When we use our senses discriminately, we are using experience wisely. We discover what we require, thereby becoming more aware of our relationship to Essence. Thinking is in tune with this Source and is either active or passive. The thinker and Essence, the causes that conceive both passive and active thought, remain alone in the awareness of each.

There is a core to everything and to know the truth behind it we must break the shell that contains it. To know the reality of life's nature we must transcend the appearance. Thus, the farther away we are from appearances the closer is the Essence.

## The Nature of Material Power

The definition of power stems from the nature of the consciousness wielding it. Power discourages someone from taking an action or prevents something from happening. There is the power of love and hate of the family, community and state. There is the prowess of physical strength and the heightened powers of discrimination and mental qualities. Power has a beginning and an ending in awareness; it cannot stand-alone. It originates in the mind and is controlled, manipulated and used for ill or good by the person or persons using it. The use of power is altruistic when it is selfless. When it is egotistical and self-serving, power is malicious and causes harm and unwanted death. Humanism is standing on the precipice of progression or relapse. As humans, we have reached a crucial point in our development, a time of immense challenges and personal development in wisdom, skillfulness and service in the use of power. Yet, we still cannot absolve ourselves from the misuse and abuses of power, especially by those in positions of trust; this is distorted power. What is there in human nature that causes a person who has gained power to use it against others? We can attribute this cause to like-minded contemporaries who have shared interests and attitudes that are not commensurate with the general population.

In order for power to be insightful, we must view its attributes as simple, not complex. The fabric of time, space and causality at its core is not complex but the human mind has made it seem that way. This foundation of Essence (time, space, causality) is the stuff of all of us. When we see our totality in this manner, we will start using trust wisely and we will use power to heal and promote well-being. When we get rid of unsavory living conditions so that everyone everywhere can live a healthy and secure life free of want, we are using power correctly. Our learned and inherited practices will be complimentary. We will be acting sensitively, creatively, and effectively for others and ourselves. One lifetime of such interests will lead to another one, on and on. Pressure and control are counterproductive to skill and wisdom. We increase our skillfulness when we use simplicity in dealing with the power of material nature. With all of our complexity, we like to think that one day we will bend the will of nature to meet our own; nothing can be further from the truth. We can use our skills to understand nature. Like a free spirit, one can only manipulate it so far until it flies away. However, if we strive to make each person free and well, we will no longer use power for destructive purpose, natural or human.

Humanism derives its power from mechanical causation and the work of nature. Psychological modifications of creativity, preservation and destructive processes constantly modify nations, races, and cultures. How we act toward one another determines the severity of the psychosomatics in persons. The history of power exposes the foibles of human nature and its inability to coincide with the concept of Universality.

A person-oriented society is better equipped to handle the issues of the social order then a thing-oriented humanity. It is the only way to eliminate racism, the misuse of materialism, and militarism.

## The History of Images

It is the individual's duty to create from the Self (energy and force) a better person. Images ascribed by others, whether they are from the past, in the present, or imagined futuristically, give us the means to accomplish what we have to do regardless of the intentions of the shapers. Good images stimulate our visual sense to produce a high quality or standard of behavior in relation to others. The bad images have the potential to produce unfriendliness, blurring and intermingling identification with reality in the use of space. In the terms of energy and force, do images survive after the demise of the observer? Images survive in hieroglyphics and in print and audiovisual recording processes. However, do they remain as the elements of the earth and space remain? It is probable that thoughts and visions created in the mind remain in some dynamic field beyond the spectrum of visual acuity and that sometime in the future the laws that govern such wisdom may open. Until that day arrives these mental images are individualistic, and another person may or may not view them. Yet, it is not a collective insight. We have the potential to develop a non-discriminatory nature that will allow us to peer in the vastness of another person's psyche. However, presently, human nature is too self-centered and untrustworthy to access such laws. Our assumptions rule us.

Everything that is above and below us in nature is under cyclic law in which the shadows of darkness and light appear in the history of the mind. Because of this law, images appear and disappear for a time, only to reappear again as surely as the sun rises and the human mind is present to see. The body is just a physical instrument drawn from the earth by our Inner Power. The elements of the earth pass through and give form to our physical bodies. Our thoughts and images come into being from the indestructible center of our humanism, the intangible Consciousness that is our most precious possession. Inner Awareness forms through the powers of nature, enlarging a vision that eventually becomes non-dualistic.

Thus, our narrow mindedness and fears evaporate. Our visions open to everything that is in the universe giving us the capacity to concentrate our energies on the task that is before us. As this strength passes through each of us, it eventually makes its way into others giving them confidence to analyze their weaknesses and strengths.

We live inside an enormous mind formed from the specific and vague ideas of ourselves. When all these aspects composed from our thoughts surface, by either our own will or others, we are amazed at the thought of what we have said and done through those aspects. We are always coming back to the point from which we started. By preparing ourselves for the revisit, we can change our previous actions so that they no longer prevent us from doing our best. No matter what the condition, we have to break away from the fictions to get to our Higher truths.

Presently, the advertising imagery of consumerism sways us. Our minds have become enormous video screens, inventions of reality seen as the objective world.

## *Initiatory Consciousness*

The development of complete freedom is a long, ongoing process that only the person who desires this state of freedom can initiate. Laws, events, circumstances and time govern this course of action. Only when a person transforms his/her Consciousness can there be a beginning. As this transformation occurs, a sense of an Inner reality becomes stronger than that of an outer reality. In the context of growth, the whole life process is constantly going through varying degrees of change. Life is ensuing from the lower to the higher; choice and free will mitigate the how and when this will occur. The initiator draws the initiate into the power and state of the initiator's consciousness. The initiator then transfers that power to the initiate. This process is similar to birth or death. The only difference is that in material life the learner starts out unaware and is subject to the confinement of matter. Whereas, the initiate is fully mature in another reality and is aware of the initiator's teachings regarding the tasks ahead.

Generated by Spiritual heat and Light, the thought processes of an initiate are vastly different from this point on. The Spiritual Sun now governs intuition instead of the earthly sun. The earthly sun stimulates duality and experiences that one gains by opposites. However, once the initiation path starts, the constant influx of heat and Light stimulate rational thinking, feeling and happiness from affection. Unconditional Love is the result of the heat of Spirituality and Truth is a condition of Light. Only through abstract thinking, can the rational substance streaming from a Sun enter a mind and bring clarity to truth and Love. Thus, the whole process of initiation by degree is important and enduring, whether it is through the progression of matter or Spirit.

When we look at the development of human life and actions, we see a history of desire and impulsive behavior. Because of these traits, there are very few higher Universal initiates on the material plane. As long as this state of craving has not gone beyond the material world and its circumstance remains, there can be no higher initiation. An initiate is in the world, not of it. A seeker thinking this way promotes the goal of initiation. However, until we are conscious in the light worlds as we are conscious on this earth world, we can never be fully conscious of the initiatory processes! In the initiatory worlds, there are no inconsistencies and differences like here on earth. The lower universe evolves through imperfections. The Higher universe evolves through Perfection. Yet, without these two universes, there would be no sense of freedom as we move into the Greater expanse. Humans in nature advance mostly unaware of their Divine surroundings, but in the initiatory stages there is complete knowing. Freedom and love are not reactions to a desire of a person, place or thing, or a desire for anything in return. Freedom and Love are responses to the whole of life, not any one particular part. When we have defeated our worries, won over hate through Love, mastered poverty or wealth by not being a slave to either, and are at Peace in the midst of turmoil, we have mastered the world of sense and matter; we no longer need to attain by degree an initiatory consciousness because we are in that realm of Light.

Initiatory consciousness is a state of being wide-awake and aware in the present without a need for the deductive reasoning of the past.

## Earthly Humanism

What wonders we would hear if the earth could speak to us! The stories it could tell about the persons, places and things it has witnessed, the billions of animals, insects and human faces that make up its memory. All have existed by fashioning their images from the earth's elements. Woodlands, prairies, mountains, hills and waterways adorn its face of life. Any human who is conscious of Consciousness cannot help but believe the earth lives and breathes as we do. Without it moving under our feet, we would be stationery. Because of this changing sphere, we have come to know that this earthly experience is characteristic of organisms that exhibit certain biological processes such as chemical reactions or other events that result in a transformation. Both the earth and its inhabitants undergo metabolism by growing and responding to stimuli. The earth provides the nutrients, and humans reproduce through natural selection thus adapting to the environment in successive generations. Currently, there is no concrete collective proof of extraterrestrial life other than that of stardust and what lives in the imagination.

As a cellular entity, life is still an ongoing process since there is no universal definition of it. In this complex human/earth existence, can one continue without the other? Is Consciousness mute and void without the memories of the earth experience? Earth is our birthplace and where we go after our life breath has ended is a belief and a mystery. However, rationality can speak if we are open to it, especially in terms of mind/memory as an environment for change inside living things, perhaps in such a way that promotes continuation. As an example, when we are asleep and dreaming coherently, it is as if we are unaware of this plane. It is only when we awaken that we are in this reality.

If there is life elsewhere in the universe, in either the now or the hereafter, it will be because we have drawn it out of the universe as we have pulled life from the earth. Time, place, person and event relate symbiotically to life, earth, and the universe! This physical world and its humanism is the central force behind our beliefs. It will continue to inhabit different people and their interpretations regarding values and thinking. Human beings perform activities that fit their needs and wants. As long as those desires remain balanced through right thinking, humanism will fulfill its proper work, to live and act well according to reason. When we think of earthly humanism, we should think of that concept from an abstract point of view while in the body. For while we are here humanism is all we have. The Inner Self is fashioned from earthly humanism, the moral soundness to which most of us ascribe. That part of us advises when we become arrogant, awakens when we sleep, and guards when trouble comes. Does the earth act any differently in its patterns of living and moving?

We start life in a vague way. As we move forward in our labors, we fit ourselves to life according to our depth of clarity in understanding it.

## Cleansing Life's Atmosphere

We are three-dimensional beings manifesting in a universe that reveals itself in patterns: relationships that exhibit duality repeating through cyclic activity. Because of the excessive pursuit of material pleasure there is a corresponding pain complex created. The pursuer(s) keep repeating their pursuits and the pain of their actions forces them to realize when they have had enough. These patterns create a continual stress not only on human life, but also on the life chain of the earth. At any given time, influence surrounds all of us. There is more negative pressure on us than there is positive in our mental atmosphere. Properly or improperly, these mental vibrations shape and have an effect on the direction in which we shape our characters. It is up to each of us to rise to our own mental keynote that will remove us from the negative plane of thinking. Only our positive thoughts can take us to the upper chambers of our better natures where we can make ourselves over. We must think discriminately and not allow the adversity of others to overtake us.

Everything on earth (mineral, plant, animal life and humans) curve back over themselves through interacting responses or cycles. Even our human activities, overpopulation, over-consumption, deforestation, fossil fuel burning, etc., are the results of our thought processes that affect our everyday atmosphere. On a global scale, these physical processes are affecting the elements between organisms and their surroundings that determine the earth's climate. Chemical or electrical atmospheric processes are biochemically related to all life and can be orderly or disorderly to the systems that serve humanity. In order for a self-cleansing stable environment to remain sustainable, we must protect these systems from the harmful ways of an over-consuming society.

When we look at our environment, including our climate, we also need to look at the mental processes of humanism. The transport and transformation of substances in the environment, the air, the land, sea, waterways, the soil and the rays of the sun are equally important to earth just as the systems of the body are important to us. Collectively we are co-dependent. The nutrients we take into our bodies circulate giving vitality to our brain cells that in turn fuels our thinking. Life and the earth both depend on atmospheric circulation. The survival and health of both human beings and the earth depend on a stable climatic state. When we are positive in regulating our material uses, our life influences impregnate the atmosphere that surrounds earth. Those positive thoughts reflect back for the use of future generations. Managing and finding solutions to humanity's many problems begin with the understanding of our thoughts. How we allow others to persuade our thinking and acting are factors that each of us must look at independently. We must cleanse these toxic thoughts on a personal level and then collectively. Toxic thoughts are human made and are as much a threat to the chain of life as are the manmade compounds, pesticides and other harmful chemicals. To rediscover life's balance and harmony a detailed examination of one's feelings, thoughts and motives are required.

The landscape of nature and human thinking are constantly changing. The light and air vary in degree and give the surrounding atmosphere its value.

## *Automatic Motion*

Does the human being have an ultimate purpose, or is life merely a play of sorts where each moment, each day and each life bleed into one another? Most of the knowledge we ascribe to, whether it is religion, evolution, or revolution, seems to be a day-to-day pursuit. Belief, faith and hope are attributes toward which we work. The lofty concepts of religion and science, ideology, technology and other systems of thought and performance are the basis of our past and present knowledge. We can never get a clear picture as to whether tomorrow will be a certainty. It seems we are ensnaring ourselves with over expectations of something outside of ourselves. When our immorality toward matter and its wasteful uses cloud our better nature, we can never sense the Truth of our core. Once we start controlling matter ethically, we will be putting human Consciousness first. The act of changing place in time and circumstance will be similar to the automatic workings of a healthy body whose systems are perfectly balanced and regulated by the forces acting on the body that give it motion, the earth. Until life is consciously aware, equal in magnitude, it will have an action-reaction cycle of uncertainty. Presently embodiment is the result of material fixation and is limited to the confines of matter that are fixed in its application of thinking and doing in the immediate environment. Our thoughts and actions will be in perfect balance when our behavior has a common thread with all persons, places and things.

At any moment in time and place, we are where our attention is. We are awake, dreaming, asleep, or unconscious. We can only be operating in one space at a time. It is possible to be aware of other places, but never experiencing them simultaneously. All of these levels represent our evolving selves. Because of matter, we seem powerless to obey our higher yearnings. These longings for something only accentuate the doubts, fears about life, thus creating insecurity, inadequacy, and the inability to think discriminately. We should never yearn for anything. Rather, instead we should learn to appreciate the world of senses not by force, but by understanding. Until we are free of the world, our needs and desires drive us forward. When we surrender to our physical, emotional and mental states, nonviolently and compassionately, Consciousness, as a condition of the Self, will reduce emotional identification. This will enable us to witness the whole of our origin with detachment from a point above matter.

When we are in the mode of disunity with persons, places, or things, the effects of that lack cloud and fog our perception with disorienting visions and images. When a cleansing takes place, we diminish the causes and effects of those deficiencies in ways only known to the Self. As we work more and more with our better natures, our past trivialities in the physical world will fade away. When one must appear in matter again, he/she will come as a new person: an intrinsic memory of all persons, places and things.

As human beings, we are a part of the whole that is the universe. When we are away from the past, time and space does not limit us. When Compassion embraces the whole of nature, our thoughts and feelings are not something separate from the rest, they are in unison with all that is.

## Natural Transparency

When light shines through it, space is the film, or transparency, through which we can view objects and even thoughts. The visual cortex is the part of the brain that is responsible for processing visual stimuli. The mind is the projector for what is being observed in light and the brain processes image information from the eyes. It is through the five senses, the sixth being mind, that humans participate and enjoy the profound nature of the earth and its many forms. It is through a physical body, made of elements, light/energy, force/matter, darkness and Light that nature unfolds in us. Light, the reflective state of matter, is the open window that allows consciousness to peer into creation's vast arena of persons, places and things and to record the past, present and future. Once the mind is fully open, nothing is ever lost. From this vantage point, we can rework the past with the present, thus improving our future.

This form we call home, the earth and our physical bodies, is the same. However, because of our detachment from the earth's more subtle nature, we connect more closely to our minds and bodies than to the earth. Nevertheless, on finer levels they are the same. What passes through earth passes through us and what passes through us passes back into the earth and the greater universe!

Our ignorance and misconceptions, a curved line mentality (inertia about energy, force and motion) keep other directional forces from acting on us. Thus, we are constantly in a feedback loop. We replay events and circumstances repeatedly until we realize a Greater Purpose. These repetitions pass through individuality then culminate in collectivism. Whether in families, nations or from a worldview, Consciousness passes through animalism into humanism that eventually moves past those venues into Spiritualism, or Clarity.

Natural transparency (spiritualism or clarity) enables one to make use of energy and its many energy systems to create a body of energy that is independent of physical existence. Consciousness is not lost; but transfers into a new body of energy allowing Consciousness to act on other planes of reality vastly different from the objective. Here Consciousness utilizes extra knowledge, resources and strengths that others commonly consider supernatural. This naturalness happens when we let go of erroneous perception and fakery of other persons and things that do not work in conjunction with our own needs and wants. As long as we employ neutrality and honesty in choice making, clarity of thought will grow and newer perceptions, so far unknown, will be apparent. It is difficult to understand the complex thought process that governs the concept of time as to where we go, how we will be, and who will be with us. Nevertheless, there is a 'here' and a 'now' that shapes and guides every person as to what his past, present and future will be and that real time runs parallel to each of us as 'energy wakefulness'. However, somewhere we allowed a scission to occur and it is difficult now to understand the differences between dreaming and wakefulness. Early human life was lived spontaneously and intimately. Every person had a body of energy whole and awakened that allowed unimpeded travel between planes of reality. In material concrete life it is difficult to maintain a clear body of Consciousness because its 'existence state' forms from specific characteristics that distinguish one person or thing from another.

In this material techno-contemporary state, Consciousness has lost the capacity to use its transparent body of energy in observing creation.

## The Flow of Life, Space and Causation

The ceaseless flow of life is Limitless in experience and is independent of the world. This stream is unbroken, transcendent and eminent if we choose to see past our everyday wishes and wants. The life we have here and the life that is there lies in the vastness of the universe. Distance and separation express this Universal Intelligence. This flow of life did not appear as one simultaneous event in the universe. Matter did not come apart and then reform itself. The events formed in the mind by scientists regarding the formation of planets and other objects started out being hypothetical. Those configurations came into being when mind started forming distances between objects. Only from ideals and the intellect does the universe have movement. When a star fades out in the universe, or a planet no longer holds life, it means that idea is no longer a part of conscious memory. Through mental observation, the human intellect cannot separate from the Cosmic intellect. When we think in terms of terrestrial intelligence, Solar Intelligence functions in human life. The objects and conditions around us have not always been familiar. They only became familiar when someone reflected on them, thus allowing others to do the same as those observations moved forward.

Ideas can remain dormant for centuries and be incomprehensible to most humans. However, once set in motion it is certain that an idea will eventually activate. Only when an ideal has become a certainty to most of humanity does it become a clear truth. As humanity becomes more intelligent within its star system, it will automatically extend itself into other adjoining star systems. As human intelligence becomes more abstract in its knowledge and information, it will be better able to understand and communicate with other intelligent beings that exist in other systems. We can only travel within our own intelligence. There is no beginning or end, oldest or newer, in which each section of the intelligence of the universe appears. Only knowledge and intelligence are moving in the universe. As we separate from one outlived idea, we move into an enhanced and better one. Whatever exists in the farthest reaches of space or in the far-away future is the same as it was in its first instance. The only difference is that events, effects and time transferred the stellar information to matter. Stars are always becoming something else, life is always becoming fuller, and the mind is always expanding which is how we explore.

When we realize that everything in the universe is in the mind and that all is contained in the flow of life, we can sense the wheel of space/time/causation and start looking at the apparent reality that is around us. Only in the workings of the mind do we have the ability to peer into the solar and higher minds above. Through this process as observers, we start perceiving our own place or reality in Infinite mind. We must constantly reinforce our minds to accept that the reality we see around us is sense related and is therefore not consistent with real reality: the Inward-going journey. When we start realizing the reality of the Self, we can begin the blending of Immortality with physical life and then mirror that reality as identity. We are in the Infinite flow. Once we have made contact with this circle, no matter where our place is, we will be making a conscious contribution to Cosmic life. We will have witnessed our own ring of Truth.

We are a moving universe in an endless stream of moving universes.

# The Beginning

What was our starting point? Are time and space necessities for something or someone's existence? Did 'nothing' have to exist before 'something' existed? Awareness forms existence. From this wakefulness, we have knowledge of something either from conversing about it, or through direct observation that should be sufficient for our existence. With that said, is our momentary existence a prelude to something longer and more important than now? The only examples we have about the continuation of existence are in daydreaming and sleep dreaming. Since both are individualistic in nature, we can substantiate neither as anything real, other than by the one dreaming.

We know life ends when we observe the death of another person. However, that is only an observation for those left behind. There is no way for us to ascertain with certainty if there is an existence for the departed, other than in our belief–imagination paradigm. An existence is only relative to the one that is doing the observing. Do recorded history and its artifacts reveal any secrets as to the origin of a starting point? Some believe the source for those events has always existed in the flow of now and we only remember them because we are a part of the material universe that presently is the source for our being awake. Realistically, the events and circumstances regarding earth, time, and space lock us in this wakeful existence. If there is an existence of an eternal, uncaused, indestructible, and incorruptible Essence that is necessary for our continuation, it can only reside in awareness as a state of observation. Because we are awake, the universe and everything that has been or will be is just there, and that is all there is. Life as we see it now is a collection of successive actions, a series of past events encapsulated in the present, all because this is where we are. Therefore, each of us has a cause in whatever existence we find ourselves. Each of us is here because of successive past actions of male/female sexual unions. Just because we are born here, and pass away does not provide any proof that we are always cognizant of this present existence. However, being in the now gives us an infinite possibility of reflecting on what was and what will be.

When we think and observe rationally, the present moment and all its histories give rise to this time and place. Therefore, we can only surmise that our field of existence is finite in the past and had a beginning. Because we cannot return to that beginning from this level, it becomes speculation as to its cause. In terms of life or awareness, the beginning of being makes no difference because, other than recognizing ourselves as a part of it, there is no way to traverse this imaginable field.

Nevertheless, starting points create all sorts of imaginative thinkers. We all began in a state of Infinite density. In that intensity space and time came into being with the matter in the universe. What was before is meaningless because we are its entirety. We are not isolated in space because we are in it everywhere. Matter is dark energy and makes up most of space. It is our life, which unfolds its Invisible light. As we think and act on the various levels of matter, we will force an infinite series of expansions and contractions that will give birth to new beginnings of life. What those beginnings will be and how we will respond to them occurs only when we are there.

We are all free agents creating an effect in time. Therefore, it is perfectly normal to believe that we will exist. We will have our beginning in another beginning, on and on in Infinite beginnings.

## The Human Seed

How could something as minute and transitory as the human contain something as vast and creative as the mind? Let us for the sake of wonderment imagine the human being as a reflective image. When we look into a mirror and see our image in another mirror that is behind us, we can see what seems like an endless line of reflections from that one image. Before each of us came into this world, we started out as a fertilized egg, a human seed no bigger than the period at the end of this sentence. All humans, animals and plants have been multiplying like this since the beginning of life and, in all probability, from the one quality that exists as each of us, the thinking self. This thinking self is more than physicality; it is an awareness that contains all the successive generations of persons, places and things. This thinking self is an array of individuals of which each of us is a part, all with quirks and foibles, an endless line of human seeds, pure potentiality, stretching into infinity. It drives each of us to develop thinking and being, to invent and build. We are more than physical matter when we hold that we are Unlimited in capacity. In order for a seed to grow into something, it must come into the light of the sun, as a child must separate from the mother to become a living breathing being. A seed cannot remain in the soil and a baby cannot remain in the womb. In order to grow into something more, the seed must reach for something greater than its garden. Humans exist because of mental cause and effect relationships that involve thoughts: the ability to create and preserve. Each level of thought can prompt a new level of thinking and doing.

When we become conscious of Consciousness, the seed of matter subordinates its quality to the seed of mind that heat and Light nurture. In time, the mind when controlled wisely no longer needs to germinate in the soil of reconstituted matter. The mind enters by will onto a newer level of action and is totally in charge of its growth/being to make things happen; it listens and obeys.

The flow of thoughts and ideas until recently have been obscured but scientists are now able to map those areas of the brain that indicate thought activity. Does it not stand to reason as a river opens out into the great ocean that our minds have a conduit into the Infinity of thought and intelligence? Through right thinking, we have the potential to unlock those Invisible currents of heat and Light, or Wisdom and aspiration, just as we do the other forms of energy. When we understand that our minds are an intricate part of that one law of vibration, we will be able to use those currents in the betterment of our daily lives. Our thoughts, the center of humanism, spread out in the same way that the rays of the sun, the center for earthly growth, spread out in all directions. Therefore, it is important that we guide and guard our thoughts because they have a drawing power of influence from others, things and circumstances.

Accordingly, we exemplify the character of the thoughts that are the sum of our actions. Our minds, depending on the character of the thoughts, acquire a corresponding appeal and once established will attract that vibration of other minds keyed to the same thought. We receive only the thoughts that are in harmony with the mental attitude held by us. When we believe in ourselves with strong mental determination and positive confidence, the unfavorable and negative thoughts of worry and failure coming from the minds of others will not affect us.

The earth in all its variations is safely enclosed in a Central Heart, and the seeds that are nurtured there are Measureless.

## *Letting It Go*

Every day the world goes through what seems like an endless duplication of events. The only apparent things that change are the nuances that describe persons and places. How we treat one another is the same as it was millenniums ago. The only difference is that there are a lot more of us to exacerbate the subtle differences. No doubt, we have improved our inventions and longevity, but our discourses and interactions with one another are still tribal in nature. Even though the quintessential qualities of human life are all around us, we have yet to grasp what it is that will make us whole humans. When we carefully study the epochs of the past, we can see that nature has always forced life, plant, animal or human to change. Presently, our minds are incapable of sensing the frames of creation that are surging in and around us. If we could, we would see what we really are: subtle copies of one another, normal and balanced, in all ways of doing. Since we cannot observe correctly, nature locks us into a slow motion viewing of occurrences.

Perhaps, when we are capable of letting go of our pain, hatred, desires, wants and the objects of our desires, we will start seeing clearly the intentions of nature. What nature is saying to each of us is, 'Do not possess!' Letting go means perceiving correctly the constructs we have allowed to influence and sway our thinking. We can only win when we let go what others have won for themselves. As long as we need bodies, we cannot remove ourselves from dualism since humanism and nature are codependent. In order for us to have being while in human-nature-earth existence, we must be selective regarding what is worthwhile and what to leave behind. We can be mindful that Consciousness is timeless and it only uses nature to gain experience.

Between the diverse and conflicting aspects of the reality of nature, humanism is slowly beginning to understand the distinction between those elements. This knowing will enable us to know what it is to be animal and finally what it is to be human. We are becoming human when our physical drives and appetites no longer control. Humankind's Ultimate nature and purpose ascend through human betterment where we view relationships as Eternal, beyond the senses of time in the material world.

Most of us progress through nature slowly. If Consciousness accelerated too rapidly, the brain (its neurons and fiber protein) could not withstand the instant surge of electrical light that frames creation and its multidimensional existences. If this happened prematurely, we would experience the incineration of the mind. When the body form dies the chemical substance returns to the elements of nature. Here the energy life separates and enters another life frame, either on this world or in another.

There is one vital Essence in the universe and that is Light or awareness within each living being. It flows according to individual wants and needs. The repetitions we seem to find ourselves in exist because of our misunderstanding in dealing with person, places, and things. The conditions of life are the reflective work that each of us has taken upon ourselves so that we may understand our place within it and thus at the appropriate place and time, let go of it.

We cannot win the world but we can let go of it and re-energize our True nature.

## *The Learning Curve*

Life is a chart that shows the rate of progression of skill and memory and the ability to recall those attributes. Memory is not always consistent with traditional doctrines and methods of culture. There is a probability of a memory that occurred before someone or something else in time that predates institutional humanism. What that is and how we could recall it is most likely individualistic.

As we discover new knowledge and information, humanism betters itself through a process of rationality and moral change. As physical beings in the now, we learn through our five senses. We read, listen, observe and communicate our experiences with others. As fully conscious beings, we learn through Intuition (reflective discrimination) by analyzing what we have passed through or will pass through. Predated memory refers to an order of existence beyond the scientifically visible universe and is illusory to physical memory.

Faith in a 'presence of self-continuum' is fundamental to the human psyche. Without a belief in someone or something, disruption and fixations transpire which can cause disease, cellular and social degeneration to occur. Whether we want to be scientific or intuitive on the learning curve of time and space, mind-body-matter, or Spirit-soul, it is important that we instill in that process idealism and magical thinking. The theory of reality as a single principle is why we see the world as an earthly form. However, we do not base life solely on what our instruments tell us. The only gaps that exist in creation are in a limited mind. It is unlikely that we came out of nothing, and even if we did, we exist now. It is up to each of us as individuals and groups to keep that existence moving forward as either matter or Spirit.

One of the most fascinating properties of life is energy: the sun, the stars, galaxies and other fields that exist in the cosmos. Energy exists because we are alive in it, changing and growing. As we pass through energy, we retain the knowledge of its vast existence. We have the capacity to learn, to gather information and to store it as memory. Through memory, we create action so we may understand the process of creation and our sense of Self within it. We have the potential to enhance memory. Thus, we should practice now to refine it as something more and better, since memory is the fundamental quality of being aware. When we choose to be truly alive by right harmless action, there is an awareness that has no qualities or features of destructive physical memory.

This process is fundamental to unlocking other pathways in the mind-brain that can take us back to that place that predates form. Imagine an enhanced memory that gives us the capacity to rearrange molecules, as well as the ability to utilize the light and heat of atoms with unfailing proficiency, or the capacity to repair cells, synapses and other system of the physical body. There is the potential of utilizing the contents of the universe in the same way we evolve through the earth and its elements.

From a physical perspective, the learning process (the scientific gathering of facts) is useful only in the context of being alive and cognizant in the material world. When we start recognizing life as reflections of Self in time and space there is only the Unseen and seen in motion. Nothing is lost, only changed. As the efforts of the theoretical and the concrete come together, we will gather a different approach in understanding the purpose of life that is our memory: our existence depends on it. Each moment, we are selecting and recalling the memories that make us what we are experiencing, consciously or unconsciously.

Energy and Light are curved, and all any of us can do is follow the memories we have inscribed on its many lines.

## The Forces of Politics

It is not difficult to relate politics to a sand box where little children play stumbling over each other. There is no developed understanding of fair play or the rudiments of social relations. This form of play involves subtle charm and trickery to gain the upper hand on one another. Usually this play involves actions that have no rules or fairness because the exploits of play are not yet self-determined. The sand box and politics are similar because the forces of interaction are misunderstood. When we compare the child to a politician, we find the child lacking in knowledge of the greater world. With the politician, there is an interaction with the world, an interface of free choice, without internal discernment. Children are innocent of the world. Political power fragments the world making those yielding this power pawns to the forces of life: forces they do not understand.

There are many means to understanding the forces of cultural necessities. Money is one type of force. With money, we can exchange wealth, but often we entangle ourselves with it. There is the eloquence of language as a way of expressing ideas. However, we cannot always translate language and ideas and we become confused as to the meaning conveyed. History is a means, too, but the factuality of times past is not always reliable because those in power often exacerbate events in order to wield control. Science is also a means of expressing facts, but the scientist can become confused with the facts and turn the force of those facts over to the controlling power.

Whatever the means employed, politics usually entangles itself with those means. Thus, society as a whole is always maneuvering away from the quality of equalization that would keep it normal in all ways. Therefore, politics as a means often prevents people from connecting to what concerns them. The retention of power is the prime motivator for the internal and external strategy of a political entity. As problem solvers regarding the concerns of common people, politicians often disengage from the wants and wishes of the populace.

Is there an internal method of understanding the forces of politics without all the hoodwinking involved? Is there a way in which politics can instill into our day-to-day living a moving awareness and Unity with the higher element of life that brings into focus the better part of our material activities? A reflective process is self-induced either through one's voluntary nature or by external forces at play. The medium in which the forces of life work and interact is through cause and effect. Behind this are the influences of hierarchical power that are interdependent, self-sustaining and are mostly unknown to us. As long as we are in physical matter, there is always a semblance of this structure at work in our day-to-day lives. Only by controlling our thought processes through an internal discourse with our better natures can we lessen these influences. Politics nurtures itself through an historical perspective and as such works from that understanding. It enforces power, not reason, which is the cause for ongoing disturbances and inequalities. There are very few philosophers in the political arena. Thus, the Light of the Inner nature is lost to the outside political world.

Human morality concerns itself with the needs, well-being and interests of the people, whereas politics is a social organization that uses intrigue to gain authority or power.

## *Getting It Right*

It seems human nature endures and endures in order to come to an understanding of getting it right. Why is this so? It is difficult for the human psyche from a personality level to accept failure. Survival, competition and an enthrallment with the senses have had an enormous swaying power over the constructs of the mind. Numerous persons and things form the processes of association that can cause problems of identity from the one to the many. As we form associations, there is the forging of identity, of wanting to be a part of a group, and the desire to help that group achieve its goals and aspirations. Often there is a feeling of preservation that some particular part will remain, even if it means giving up self-will and turning it over to a cause! Frequently a leader who aspires to serve the greater good, once placed into a leadership role, will succumb to the forces already imbued and forgo the earlier ambition. A leader's desire to do the right thing rarely overcomes the persuasive nuances of power. Sadly, what comes forth is damage, not only to the infrastructure, but to the human mind as well.

The relation we have with things, and the importance they have in our lives regarding comfort and pride in achieving those goals, plays an important part in blinding the mind to what is right. From that comfort zone of apathy, one rarely places his/her being into the shoes of those who are unable, either by the lack of opportunity or mental constructs, to be in their place. Enhanced materialism fuels the inability to feel normal and passionate for humanism as a whole. Thus, balance and equal treatment are only aspects to which the masses longingly look forward. To belong to a group is an intrinsic human need like the need for food, shelter, security and freedom. Therefore, it is very difficult to be self-reliant apart from society. Because of the need for belonging, most humans will not step away from the culture or society into which they were born; it is easier to go along with the interests of the existing social hierarchies. When we fail to act in a holistic and humanistic manner, isolationism creeps into the imagination, intelligence and character. Consequently, the world and communities become unbalanced and a separation occurs between groups of leaders and those they represent.

In order to understand fully the intricacies of the life process, it is fundamentally important, at moments, to step away from the pecking order to gain a rational view of understanding the world of humanism. Where there is oppression, exploitation, and domination, there can be no freedom of choice. A society will never 'get it right' unless all members have the ability to rise to their full potentiality. Only by understanding the world from various points of view will we understand fully the causal factors related to social interaction. Idealistically, the vision of a humanistic society should be fashioned in such a way that the only priority would be the Will of the people. In such an interactive collective society, freedom and progress would bind all citizens together.

Each generation will see and do things in a different way according to the standards or principles to which they aspire.

## Three-Form Existence

Do we need to have a physical form in order to know existence? Can we know existence through the aspect of thought only? In the physical world, reality is related to objectivity, the thing being perceived, or the manner in which we take in reality, actual being, as opposed to the imaginary or idealized. Existence is only factual if someone perceives a type of existence. When two or more persons perceive the same thing, or object, then there is a direct actuality of something without the impressions or references to someone else's ideas.

In the terms of mind/thought, is there a way of life independent of concrete perception? As of yet, that is not a practicality because there is no way to witness, perceive, or know of thought waves, especially when they leave the body of form. However, that does not mean those wave forms do not exist. The energy of electricity has become factual only in the last century. Before that, only static emanations and lightning allowed this energy to be visible. It is quite probable that the human form has an electrical form surrounding it; we just lack the instrumentation or sight to feel and realize it. Some believe that all is electricity and that when we touch something what we are touching is the space between the two objects, or the electrical field of those objects. All of the things created from nature except plant, animal, and human have been shaped and formed out of the inventions perceived in the mind, starting from the club all the way up to our present techno-concepts. Three qualities, mind, emotion, and form exist as one body. Presently we live in a reality of height, width and depth, real world objects, of which the body is three-dimensional. Most likely, until we have mastered the form nature, other dimensions beyond the physical will remain an ideal for which to reach. If the emotional and mental worlds become actual realms of their own, it will be because we have reformed ourselves to live and move within that perceived reality of mind and emotion. We will have inculcated a fourth dimension into our three-dimensional consciousness, the dimension of time that will specify completely the location of any event that relates to existence.

Some theorize that the universe has an infinite number of dimensions and because we have just begun using the mind at only one-tenth of its full capacity, we are only on the threshold of multi-dimensional awareness. We are all travelers moving through dimensions of time and space. Sometimes we travel one by one, other times together. We go in different directions or we share time and space with one another. Nevertheless, the energy waves of time and space have their own sources of knowledge. Only those traveling on the same wave of experience fully understand this. We rest, we share and we experience. As to what form that association takes depends on the mental and emotional content of the relationship.

Recognizing this dimensional energy is the first step toward a full Consciousness that has the ability to move beyond the three-dimensions. A gateway opens to the sky where the internal structure changes. Forms come and go like drifting clouds. There are no erosive processes. Every dimension needs an informational dimension to give it validation within the system; this is what our minds and emotions do. When we step away from our three-form existence, we are preparing ourselves to move beyond the thought processes that enshroud the three-dimensional earth.

We are dimensional beings projecting dimensions from darkness into Light: one, two, three, and four, on and on.

## Different Directions

The line or course along which a person or thing moves is determined by force and energy which is either by an act of nature or the will of mind. The five senses and the mind create a reservoir of negative and positive thoughts. Each of us is born, lives and moves because of such thoughts. The experiences and the environment into which we are born determine how each of us evokes those thoughts and memories. The re-creation of the events and feelings of the past are from the choices made within or those influencing us from the outside. A sudden onset of pain or joy can cause memories to surface. If memories are devoid of emotion, it is possible they can be animalistic or dictatorial depending on the strength of will. The more the body responds to the strength within, the stronger the will becomes.

No matter who or what we meet in life and interact with, whether animal, plant or human, each has a path of direction. While in a body, we may feel and sense a similar direction with another person; but once that thinking, feeling and sharing human being has moved beyond sight, memories and feelings in our physical existence are all that are left. We link memories to the personal feelings that exist in the mind, as those personal feelings are dependent on the mind.

The attributes of nature form our objective side: the knowledge of experience and actions. Reasoning forms the subjective side and is the basis for our Intelligence. To a certain degree, both the subjective and objective planes are going in different directions. Nature is non-conscious but the Self within is conscious of nature because there is a reciprocal concurrence between nature and the Self. Knowing this, the objective and subjective are so equalized it is difficult to say which of the two has priority while in physical form. As soon as we identify with either the subjective or objective aspect, persons, places and things vanish through a change in direction. Nature is not aware of any concept of the subjective. However, the mind analyzes the concepts of nature, its consequences, quality, or condition. It seems that nature is not aware of intelligence, yet, as intelligent beings, we are aware of nature. In the course of the direction that each of us takes, do we add to nature, and how does nature present itself to us? It is natural to take from nature and add that understanding to intelligence. As a result, Consciousness and nature are two poles: Spirit and matter. Working from different stages and constantly intertwining, these poles seek each other, mixing all natural laws into laws of intuition and thought.

Matter, the invisible stuff of nature, is absorbed into the form thus animating it with its energy. Through lawfulness, the outer coverings of nature reconstitute into the mind. Thus, the lines of light from which Consciousness is optically relayed as gravitational reciprocity of motion, force and energy emerges as life, quality and appearance. The whole of nature transforms itself as intelligence. The highest aspiration of nature is to become aware through the highest order of reflection: humanism. Consequently, what we recognize as the First Cause in ourselves as intelligence and consciousness is nature. Then, whatever direction we set out from, matter or consciousness, it is apparent that those directions are mutually necessary for progression. Matter and Spirit, though different in appearance and disposition, are intrinsically of the same Essence.

When we look outside of the mind, we are teaching ourselves through nature's complementary or opposed activity.

# The Spirit of Minuteness

Some theorize that creation began as a Singular moment, a first word or an ideation of a beginning: an awareness of livingness. Otherwise, none of us would be here thinking of the past, in the present or a probable future. We can base the future only on probabilities such as existence is! Since theorizing is an ongoing process, is there a theory waiting that puts forth, "This is the final theory?" The heavy thinkers of life have categorized the Invisible with such names as the atom, electron, quark, neutrino, lepton, photon, the void, or vacuum, and the ether, etc, all burdened by theoretical pieces of something subatomic.

The language of life has many faces that come and go. There are no indicators, other than thought, that there was a beginning. No doubt, each of us had a beginning as a fetus, then as a baby, and as an adult. Beyond that, it is what one remembers. Viewpoints about the future are a matter of opinion. Scientists are delving into the density of smallness in an attempt to discover the causes of existence.

Humans are a curious bunch of atoms when it comes to their surroundings. They could never accept just picking the fruit off the vine; they had to ask, "Why?" We are not just content enjoying the magnificence of the universe. We have to tear it apart and turn something small into something big and make a Big Bang out of it.

The underworld can be a terrible place, a world where 'angels fear to tread.' If science becomes fearless of that void and enters it before we condition the mind to accept such light, the human race could get a bad burn. Experimentally when we enter the dimensions of the extremely small, we had better have a flawless plan. Otherwise, there is the potential of ripping the fabric of time and space. All it takes is one little spark going in the wrong direction, Bang, and we are back in the primordial soup pot. Through science, we know that particle worlds exist.

Particle history began with the philosopher Thales in the Greek colony of Miletus. He wondered if it could be possible to trace back the multiple objects of the universe to a single basic substance, an underlying simplicity. We are still at it today only we use super colliders that bang elements into one another at the near speed of light. The big question that scientists need to examine in all of this light research is, "What will it do to the neurons within the human mind once that underlying particle is let loose?" We are traveling at the speed of light; it is in everything we do.

From thinking and doing, the human mind brings about all research. Mind is what gives the universe being. If there is one Creative particle, we could theorize that a single human could correlate to that particle. If one awakens, it awakens the other. Do we then have benevolence or malevolence? The races of human kind should be equal when such a discovery occurs, or the fallout could be far worse than the side effects from the release of the atom. We are still burying the waste from that discovery, which has a lifespan of twenty thousand years or more. In the finality of the mind, there is no inside, no outside. The mind cannot visualize its totality anymore than it does the atoms and molecules that make up its physical form. There is only awareness expanding which depends on the Spirit of wakefulness.

All life whether particle, person, planet or mind is constantly expanding.

## The Truth about Everything

Is there a culmination of everything where all of life comes to a final point of activity? As of this writing, the world population count is seven billion. If we were to ask each person the aforementioned question, each one would most likely have a different answer. The eyes and senses that behold life, existence, and everything else, evaluate perception from an individual mind level of understanding. Therefore, if there is a greater opportunity to witness persons, places, and things, there will be a greater measure of evaluation of the environment's array.

The physical aspect of the mind is one of its many related abilities. However, in terms of the physical body, scientists cannot fully identify or explain the mind. Intelligence and Consciousness are the conduits for awareness located in the brain. These conduits witness physical life from a set of views based on two states that are complementary or opposed to each other. These two aspects, matter/form and energy/mind, under different conditions are projections of related abilities. Therefore, each person is a reflection of his/her place in time. If the umbrella of truth that clarifies the One Reality should unfold, individualism could not express itself.

Therefore, the meaning of life, as we understand it presently, would no longer exist.

From whatever ideology we look at truth, if we try to see it from our present place, we will certainly fall on our faces. We can liberate ourselves from encrusted truth only by keeping our minds open and critical to tradition. There is no special technique to thought, other than one's own. In our attempt to bring order and structure to life, as we now perceive it, we have limited the potentiality of many in the population. We have mystified thought in our pursuit of truth. Through personality cults, we have divided and controlled truth through a series of schools and movements. Simply knowing views and theories of recognized persons and institutions is not what truth is about. When something continues without interruption, we are adding to truth. When there is a renewal of an action, event, or process it becomes a fact in consciousness. Our senses of mind continue forward. Belief and truth are counterproductive; they become obstacles to one another. Truth makes things equal, whereas beliefs divide.

To discover the truth requires an open mind that knows with certainty: 'I am everything. For anything to exist, I have to exist. Therefore, things that are real for me are of my own interpretation of the things from the outside world. The inside world is my own and cannot be viewed by another living being.' When we look at living squarely, we can only face it second by second. Observations tell us that in a second we could be lifeless to another face. Is there anything then, or do we merely awaken from a dream? No intelligence alive today would base its life on that belief. However, what is the truth? We can dissect the truth of the past through how we perceive truth in the here and now and even into the hereafter if we are awake. Truth is being mindful of wakefulness in the life we have now.

## The Earth Leads to Everything Else

When it comes to the Earth there is a lot to think about, such as how minute it seems as the earth travels around the sun in an oval track of 93 million miles and at a speed of 18 ½ miles per second, a mere point of light among an unfathomable number of points. As physical beings, our very survival depends on this blue/green sphere. The issues it faces today can overwhelm the mind. Nevertheless, we have to face the fact that we are its crew. Like the crew of Apollo 13 who had system failures we, too, are going to have to think comprehensively and in harmony to keep our ship safe. The safety of our earthly home depends on how we face the threatening issues we have collectively created. Sadly, the issues we face are not by accident but by over-population and consumption. We simply did not think of the cause and effects we were creating just to assuage our cravings. Our nationalistic rituals and the roles played by leaders in academia, government, business and religion are going to need a revamping if we are to remain a viable creative species for planet earth. It is evident from studying prehistoric times that nature has a way of setting causes right. Surely, there are focus groups of bright creative people with specialized tasks who have the insight to sway the ruling elites out of their stupor and awaken them to what lies ahead. We need to evaluate and change our standards of living and doing.

When our children cry and cling to us, as parents we do our best to soothe their tears. However, there are hosts of species clinging to the earth that are unable to speak for themselves. What are we doing to soothe their cries? We defile the pleasant rippling streams and oceans where fish swim. We rob the habitats of the wild birds and animals who abide in forests of green. We have massacred a million dreams and cast our poison in the air we breathe. In our glee, we impregnate our landscape with urban sprawl. How long can we thrive in a sea of concrete, plastic and fumes of coal and oil? With hardly a thought of wind and sky, we pass over fields of green and blue with our machines like the mighty buffalos and cranes once did. Is our quality of life becoming a reflection of the elements we intermix? From seafloor to space, we have planted the waste of civilization: discards that we are yet to reckon with. The citizens and cities of the earth have become more decentralized and politics have shifted from the interests of the people to corporations. From the hands of the few, the many depend. Production, consumption, and over-procreation are the norm. We allocate commerce and scientific research to the main stream and we subrogate happiness to the motivation of money.

What we have morphed into is a world skewed by economic self-interests where managers, accountants and politicians administer the systems of government with a free hand and with very little oversight. Such leadership has become the beacon for the evolutionary right of the strong and self-righteous, a moral superiority of personal beliefs and actions from which the average person is exempt. The principle behind this type of immoral thinking is divide and control: a set of principles that guide a series of controls that reduces the power people have regarding community standards. Through community, we have our primary existence that leads to everything else. Therefore, we have to keep asking our better natures what kind of crew we want our children to become.

## Simplicity: the Art of Living

We cannot find simplicity, the real quality of something, in a laboratory, a test tube, a Petri dish, a vacuum, a quantum approach, an event horizon or in an established set of rules, laws and regulations that govern. Simplicity is a sudden epiphany of time, place and circumstance where everything is normal, balanced and equalized. Simplicity and matter are counterproductive; they are opposites but symbiotic which is necessary to gain unity. Friction by fire removes the impurities from the lesser atomic lives so they can progress onward in greater expressions. This counter direction transforms matter. The blending of elements is a mental process: air (ether) transforms matter into plant, animal and human forms.

Presently, we consider matter as only three-dimensional. However, when the senses are coordinated and balanced, higher dimensions can be accessed thus coloring and coding the lesser substances (earth, air, fire, or water: the fundamental constituents of the universe) with their value. This leap of understanding is devoid of time, ego and place. In this new understanding, there is nothing to discover about life because life is the builder. The plans, values and structures are already in place for us to witness. If there is a difficulty, it is in the impressing of others because the ego is a difficult thing to impress.

Life is an imbedded chemical process, an array of organizations of which the human being is one. The human being by far expresses a higher degree of autonomy with respect to its environment than any other atomic form. Intelligence, or electrical Light, is the Universal Principle that governs the cosmos, circulates through the metabolic components, the breath of life. Along with this air, there are the components, or code structures, that shape life through slow, but infinite processes. These series of actions have a specific aim that involves a large number of simultaneously existing dimensions of which a certain number of humans are aware of as Intelligence.

Some believe that there are thirteen fully aware humans: six who work with matter, six who work with Light and one who synthesizes both matter and Light. Light represents simplicity; matter represents difficulty. From these beacons, differential states of being exist. Each individual in the human equation moves through the complexity of material substance or the simplicity of the unchanging Essence as it passes through the living force of those thirteen beacons, or diffused grades of differentiation. Because of these established differences, the generalized forms will in time change into more specialized forms that are pleasing to their better nature. Life as we know it came about because of a successive set of organizations, from simple systems to increasingly complex systems. Therefore, as these systems, the simple and the complex, rotate counterclockwise to one another, they exhibit differences with the terrestrial natural life process. Because of the synthesizing influx of Light, they will start formulating a Universal sense of simplicity with the complex. Thus, life will not focus on the reconstruction of concrete history, as we know it; but it will focus on the specifics of the present and future.

In the finality of Being, we discover that all achievement, the Ultimate expression of art, is in Simplicity.

## Free-Flow Interchanges
## (Ballroom in the Sky)

No word or symbol can fill the inquisitiveness of a free flowing mind. The flow of creation and all the good that is upon its firmament are what a mind remembers from the things long ago to the things to be, as each life passes into the next. We know the creation of the universe came from an immense power and force beyond imagining. We know there is greatness out there. All we need to do is open our minds and create a state in which we are able to act and live as we choose without being subject to any undue restraints or restrictions. Free-flow succeeds not because it is there in its completeness, but because of the asserting existence of a person's self-chosen mode of morality with respect to the rest of the world. In this free humanity with its interchanges, there are no restrictions in rights and enjoyments of civil liberties. It is a reassurance that the universe is a safe and rewarding place. It tells us we are points of Light in a vast cosmos where beautiful things are happening and where movement from one idea leads to another. It is transaction without the negatives of cause and effect: a free-flow of inquiry without congestion. In the free-flow interchange, events relate to one another but do not cause the other. A relationship between ideas structured in their own logical goodness allows relationships to arise without a causal nature. Out of themselves, these relationships can manifest as simultaneous happenings that have meaningfulness where the cause and the effect occur together creating a permanent memory that shares the same place and time. This occurrence of memory looks forward not backwards.

Free-flowing awareness is always progressively in touch with the ultimate interior design or pattern of other things of the same type. These inherited parts of Consciousness have a commonality as to behavior, dreams and aspirations. From this lineament, we ultimately uncover the true contours of related experiences, or parallel events, reflecting the governing dynamic cosmos. When we are wide-awake and aware these exceptional acquaintances are within and around us as free-flowing energy systems.

The free-flowing interchange is where persons, places, and things meet to evolve and to bring into place the higher meaning of Consciousness. Imagine entering a grand ballroom where exotic persons are dancing. You step out onto the dance floor, alone, and suddenly from nowhere a beautiful counterpart to your imagination embraces you and the two of you dance and whirl around in perfect time like the orbiting of the planets in the solar system around the sun. Once one experiences this free-flow of life, one cannot let go. This attraction helps one to evolve to a state of Higher consciousness.

The more conscious we are of the free-flowing energy, the more it will appear to help us manifest positively and to encounter aspects of the Soul in a meaningful and remarkable way. It is how the free-flow works and it is why we are here. Our true being has two sides that equally assume and demand that we seek out one another in the flow of life. Hence, one cannot set out to do something without being attracted to the other. The highest consummation of this attraction is the complete merging of Intuition and thought.

Human yearning flows in thousands of forms, fertilizing the earth and beyond.

## The Room (Womb) at the End

A small room or port of entry exists between the outer world we are leaving and the interior one into which we will be going. There are many theories and ideas as to what this port is. Some believe it is a vacuum of nothingness while others believe this port is a passageway to another form of existence. Whatever the case may be, it is an individual one. But if we are rational about life, memory, or Consciousness as existing, we would have to think that we exist now and because of this actual state of being, we must exist as 'everything' or there would be no purpose for this particular place or situation. We are always entering this region whether sleeping, day dreaming, imagining, creating or passing over. This portal is a distinct part of us that has a specific function just as the systems of the body do. We are not always conscious of the workings of our body systems that are involuntary. Nevertheless, they keep us living and moving on this world of form. Knowledge acquired is our Consciousness. Thus, the more familiar we are with the properties of being, such as an object, an ideal, or a symbol that exists, the more confident we will be about the certainty of a continuum. Knowing, thinking, learning and judging make us who we are: self-aware, choice-making Consciousness. We are solitary beings performing a part among many in the Essential nature of something all-important that is beyond the limits of material experience.

When we carefully look over our actions from childhood to adulthood, the point of view that we hold with persons, places and things gives the world its actuality in time and space. We are always viewing reality from a former state, a state of coexistence that has substance in the current state of awareness as an individual. Because of life we have an awareness that existence depends on many processes of which this wakefulness is just a component. As we start on the downside of our outer journey, we should begin the process of imagining how we want our next existence to be. The atrium or room at the end is most likely void of the imaginings of others. What happens is unknown, just as it is in the womb, the place of our origin for this world. Nevertheless, development and growth are happening with every heartbeat the mother makes.

The 'Heart of Universal Essence' beats the same way. The earth and each of us came into being from its activity. The energies that we feel pulsating around us are also pulsing in and through our own body systems. Unknowingly, we attune ourselves to the multi-dimensional vibrations of existence and from them we have the ability to tune our better natures. The earth and the greater systems are always in the process of attuning to those who desire alignment with them. The purpose of the room is to awaken and reconnect to a Greater Purpose than the one before. Here clarity is rekindled and sparked with those connections that are the Truth of existence: the images forged and fertilized with matter and its many aspects. The imagery of the heart and mind compose a different spiral for ascending or descending into matter. The invocations and attunements we make while living now are vital to our being aware of the next steps we take afterward. The linking at the end is not one of fear. It is one of strength and knowledge of another beginning. It is here that Truth of being and purpose always manifests fully and everything that exists passes in equal circles of time and being.

The Self, through the choice of selection, then action, is in continuous formation.

## *Withering of the Bloom*

When a person or group denies another the right to be normal mentally, emotionally and physically, they are reverting to a less mature state. These denials often involve forms of behavior that are vocally abusive. Laced with intimidating aspects of fear, this type of coercion is a reversion that is generational in shared interests and attitudes. Such behaviorists have no interest in anyone outside of their pool and believe that improving the qualities of others will take away their gain. Anyone attempting to change the characteristics of wealth and property is an antonym to their way of doing. However, such behavior can lead to disturbances in a person's emotions that can step them backwards with the loss of control as to their own destiny. In reality, they are only impairing the quality of their future by not improving the property and welfare of everyone, the basic or essential attributes by all common members of a class society. As a result, there is division between the reality of change and the literacy that meets the demands of modern life. In this disconnect there seems to be a stronger belief in lies that comprise modern culture and everyday life instead of those beliefs that meet the honesty and demands of modern life. Thus, there is an ongoing entrapment of tradition.

According to our will, the events and circumstances of life will make us stronger or weaker. We know that every event follows a prior event that caused it. Consequently, this second event will be pleasing or unpleasing according to its cause being resistant or accepting. Events result from the goodness or degeneracy of the mental events that occur with them. Accordingly, each of us is responsible by choice for any action born from others or us. Whether skillful or of an incompetent nature, any person who commits acts bears the fruit of that action. Any behavior that expresses something forceful through a visual or vocal means, produces pain and quells joy can lead to an unethical action. We know that every human life has a DNA pattern and from that, we produce. This is the physical way of being and doing.

How we act when we disseminate information will determine the bloom of the tree of life for social betterment or illness. Often individually and as a society, we do not give away enough of our resources or ourselves to keep society healthy and prosperous. Nevertheless, we can learn much from our ancient and modern habits. However, to give those actions and patterns merit we must adopt the general disposition that everyone is the Keeper of all. Failure to identify and eradicate incorrect opinions hinders human betterment. Because the concerns of people come under the control of others who influence events for personal gain, it is difficult to clarify cause and effect. Unfortunately, habits of self, absent of commonality, rob people of their freedom for that which is essential.

Love must win over hate. As inhabitants of the modern world, we can overcome avarice by being generous in our actions. We must break the chain reactions of narrow-mindedness by a broader view for everyone, everywhere.

## $E$ = energy = me the force, which = $I\,AM$

We go through life trying to figure out the how and why of it. We look to science and religion to try to unlock the mystery of life and existence. Along the way, we invent theories and have round-table discussions of those speculations. In due time some of those ideas are given over to facts and as a result life for many is improved. However, many are also untouched by those realties. Along with this truth come new diseases, pollution, and hunger and nature degradation. There is also a demise of self-awareness. The vast majority of people need talking points and opinions from others just to make a decision about events and circumstances. Public opinion, under the tutelage of groups regarded as individual by law, steer people in the direction it wants them to go. True knowledge can only come from self-inquiry.

The Self, the thinking 'I', provides the clarity from which we see the one foundation from which everything else is built. From that point, we discover the truth about ourselves. The Self prevents each of us from falling into deceptions fostered by the myths of past cultures. One thing is required to cause and connect the many things we experience and that is the Self within. This Self forces us to describe reality from the one substance, space and its wave motions (thought) that form matter. Regardless of the lens, we see reality through there is one thing that is common to the many things: space. Though life is of many minds, we commonly experience the one Universal space. With undue reliance on science and religion, we have lost our footing with nature. We are becoming more and more unbalanced by the manipulations of its elements and laws. Nature and mind are not always in harmony. For many the mind has become so complex that the structure of simplicity can no longer guide. From the view of the Self: the simpler, the better.

Physicality does not exist in space. The objects we see are spatial extensions of the mind. Their field of strength is due to the inculcating of the mind by societal imprinting or the energy of thought passed on by those individuals whose wisdom or development are equal or greater than the one doing the thinking. The Self, the critical thinker, is free in the exchange of ideas, in spite of the sphere of cultural life those thoughts came from.

If the human species is to survive, it is going to need a new wave of thinkers that can synthesize the complex with the simple. Human behavior makes the world complex. Our myths, customs, desires and collective programming to want more are the causes of nature's negative complexes. Nature/space and its wave structure interconnect with our thoughts; it is how we relate and understand everything around and in us. We have in us the capacity to realize the solutions to our problems. All we need do is equalize our knowledge around service, economics, and impartial science that will strengthen our institutional infrastructures. The energy of the mind that realizes 'I Am', allows the imagination free reign. However, we must constrain our senses by not believing what others claim to be in our best interests. A few bad complexes can create deception and harm to society and ourselves. In the end we may find that the better nature of 'how and why' was not a process from the one to the many, but was a means to meet the needs of a select few. It is up to each of us to unlock the hidden Causal connection of our visible senses. We can find reality only in the Self.

From a distance, the interconnection of all things enables us to see the earth as one form. In general, we cannot view substance and its Essence until we develop the same mind set.

## The Ladder of Progression

Whether we are aware of it or not, we are always moving forward. The hands of a clock were never set to run backward, nor have we alerted ourselves to be aware of the nature of time or the distant voice that calls us forward. Nevertheless, those aspects of past/future have their place in the time of now. Somewhere, half-past life, we start looking in the direction we need to go. We make great effort to use our minds, emotions and resources of life fully. Each of us has the capacity to review our better nature and thus do away with what is unpleasant. Success in this endeavor must start in something solid before we make the necessary steps that will take us from the bottom (the starting point) to the middle (the reflective aspect) and on to the top (our place of acceptance). We are progressing when Compassion rules our thinking and Wisdom checks our actions. When we sense an action that is beneficial to us and to those near and close, we persevere and strive to preserve the ways in which something or somebody moves us. Progressive movement takes us outside our biases, opinions and cultural concepts to a state of thinking that utilizes logic and common sense. It is a place of understanding where the past, the present and the future help us project our own conclusions. As we move through the present by reflecting on the past and its associations, and if we are honest with ourselves, we can see a redundant pattern. Progressing from one truth to another through clear thinking, we sense and know what we no longer need. In this manner, we step forward in our newness; we go where the majority fears to tread, to a place that outweighs cultural concepts.

On the bottom rung of the ladder, personality life and its enticements enthrall us. Enraptured with the world the aromas emanating from its atmosphere capture us. At this stage, places and things take precedence and the individual components of a person's physical, mental, emotional and social conditions are central. In consequence, the consideration of all factors that makes up totality eclipses rationality. However, it is in rationality that we adapt the methods of human goodness. On the middle rung, we are taking steps that at times seem to be as if we are walking on a razor's edge. We know we cannot return to the past, and we cannot be fully in the present. Therefore, we experiment! We start looking at our disconnects by asking questions that will help us relate better to the broader way of being and doing that will benefit everyone. Forward momentum does not mean that everyone will be the same, think the same, or get the same material necessities. Rather, forward momentum dulls the razor's edge creating a level walkway. We can then live a reasonable life. When we finally arrive at the top, we know the direction in which we want to go. We are in the Clarity of our place of acceptance. We are fully capable of adding additional rungs to our progressive ladder that are of our own making. We understand the basis of our thinking and doing. We reject the foundations of authoritarian thinking that restrict personal exploration. Thus, we embrace a journey focused on the fundamentals that make up our own independence, concepts, and actions. Often these underlying principles leave us alone in our conclusions. Only when we think outside of the box can we find other explanations and different possibilities for moving forward.

Truth becomes the means of developing open-minded ways of understanding our continuum.

## Levels of Reality

Existence is. Actual being or happenings are dependent on wakefulness: being cognizant of surroundings. In third-dimensional existence, there are periods of rest and sleep needed for the physical body to remain mindful of its environment. Once the third dimension abdicates, the thinking power that manifests the physical world (infinite dimensional existences or the self that abides in the heart of all things) is always awake and fully aware because there are no false or unreal experiences with which to contend. Consequently, the reflection in Consciousness, the flow that directs perception of one's true nature, is in the pathway or channel where the experiences and affections of joy and happiness are constant and attainment of knowledge is ongoing. This gathering is dimensional in measuring the characteristic and energy types, the specifics of all knowledge. At this level of reality, we can only have knowledge of something by observing it or hearing about it. We will remain inferior to the higher dimensions as long as we stay behind and enthralled with the self-restrictions of the subject/object world of the third dimension and its outward-turned consciousness. To go beyond restrictive dualism a channel of compassionate communication must be set up with the Self, the higher senses, and the lower ones of action, the determinative mind that controls the sense organs. In time this reflective exchange of what to do and what not to do will allow the fourth dimension to come into view and equilibrium will rule the viewed existence.

When we achieve Inner insight, the levels of existences are infinite. Our third-dimensional work, play, knowledge gathering, etc., need not be limited to this reality. Unless we set aside a time where we can be imaginative and creative in expanding perception, we will not sever the knot between Pure Consciousness and the insentient body (the ego). We will remain tied to the play of a one-pointed mind. The body, the aspects of the lower mind and the Self, the purity of mind, through a play of waking, dreaming and sleeping equalize good and bad action in equal proportions until the manifest world (the veiling and projecting power of existences) becomes an observed reality of play. The body/mind then identifies with its next stage where the knower becomes convinced of infinite Consciousness. Infinite Consciousness does not mean the play stops. As infinite Consciousness, each dimension of being has its own here and now familiarity to work with, but the workings are of a benign nature. There are no malignant forces with which to contend. Other appearances and substantial forms aid the transcendence that comes naturally and is present always. Similar to the universe, both the inner and outer worlds are in a constant state of expansion. Forces and energy systems of creation are always impersonal. It is Consciousness that remembers and repeats the causes of existences. It is up to the Self and ego to determine what is invalid and valid in negating all names and forms in order to arrive at the fundamental phenomenal existence. As the Self absorbs the ego, another higher waking state of inquiry absorbs the self. The processes that direct life, its energy and forces, are within and around us. The Essence of being, its Love and self-direction, is fully deserving and fully controlled. For the circumstances of any reality to remain real, they must be equal in their identifying nature.

The first step is to deal with the existence of the reality of the now in which we exist. Only then can we step into another level of reality.

## The Actuality of Events

The events of objects and persons originate in twos. First, there is the cause followed by the second (effect) which is the direct consequence of the first. Cause and effect include objects, processes, properties, variables, and facts that occur together in a meaningful way. Just as we group events by cause, we can group them by meaning also. What we experience is subject to conscious and subconscious influence. Consequently, the subject matter at the human level is made of a complex mental construct, mass and energy, gravitation, and circumstance that are equal and beneficial. When an event is set in motion, we must establish positive thinking that will bring about the effect. Visualizing the issue as a positive relationship in time and space allows the most fundamental levels of creation to come on line and side with what has been set in motion.

When we have a sense of ease with the rules of conduct regarding events, it brings about growth, balance and understanding regarding what we initiate and what is to follow. Cause and effect establishes justice because it renders equal payback. Only the mind tuned to self-responsibility can bring about justice, unity, harmony, and truth. With this attitude of wholeness toward existence, it leads to the one Great Truth, the perfect Self which measures unerringly. Through action and constant change, we bring things into being. We solve misunderstandings so we can move forward toward fulfillment. The hills, valleys and waterways of consciousness and its activities push us from darkness into the One Light. Although the light is the same for all, its variety is individual as the rose is different from the violet. No matter what we pass through, we cannot help but be true to our own personal nature because activity teaches us to flow in conjunction with our own desires.

We each choose our own line of growth and there are as many lines of growth as there are stars. None of us is the same, but we do move along the same lines. Our past, present and future desires create the threads that culminate in our present: the central focus. The nature of our desires has no power to check the action of this or that. Desire brings to maturity the bitter as well as the sweet. It does not matter whether life is pleasant or unpleasant; our place in it is to bring to realization the results that follow from what we think and do, for we hold their nature, their effect and their purpose within ourselves. To move outward events forward in a positive direction, we first must understand and check the essential nature of our Inner life. The Inner life, the stuff of the mind, gives covering to the effects of action. In dealing with any kind of action, we must look at the multiplicity of events and their domino effect. Even trivial action has merit for it quite often allows us to see into the depths of things and understand what is factual. When we use our past as a sounding board, we are fashioning our future and our responsibility to it.

The mind is the Cause of and fashioner of everything. How we act with mind determines what will follow.

## Imperfect Perfection

Life and appearance move through an environment expressive of incomplete action. At times, the surroundings appear perfectly normal, balanced and equal. Then circumstances change and vertigo blows in and restlessness appears influencing life and its activities. Life is hereditary by nature and its core is information gathering. Our state of awareness depends on the type of knowledge acquired or supplied about something or someone. Life propagates through this linear array of collected data. This information dictates the interactions of persons, places and things and carries out the process of replication and transcription. On a macrobiotic level the stuff we are made of (atoms, cells, and molecules) are always rearranging in pairs. This mixture of life and appearance constitute our perception. The good and bad properties of this mix are prevalent in the natural order and remain neutral regardless of their use. There is consistency in mineral, animal and plant forms. However, when we bring in the human equation we get volatility of mood, temper, or desire and everything suddenly changes. Outwardly, when we look at the world and its place among the stars it seems perfect in all ways. It orbits the sun and remains in place among the other planets. We know our bodies evolve on the stuff of the earth because its elements are in our blood. However, where did this mind and its seeming imperfection come from? Fundamentally, life and appearance are perfect; the discrepancies in the mind make them imperfect. The laws established in nature in a formal sense are perfect and if we followed the laws established by the mind in the same way, there would be no imperfection.

To a certain degree when we look at human relationships and the changes those relations take we often attribute them to earth changes: the changes of energies connected to the universe. We rationalize our imperfections onto something else and we give those actions various names and beliefs. When we become imperfect in one relationship, we move on and attempt to become perfect in another. However, if balance is not attained the lessons will go on until we figure out how to master them. We justify our behavior by saying, "We are imperfect beings". Only the Creator knows Perfection, but who is that other than the Self? There is no doubt that we live on a polarity world of vicissitudes, male and female, and we must share ourselves with others to learn our lessons. However, we do not have to keep repeating life's lessons, yet we keep on saying we are imperfect beings struggling to be perfect. It is easy to judge others when we see no further than the tip of our noses. Different tempers, points of view, judgments, opinions, laws and customs pervade the world. In spite of this, when we look with impartiality, we can see that nothing is perfect and everything is Perfect.

## One Page, One Life, and One Story at a Time

Every life is different. Each one of us is different in mannerisms, voice, looks and degrees of intelligence. Since the dawn of intelligence, life has been operating this way. There may be similarities in time and place. Mostly though, everyone one has their own page number when it comes to individuality. A person born to this world comes into an arena of great influences. Families, schools, peer pressure, relationships, group settings and ideology, art, poetry, plays, music and forms of government all compete to shape the story of that person.

History reveals acts of all shapes and types that tell the story of a person's time and place. The annals of history inscribe some stories well. Others go unnoticed and never record person, place or time. However, when it comes to Consciousness every numbered page has a meaning. We can view consciousness like time; a dimension of nature where things rearrange themselves, and in that respect no story is unread. As the reader scans this information, he/she is relating or not relating to what is on the page. As each of us goes through the living process, we encounter other persons, places and things. In our course of action the past or future are only mental views. The observable things of the present are the conditions that pass from generation to generation, the source for the now. The future arises as an extrapolation of passing through the present. The past, present and future are the backgrounds for time that everyone has a certain amount of now.

As human beings on a world of form, we are always operating from the past. Our communication systems give us this consensual coordination of behaviors. Because of the close encounters that can be good or bad, we develop reoccurring conditions that give rise to our observations and acts as human beings. Unknowingly, we are always responding involuntarily to indirect stimulus, or shadows of others. Is there an independent place of knowledge outside of us that can explain our human experience? Any notion of an independent reality beyond the now is merely a supposition or principle taken from a self-evident point of view. Any domain of entities that exists independently of the observer in a future determined existence, as structure determined systems, is a generated belief in the event to be lived. There are as many domains of Consciousness as there are humans.

Human experience is the basis for our lives. Because everyone has a narrative, we are aware of life in experiential stories. We operate as one life at a time among other lives in domains of arrangements composed by others. Each of our worlds, individual or group, operates in us as other known experiences as we live in what is happening now. As we become more aware we realize we are living what has already happened. The only differences are in the nuances, the subtle shades of meaning, feeling and tone. We become aware that life is an imitation of sorts passed down in language and art. As we attend to our daily living, we cannot help but notice that we identify something because of a page, a life and a story that came from another domain of knowledge. We owe our lives to others and their behavior toward us. If we are not aware of this now, we cannot be aware of other entities in other domains of existences that will be our future. It is because of these circumstances in time and place that we give meaning to our being and our never-ending quest for self-awareness: one page, one life, and one story at a time.

In a single story, there are thousands of voices.

## *The Song of Life*

The whole of life, the universe and everything in it, from the grandest of objects to the smallest, is swirling to the Song of the Heavens where opposites attract. For earth bound humans it is one where the ovum unites with the spermatozoa to produce a zygote that may develop into an embryo that may eventually become a human. The Song of the Heavens is more than physical eroticism or the moment of sexual release. Though that feeling in some ways mimics the force and energy behind creation, it is not the full essence of that conception. Symmetric beauty that relates to the balanced proportions of two halves relating to a whole can produce a feeling similar to that produced from sexual pleasure. The only difference is that no offspring results; the origination becomes internal in the emotional and mental realms of the observer. However, the ecstatic feeling of physical creation is limited because matter encapsulates the physical, emotional, and mental properties of a human being. There is a common belief that sexual enjoyment is counter distinctive to spiritual development; in higher thinking, nothing could be further from the truth.

Sexual visions exist within the Self and have a direct connection with Essence. It is an exchange that consists of consensual sex play in which the observed and observer are equal. Mutual love, trust and respect is the motivation in this drama. Only by experiencing visual emotional arousal on a backdrop of erotica can one master the dominant qualities of the personality. Ultimately, it is through this process that we can eliminate the dominant side of pleasure. The more we exercise this power, the stronger becomes the character until any violence is absent in desire. Cultural changes that allow for this freedom of sexual expression will advance in the long-term because it will influence the family, promote the equalization of the sexes and lessen population growth, a byproduct of self-responsibility.

Throughout history, cultures have used sex in all sorts of ways to maintain control over the population. If there was a sordid side to sex play, it usually came from the upper rungs of society who held those seedy qualities unto themselves. Sex expressed itself one way for the rich, another way for the poor. As generations passed, those morasses have only weakened and distorted the visual beauty of the Song of Life.

When we view non-restrictive sexual norms as positive in adult relations, we eliminate sexual oppression and inhibition, and Love is normal and balanced in expression. Until our emotional and mental bodies view the physical act of sex as essential to our enlightenment and spirituality, we will be incomplete with our core of being. We will be limiting our true harmony and place of beauty where sex and heart beat as one with the force and energy that set us in motion.

## The Busyness of Doing

No matter how hard we try, we cannot keep from doing. Our hands, our minds, and emotions are always working, thinking and moving objects, thoughts and feelings around in a complex set of events and circumstances. Creating and shifting, we go about our days and nights, sometimes amazed, other times perplexed as to what to do or not to do. We make decisions and then second-guess them. When there is no agreement, we put these decisions off until another time or day, as if somehow, that time will resolve the issue. However, if we look reality square in the face and see it for what it is, life in motion, we will realize there is no such thing as tomorrow, only events and circumstances created by none other than ourselves. We have filled the space in-between the event and circumstance with this thing called time that sequences events and compares the durations of events and the intervals between them. This ability to sequence and compare events is what gives us the momentum to live, move and have being. We are always doing something; we work, play, argue, and love one another. We kill. We cheat and take advantage of each other. In our creativity, we produce art, literature and develop advancements in science that we can use for or against us. When the sun rises, we rise and keep doing; when it sets, we retire and keep on doing in our dreams. Even the systems of our bodies keep busy, mostly without us even being aware of them. Are we innately afraid that if we stop doing we will stop being?

This event called life is just a learning field and we are still learning how to plow the field. It seems what we want to cultivate and how we nurture is still experimental. We are not yet equal in acquiring knowledge. If that were the case, we would be moving the universe; instead, we move in it, which is why we keep busy at doing. In this confinement of busyness, we have lost the ability to be in the wholeness of creation. We no longer play and see through the eyes of innocence. Rather what we have done is to succumb to the ideas of guilt. We have allowed overseers to rob us of our self-esteem, and we have done it with enthusiasm. Eventually, because motion vivifies life, we will become our own supervisors engaged in our own constant activity.

It is necessary that we will always be doing something, even if it is doing nothing. Therefore, life can be both empty and full at the same time. It is what we make of it and nothing more. In this play of awareness, we can involve ourselves in all sorts of activities. The types of persons, places and things we allow to influences us will determine the beauty and symmetry of the planting.

It is busyness and doing that keeps our candle lit at both ends.

## Useful Information

The quality of our mental discrimination determines how we use information gathered and the practical use we make of its knowledge. The ability to appreciate good quality or taste in our understanding of persons, places and things is essential to the creation of positive cause and effect. The more we use positivism the greater the value of time and place and the right use of life and its assets. Thus, our actions will be relaxed and beneficial whether they are community related or of a personal nature. Our systems of action will be normal and balanced when we take the information gathered and use it in such a way that the interactions produce a good or advantageous effect. When we carefully review the years of past actions, we can visualize and disclose periods of time and place where activity produces useful results or benefits.

Everything begins in mind, and mind shapes everything. We are the instruments of mind and it acts according to our wishes and dreams. Mind is only as perfect as its instrument. Our state of Consciousness increases in direct proportion to our gathering of knowledge. Our experiences, observations and reflections designate the outward world and the world within. Therefore, everything that we possess has its origin in Consciousness and is the sum of our thoughts, mental pictures, words and actions.

From a particle of dust to a man/woman, force and form make up everything in the universe. When we understand that, we become this Creative Power, we possess it. We are on our way to understanding, controlling, and directing this power and in so doing we act on the forces and forms in the objective world. When we possess creative power, we have the understanding to maneuver around persons, places and things unencumbered. When we think clearly and difficulties do not burden us, we are more apt to help both others and ourselves. The sun involves itself with our world by shining on it. We should see ourselves in the same way. We always relate to the things we desire. From the Original Cause, the mind sets those desires in motion. There is abundance for everyone as nature has attested. If there is a lack on anyone's part, it is because we have not come into the realization of the Universality of all substance.

We will harness the results of this universal thinking when we act in accordance with the understanding of the laws of creativity and make them applicable to everyone as nature does. In the human equation, relationships involving mutual exchange of goods, services, favors, or obligations produce everything in creation. Thoughts of equal abundance put a new face on us and the world as a whole.

Only by having a positive mental attitude and a harmless sequence of cause and effect can we have a healthier relationship with the environment and others!

## The Other Half of Time, Person and Place

Time is what puts us in the now. Place is where we are in the now. Person is the other awareness that resembles our thinking and doing in a reflective way. A complete and whole person's energy is not fully compatible with physical time awareness. Therefore, it is reasonable to believe that the form side of matter and the spiritual side (Spirit) exist as a body of matter/form, and a body of Spirit. The form side, or personality, is experiencing the duality of matter and the spirit side, the soul, which is not in manifestation, extracts the better parts of that duality experience in order to expand its awareness of time and place. Most likely the person whom we love the most (parent, brother, sister, husband, wife, or friend) is a reflection of our soul nature, especially if those affections are of a kindred kind. If those similar qualities or interests are not there, these relationships are of a third dimensional kind and not multi-dimensional. The Essence of our selves is Spirit, or pure energy, representing the will to manifest through love and nurturing. The Soul is the vehicle for Spirit that gives meaning to morality, our ideals, conscience, and intuition. While we are on earth, the personality is the body form that houses Spirit and Soul. The personality controls our feelings, thoughts and subconscious reactions. Because physical matter confines us, our earth bodies are extremely dense. The Light of our Spirit/soul Essence is within and does not walk upon the earth except as a personality. Our spiritual Light manifests in the brain, the heart and navel area of the physical body.

When we visualize our earth experience as a form of guidance for our actions, we are pulling down our True Essence. We all are born on this world, not knowing, innocent, but it is through our experiences with forms that we light or dim our divine spark. Many believe that perfection on all levels can only come through experience. It is the light and beauty of the Soul that improves and refines the personality. Therefore, it is common, from a timeless place, for the Soul to show itself to give worthiness to its personality for this experience and the ones that are to follow. This deserving respect can come in dreams, or through enhanced creativity that nurtures the brain and heart to be morally upright and good to all with whom we have contact.

The circumstances of our present place are just reflections of what we need to understand. The time and place for this Inner occurrence will differ and depends on aspiration and will. Developing good qualities, good intentions and motives is the surest way. No matter how we look, feel and know what our truth is, we are all derivatives of this sacred Light that reflects itself in and through each of us. When we do our full duty and effort to remember it, it will show up in unexpected ways as the other half of time, place and person. When we are aware of the affection of the Soul, our struggles in the currents of life will lessen and our influences will be more efficacious. This is the spiritual way of evolution for Consciousness.

In Passing through the Fire, the Original Cause, we become fragments of the effects dispersed: the splitting of one into two. Consequently, we are in search of the other half of time, place and person in earth and that which is to follow.

We cannot change the minds of others, but we can show that there are other alternatives to what they believe. When we allow others to weigh the evidence of other possibilities for themselves there is the freedom to make the choices they deem right. The more one is prepared to see, the more one sees. Just because we do not understand something, or we ignore facts, does not mean it ceases to exist. There are more things in the unseen than the mind can dream. We live on the world to give it meaning so that we have purpose.

Humanism is the beginning and the end of a thing sensed by the intellect. The cause of life and all its flowering and depths of despair that was the past and is in the present, or to be in the future, is in mind: a system of thought that is based on the values, characteristics, and behavior that make-up a human being. Without this mental knowing existence would be an unknowing nothingness. Nevertheless, nothingness of the mind is the quintessential force for newness that permeates the invisibility of space, the gravitational force for wanting. Humanism and its struggles between good, bad, more, less, and the feelings between the sexes, unravel in the mind in order to manifest the physical world. Everything seen and experienced is a necessity delivered by the mind. Through mind, humankind creates the tangible tools that allow it to peer into the vastness of the construction of the universes. Mind also has the ability to turn inward on its self and see how it forms its Innerness. Before these inventions, humankind could only see the immediate, or imagine how something might be. Presently, mind is singular in its observations. No two people can see the same thing that is not material. Wanting is what keeps the mind weak. A mind filled with wisdom and wanting nothing is strongest. A wanting mind is the most dangerous. Inevitably, in terms of time and space mind is brief and has a final flowering, the natural result of achievement expressed in a person, a society, or world. Then as quickly as it started, in a flash the flowering flies away and becomes a new system of knowing.

Life is an Intelligent Heart speaking through the eyes of the Inner race of humankind. Existences come and go, showing the way through the Fire.

# Summation

In the final analysis of our earthly experiences relating to persons, places and things, we will gather together the composition of our thought-form constructions, for that will be all that is left when we are no longer in a physical form, the creation of the Spirit. Man/woman, united as one lofty principle in the infinity of Spirit, will address the varieties of the past in a ceaseless stream of perceptible forms that existed before. From this stream the abstract qualities of creation (beginnings, the point in time and space at which everything started) will be realized. The wind that pushed the earthly path stills, and the parallels of every level of existence stand open in this aloneness of being. In this unattached state, one releases all past choices, reserving only self-knowledge. In the embrace of Eternity, we sense wonderment at the unending Presence that envelopes Consciousness.

The living of life, whether it is the now or hereafter, is a preparation for the changes that occur in time, place and circumstance. All the seeds scatter as we move through one experience to another. The seeds that have beginnings and endings are the things gathered while living. Through this manner, the properties of Consciousness recur as matter or Spirit, always allowing the new to refurbish the old with better ideas and concepts that propel the next experience. Re-energized, thinking recreates self-knowledge out of previous knowledge. While the experience is fulfilling within itself, there is no permanency of Infinity to sustain physical life as it passes back and forth from the visible to the Invisible. Therefore, there is always movement from one level of change to another. During this change, there is more faith of the Self in its collection of knowledge, even toward things not known at the time of putting down. Assuredly, a certainty of fullness prepares for another continuation. Thus, we see more clearly than before that life and awareness take shape from choices made in thinking and acting on the changes that come up, one life at a time.

In search of myself, I am living one life at a time. With Infinite time by my side, I seek out my guide. In my mind, I see things outside of the ordinary. With eyes wide open and Infinity on my side, I clearly remember each yesterday in today's memory. As I gaze into tomorrow, I see that all that matters from youth to Truth resides there. The growth that fashioned the lives one at a time, I do all I can to shine in the flow of Infinite Time.

To get it right my story recites the signs that fill the Light and invites the Soul to come around in all Its might and commission the White Light of Heaven's defender to align all that is Divine, one life at a time.

There are no endings, only beginnings; existence, within and without, is ongoing. All that we see and sense is in the Imagination and in Infinity's Light, one tiny part at a time. The world, space, and time are impersonal to life; they give no status as to persons, places and things. All they do is provide the laws for us to discover, understand and to guide our lives. Life goes on!

## *Precious:*

In the precious time that we have let us show Humility in the knowing, that it had meaning and purpose. Even though we thought we had not seen the Miracle that surrounded us, It was there, in us, all along; we were just too busy to take notice. Our Beauty, Strength and Truth were there guiding and watching. No judgment came to us, just an Invisible hand to pick us up when we fell or failed in our actions. The Awareness that is in us is uniquely individual; yet it is common in all of us. It lingers on the smile of a face, in the touch of a hand, or a warm embrace to fill togetherness. The Golden Sun, watching and shining above us, is common to all who stand in its Light. Whether a human being, a planet, or a solar system, the screen of time spreads out across the universe to gather what is to be Truth. From the vivid images we paste there, we will choose the view that is to be. When we treasure the situations and places we were in while upon this earth, we will understand their purpose in us. Then, gradually and graciously, we will let go of the thoughts and actions that kept us from seeing our proper place in the Love we each had.

There are no beginnings or endings, only Life expressing itself as Consciousness in Light, time, space, matter, Spirit, and Fire.

## Epilogue

## Conscious Imagination and Thinking

Imagine you are standing and looking at the sun directly above your head. Now visualize a set of silver clock hands directly in front of the sun with the hour hand pointing toward the number twelve and the minute hand at two minutes to twelve. Now imagine your body as a conduit for the sun with the crown of the head touching the bottom of the minute hand and the feet touching the earth. Consciously imagine in this Timeless Now of two minutes to twelve every single human being on earth standing together in Humble Adoration. Now lift this conduit of human imagination into the clearness of space and see there in Perfect alignment the Milky Way galaxy, the sun, moon, earth and all the planets, stars, galaxies and solar systems that exist in time, space, matter and Spirit. Now visualize the minute hand aligning with the hour hand at twelve with the dark core of the Milky Way. At this junction, realize we are all Precious Beings passing through the Fire. In this quintessential Stillness see the dark drift of the Milky Way slowly open and spread its breath of Invisibility across our visible sun. As these waves of energy and force pass through the sun, know that they come to comfort and realign our thinking with our True Essence. Serenely imagine these Invisible waves spreading out from the sun into our conduit radiating and vivifying the atoms, molecules and cells of our bodies and planetary systems with a new way of understanding our place among the stars of persons, places and things in the Universality of Life. Muse over this wonder: Light the Fire, Cleanse the Mind.